The Universal Right to Education
Justification, Definition, and Guidelines

Sociocultual, Political, and Historical Studies in Education
Joel Spring, Editor

Spring • The Cultural Transformation of a Native American Family and Its Tribe 1763–1995

Reagan • Non-Western Educational Traditions: Alternative Approaches to Education Thought and Practice

Peshkin • Places of Memory: Whitmangs Schools and Native American Communities

Spring • Political Agendas for Education: From the Christian Coalition to the Green Party

Nespor • Tangled Up in School: Politics, Space, Bodies, and Signs in the Educational Process

Weinberg • Asian-American Education: Historical Background and Current Realities

Books • Invisible Children in the Society and Its Schools

Shapiro-Purpel (Eds.) • Critical Social Issues in American Education: Transformation in a Postmodern World, Second Edition

Lipka/Mohatt/The Cullistet Group • Transforming the Culture of Schools: Yupgil Eskimo Examples

Benham/Heck • Culture and Educational Policy in Hawai'i: The Silencing of Native Voices

Spring • Education and the Rise of the Global Economy

Pugach • On the Border of Opportunity: Education, Community, and Language at the U.S.–Mexico Line

Hones/Cha • Educating New American: Immigrant Lives and Learning

Gabbard (Ed.) • Education in the Global Economy: The Rhetoric of Reform

Glander • Origins of Mass Communication Research During the Cold War: Educational Effects and Contemporary Implications

Nieto • Puerto Rican Students in U.S. Schools

Benham/Cooper • Indigenous Educational Models for Contemporary Practice: In Our Mother's Voice

Spring • The Universal Right to Education: Justification, Definition, and Guidelines

The Universal Right to Education
Justification, Definition, and Guidelines

Joel Spring
State University of New York at New Paltz

LAWRENCE ERLBAUM ASSOCIATES, PUBLISHERS

2000   Mahwah, New Jersey   London

Lawrence Erlbaum Associates, Inc., Publishers
10 Industrial Avenue
Mahwah, NJ 07430

Cover design by Kathryn Houghtaling Lacey

Library of Congress Cataloging-in-Publication Data

Spring, Joel, H.
The universal right to education : justification, definition
    and guidelines / Joel Spring.
        p.   cm. — (Sociocultural, political, and historical
                studies in education)
Includes bibliographical references and index.
    ISBN 0-8058-3547-4 (cloth : alk. paper) —
    ISBN 0-8058-3548-2 (pbk. : alk. paper)
1. Right to education. 2. Human rights—Study and
    teaching. I. Title. II. Series.
LC213.S67   2000
—dc21
                                                99-059806
                                                        CIP
Books published by Lawrence Erlbaum Associates are printed on acid-free paper, and their bindings are chosen for strength and durability.

Printed in the United States of America
10 9 8 7 6 5 4 3 2 1

Contents

Preface   ix

1   Justifying Human and Educational Rights   1

    Universal Justification, Definition, and Guidelines   2
        for the Right to Education
    The Right to Education   3

    Finding a Justification and Definition for "Everyone Has   6
        the Right to Education"

    "Is There Anything Surprising in Systems Antagonistic   9
        in Theory Converging in the Practical Conclusions?"
    The Socialist State and the Universal Right to Education   11

    Cultural Differences and Universal Rights   13

    Conclusion: Searching for the Meaning of Education   16
        as a Human Right

2   Justifying a Universal Right to Education For Indigenous   19
    and Minority Cultures
    Colonialism and the Development of a World System   20

    Minority and Indigenous Cultures in Multicultural   23
        Societies
    Elkin's Manifesto on Cultural and Educational Rights   25

    Human Rights and the End of the Colonial System   27

    The 1960 Convention Against Discrimination in   29
        Education

v

A Universal Covenant of Linguistic Human Rights   30

Are Cultural and Linguistic Rights in Conflict with   32
    Universal Human Rights?

The Educational Rights of Indigenous Peoples   35

Conclusion: Justifying the Right to Education in the   37
    Context of the Genocide of Indigenous Peoples
    and Colonialism

3   The Right to Education in a Global Culture and Economy   39

The Evolution of a World System   39

McCulture and the Hybridization of World Cultures   42

Economic Development and the Instrumental Use   45
    of Culture

Development, Cultural Freedom, and Justification   47
    of the Right to Education

Global Ethics and the Right to Education   47

Biodiversity, Education, and Human Rights   50

Conclusion: The Right to Education for the Privileged   53

4   Universal Justification for Education and Children's Rights   55

The Condition of the World's Children   55

Children's Rights Assistance and Protection Rights   60

Convention on the Rights of the Child: Liberty Rights   64

Cultural Differences and the Best Interests of the Child   65

Sub-Saharan Africa: Children's Rights   66

India and Sir Lanka: Children's Rights and Education   70

Children's Rights and Educational Exploitation   72

Conclusion: Justification for the Universal Right   74
    to an Education and Children's Rights

5   A Universal Concept of Education: Human Rights Education   76
    and Moral Duties

The United Nations' Decade For Human Rights   78
    Education

Protection of Human Rights as a Claim Right   86

The Moral Imperative of Human Rights: Guilt   89
    and Shame

All Human Beings ... Manual for Human Rights   89
Education

Democracy and Education   90

"Nationalistic" and Uncritical Human Rights Education   93

Culture and Human Rights Education   97

Critical Thought and Human Relations Education   101

Let Our Children Dream About a Perfect World of Rights   104

Critical Dialogue About Human Rights Education   106

Conclusion: Universal Guidelines for Human Rights   111
Education

6   A Universal Concept of Education: Guidelines for Literacy   114
    and Numeracy Instruction

    Universal Guidelines for Literacy Instruction   115

    Universal Guide to Numeracy Instruction   120

    A Universal Concept of Education   127

    Conclusion: Literacy and Numeracy as Methods   129
    for Reflecting on the Good Life

7   Mediating the Effects of World Culture and Economy   131

    The Meaning of Cultural Centeredness   132

    Centering a Culture: Language   139

    Cultural Centeredness and Cultural Values   143

    Cultural Centeredness in a Managed Culture   146

    Economic Unity and Understanding the Global Economy   147

    Economic Morality: The Search for the Good Life   149

    Conclusion: Culture and Economics   155

8   Summary: The Universal Right to Education   157

    Justification   157

    Education and Children's Rights   158

    Liberty and Education Rights   158

    Nondiscrimination and the Right to Education   159

    Culture, Language, and Education Rights   159

    Environmental Destruction and the Right to Education   159

Human Rights and a Universal Concept of Education   160

Universal Minimum Guidelines for Literacy Instruction   161

Universal Minimum Guidelines for Numeracy   162
Instruction

Cultural Centeredness, Moral Economy, and Social   162
Imagination

Notes   165

Index   179

Preface

My original intention was simply to explore human rights education, which I thought had lost touch with its primary mission. However, I discovered that no universal justification for "the right to education" was provided when this idea was proclaimed in 1948 in Article 26 of the Universal Declaration of Human Rights. Indeed, no one had even bothered to define the meaning of education in the "right to education" except to say that everyone was entitled to elementary schooling.

Being interested in differing cultural concepts of education and human rights, I decided to examine the original debates about the Universal Declaration of Human Rights to see how the writers had handled the issue of cultural differences. I discovered that because of the Cold War and the ideological tensions between so-called capitalist and communist countries, it was impossible to arrive at a common justification for the Universal Declaration of Human Rights. Rather than stall the process by trying to overcome impossible ideological differences, the writers simply agreed that all national ideologies would *eventually* evolve into an acceptance of a common justification. One result of this disregard for finding a truly "universal" set of human rights was the refusal of the U.S. Congress in the 1950s to ratify the Universal Declaration of Human Rights.

Without a universal justification for the "right to education" and a universal definition of "education" as provided for in this right, the right is very difficult to protect and implement. Consequently, I took on the task of finding both a universal justification and a definition. To demonstrate the results of this search, I decided to apply my universal justification and definition to instruction in human rights, literacy, numeracy, cultural centeredness, and moral economy.

In chapter 1, I examine the discussions leading up to the writing of Article 26 and the Universal Declaration of Human Rights. These discussions provide a framework for examining the problem of reconciling cultural differences with universal concepts. In chapter 2, I expand on the topic of education and cultural differences by finding a justification for education that is applicable to indigenous peoples and to minority cultures and languages. The justification for education for indigenous and minority cultures is, in chapter 3, applied to all people in the current global economy and culture. Realizing that the right to education is inseparable from children's rights, I justify children's rights, in chapter 4, by the universal right to education. In turn, I apply children's liberty rights to the concept of education. This mix of cultural, language, and children's rights provides a universal justification and definition for the right to education. In chapters 5, 6, and 7, I use the justification and definition of the right to education to create universal guidelines for human rights education, literacy and numeracy instruction, cultural education, and the study of moral economy.

—*Joel Spring*

1

Justifying Human and Educational Rights

"Everyone has the right to education," proclaims Article 26 of the 1948 Universal Declaration of Human Rights. Is there a universal justification for the right to education? Is there a universal definition of education? Are there minimum guidelines for fulfilling the right to education?

Answers to these questions are of more than academic interest, in view of global educational problems. One sixth of the world's population—nearly 855 million people—is functionally illiterate, while 130 million children in developing countries are without access to basic education. According to the 1999 United Nations' report, *The State of the World's Children 1999*, "Girls crowd these ranks disproportionately, representing nearly two of every three children in the developing world who do not receive a primary education (approximately 73 million of the 130 million out-of-school children)."[1]

In the current world economy, educational deprivation has dire consequences for human welfare. Since the 1970s, income and wealth are increasingly related to years of education as wages increase for jobs requiring technological skills and wages decline for low-skilled jobs.[2] Also, education contributes to health: Population movement and crowded living conditions have enhanced the conditions for the spread of infectious diseases. Rudimentary health education programs can make dramatic improvements in mortality rates. The United Nations Children's Fund estimates that a "10 percentage point increase in girls' primary enrolment can be expected to decrease infant mortality by 4.1 deaths per 1,000, and a similar rise in girls' secondary enrolment by another 5.6 deaths per 1,000."[3] In addition, education can provide citizens with the tools for resisting totalitarian and repressive governments and economic exploitation. Under current conditions, education does contribute to human welfare.

A major difficulty in formulating a universal justification and definition for the right to education is the existence of multiple languages and cultures. This issue was discussed but left unanswered during the writing of the 1948 Universal Declaration of Human Rights. As I explain later, human rights were simply proclaimed without an agreed-on universal justification. In fact, the right to education was announced as if all people shared the same beliefs about learning and development. Article 26 of the 1948 Universal Declaration of Human Rights states:

1.   Everyone has the right to education. Education shall be free, at least in the elementary and fundamental stages. Elementary education shall be compulsory. Technical and professional education shall be made generally available and higher education shall be equally accessible to all on the basis of merit.

2.   Education shall be directed to the full development of the human personality and to strengthening of respect for human rights and fundamental freedoms. It shall promote understanding, tolerance and friendship among all nations, racial or religious groups, and shall further the activities of the United Nations for the maintenance of peace.

3.   Parents have a prior right to choose the kind of education that shall be given to their children.[4]

UNIVERSAL JUSTIFICATION, DEFINITION, AND GUIDELINES FOR THE RIGHT TO EDUCATION

My formulation of a justification for the right to education begins with an exploration of the original debates about the 1948 Universal Declaration of Human Rights. Two important educational ideas emerged from these discussions. One was the difference between authoritarian and nonauthoritarian school systems. This distinction is important for defining a universal concept of education. It is also important, as I argue throughout this book, for unlocking the social imagination of all people so that they can think about alternatives to current political, social, and economic systems.

The second important idea was the educational rights of cultural minorities. Delineating the educational rights of cultural minorities is key to providing a universal justification for education that is applicable to all cultures. In chapter 2, I discuss the educational rights of minority and indigenous cultures in the context of the evolution of a global economy and culture. The meaning of *global economy and culture* is complex and requires discussion of the origins of a world system and the relation between global and local. At the end of this chapter, I present a list of rights under the title: "The Right to Education for Indigenous and Minority Cultures in Multicultural Societies."

The right to education for indigenous and minority cultures provides the basic framework for a universal justification, as I discuss in chapter 3, for education in a global economy and culture. In chapter 3, I elaborate on cultural and educational rights in the context of the 1960 Convention Against Discrimination in Education, global ethics, and the relation between environmental destruction and the right to education.

An important consequence of a universal justification of the right to education, I argue in chapter 4, is the protection of childrens' rights. Exercising the right to education requires that children have the right to adequate nutrition, health care, and housing and the right to protection from exploitive labor and physical abuse. These basic rights must be met before children can exercise their right to education. In addition, children's rights include freedom of ideas and expression and freedom of access to information. These basic intellectual freedoms highlight the right of children to nonauthoritarian school systems and to an education in human rights. Chapter 4 concludes with a set of principles that provide a "Justification for the Universal Right to an Education and Children's Rights."

Because the right to education includes the right to education in human rights, I analyze in chapter 5 existing human rights education programs and then propose universal guidelines for instruction in human rights. In addition, I propose that all children be taught that they have a moral duty to actively protect the rights of others. Based on the universal justification for education and children's rights, I provide in chapter 6 a universal definition of education including basic guidelines for literacy and numeracy instruction. These guidelines are intended to protect local cultures while preparing students to decide on the advantages and disadvantages of the global economy and culture. These guidelines are also intended to provide minimum guidance in the organization of school systems. In chapter 7, I provide educational guidelines for preparing students to mediate the effect of world culture and economics. In the next section, I begin my search for a universal justification of the right to education.

THE RIGHT TO EDUCATION

Can a "right to education" be justified for all the world's peoples regardless of differences in culture, religion, and political and social circumstances? If there is a justification for a universal right to education, should education have the same meaning in every culture? Is there a universal concept of education that is applicable to all cultures?

The rush to compose the 1948 Universal Declaration of Universal Rights left little time to debate these questions. In fact, while recognizing major differences in cultural and political concepts of rights, participants set aside their disagreements to produce a document that might in the future stop the spread of the nationalism and racism that led to World War II. Unfortunately, future generations were left with a hollow document waiting to be given meaning and direction.

Despite efforts since 1948 to implement the "right to education," there is still no universal justification for the right and no universal concept of education. The boldest initiative to ensure the right occurred with the 1990 World Conference on Education for All (EFA) with its rousing theme song,

> Education is the right of all
> For you and for me
> It's action time and time is now
> Let's all heed the call
> Join us, come with us,
> We are on our way
> To Education for All
> By the year 2000.[5]

While delegates joined in singing this hymn to education for all, they were bitterly divided over political and economic educational goals. As a result, there never emerged from their discussions an agreement on a universal concept of education. Sponsored by the United Nations Educational, Scientific, and Cultural Organization (UNESCO), the United Nations Children's Fund (UNICEF), the United Nations Development Programme (NDP), and the World Bank, the World Conference on Education for All, meeting in Jomtien, Thailand, on March 5, 1990, was characterized by an array of conflicting educational purposes. Some delegates wanted the right to an education to be linked to individual liberation and democracy. These delegates declared, "Education is the crucible for democracy and liberty.... Education for All must be oriented towards individual liberation from every form of domination and oppression."[6] In contrast to those advocating education for individual liberation, some delegates wanted basic education to stress moral and spiritual values. Moslem countries were particularly concerned about the ethical and moral aspects of education. As Professor A. Boutaleb observed, "The first revealed word in the *Holy Qu'ran* is 'Read.'"[7] For Moslems, the fundamental reason for literacy was for learning the teachings of the *Qu'ran*. Crown Prince Hassan of Jordan, the leader of a monarchical and antidemocratic nation, stated,

"Education can and should be made to implant human values that should manifest themselves in the endeavors of groups and individuals, and in the struggle to improve the quality of life."[8] Delegates were divided over the economic purposes of basic education. For some, a basic education should include, along with literacy and numeracy, skills for living and increasing national economic growth. Others warned against defining education according to economic outcomes because education for economic development does not necessarily include education for democracy and individual liberation. The most daunting problem for delegates was reconciling a universal declaration of the right to education with cultural differences, particularly those of indigenous peoples.

In an effort to achieve agreement despite significant political, economic, and cultural differences about the meaning of education, the Preamble to the World Declaration on Education for All was written in such a manner that any group can find support for its vision of education. Of course, one could argue that all preambles are filled with high-sounding words waiting to be given meaning. The Preamble states as a justification for education for all:

Recalling that education is a fundamental right for all people, women and men, of all ages, throughout the world;

Understanding that education can help ensure a safer, healthier, more prosperous and environmentally sound world, while contributing to social, economic, and cultural progress, tolerance, and international cooperation;

Knowing that education is an indispensable key to, though not sufficient condition for, personal and social improvement;

Recognizing that traditional knowledge and indigenous cultural heritage have a value and validity in their own right and a capacity to both define and promote development;

Acknowledging that, overall, the current provision of education is seriously deficient and that it must be made more relevant and qualitatively improved, and universally available;

Recognizing that sound basic education is fundamental to the strengthening of higher levels of education and of scientific and technological literacy and capacity and thus self-reliant development; and

Recognizing the necessity to give to present and coming generations an expanded vision of, and a renewed commitment to, basic education to address the scale and complexity of the challenge; proclaim the following.[9]

Oddly missing from the Preamble is any justification of education as necessary for the protection of human rights. Of course, human rights education would undermine the effort at "education for all" by threatening oppressive governments or economic systems. The only reference in the actual articles of the World Declaration on Education for All that comes close to human rights education is the suggestion in Article I, Clause 2, that education "empowers individuals ... to further the cause of social justice."[10] *Social justice* is never defined, although it could have been through reference to Universal Declaration of Human Rights.

Clause 1 of Article I of the World Declaration on Education for All is the only clause that provides a definition of education. The other nine articles are devoted to establishing the conditions for education and the methods for implementing education for all. Article 1 states:

> 1.   Every person—child, youth and adult—shall be able to benefit from educational opportunities designed to meet their basic learning needs. These needs comprise both essential learning tools (such as literacy, oral expression, numeracy, and problem solving) and the basic content (such as knowledge, skills, values, and attitudes) required by human beings to be able to survive, to develop their full capacities, to live and work in dignity, to participate fully in development, to improve the quality of their lives, to make informed decisions, and to continue learning. The scope of basic learning needs and how they should be met varies with individual countries and cultures, and inevitably, changes with the passage of time.[11]

In addition to *not* identifying the specific content of a universal education—there is a vague reference to literacy, oral expression, and numeracy—there is no reference to human rights education or to a specific means by which education will be adapted to "individual countries and cultures." For instance, it was not the intention of the writers of the Universal Declaration of Human Rights that the "right to education" would be used to justify school systems that supported dictatorial governments practicing torture, engaging in random acts of violence, and economically exploiting a subjugated population. The writers of the Universal Declaration of Human Rights did not envision a literacy campaign that would result in political prisoners being able to read their own death warrants.

The World Declaration on Education for All fails to provide an adequate and complete justification of the right to education and definition of education. In part, this is a result of the inability of the writers of the 1948 Universal Declaration of Human Rights to reconcile their differences.

FINDING A JUSTIFICATION AND DEFINITION FOR "EVERYONE HAS THE RIGHT TO EDUCATION"

My search for a universal justification for the right to education and a universal concept of education begins with the original debates over the 1948 Universal Declaration of Human Rights. I use the accumulated debates since 1948 about education and children's rights as a starting point for articulating a justification and concept of universal education.

Two important conditions, I believe, are required for a universal justification for the right to education. First, a justification must protect the right to education for all people, notwithstanding differences in culture, language, and religion. Second, there must be a definition of education that is appropriate to all cultures, languages, and religions. None of these conditions was met when Article 26 was drafted.

These two conditions were only partially mentioned in debates leading to the drafting of the 1948 Universal Declaration of Human Rights. In addition, there was little agreement on a justification for universal rights or even an agreed-on definition of "human right." During the writing of the Universal Declaration of Human Rights, disputes cut across cultural and political lines. Directing the effort, John Humphrey, Director of the United Nations' newly created Division of Human Rights, wondered whether the competing sides could ever agree on a declaration of rights. Leaving his academic position at Montreal's McGill University Law School in 1947 for the untested waters of the United Nations (UN) human rights efforts, Humphrey found himself embroiled in a dispute over the nature and protection of human rights between advocates of Asian and European social concepts and capitalist and communist economic ideologies.

The 1947 opening session of the Human Rights Commission was the first attempt in human history by an international group to identify and agree on common values and beliefs shared by the world's cultures. After Humphrey organized the Human Rights Commission, Eleanor Roosevelt, the U.S. champion of human rights, was elected chairperson of the Commission, with P. C. Chang, China's representative to the UN's Economic and Social Council, elected vice-chairperson. At the opening session, the major philosophical division was between vice-chairperson Chang, who was a Confucian scholar, and the Western–liberal-thinking Charles Malik of Lebanon. Humphrey recalled, "Chang and Malik were too far apart in their philosophical approaches to be able to work together on a text.... Chang suggested that I put my other duties aside for six months and study Chinese philosophy.... This was his way of saying that Western influences might be too great, and he was looking at Malik as he spoke."[12]

Europeans claimed a human rights tradition that originated with the English Magna Carta and was expanded on by 18th-century philosophers of the European Enlightenment. However, European representatives could not agree on the final outcome of this human rights tradition. They were divided over concepts of individualism versus collectivism. Charles Malik represented the individualist interpretation of human rights. Humphrey summarized Malik's views:

- The human person is more important than any group to which he may belong.

- His [/her] most sacred and inviolable possessions are his [/her] mind and his [/her] conscience.

- Any pressure on the part of the state, religion or race involving the automatic consent of the individual is reprehensible.

- The social group to which the individual belongs may, like the human being himself [/herself] be wrong or right: The human person alone is the judge.[13]

Valentin Tepliakov, the Soviet Union's representative to the Commission, and labor leaders from European countries immediately attacked Malik's individualist philosophy. Humphrey summarized these opposing positions:

- The human person was essentially a social being.

- Unrestricted individual liberty was impossible in any modern community.

- In an organized society, groups could not be prevented from putting pressures on individuals.

- [There is a] coexistence and closely knit interdependence of the state and the individual.[14]

Cultural rights also represented a major stumbling block for the Commission. The problem was the difference between discrimination and protection of minority cultures. In the process of creating the Commission, Trygve Lie, Secretary-General of the United Nations, proposed two separate subcommissions to deal with discrimination and minority cultures. These subcommissions would play a significant role in investigating educational discrimination. Lie made the following distinctions between the two subcommissions:

- Discrimination: "the prevention of any action which denies to individuals or groups of people equality of treatment which they may wish."[15]

- Protection of minority cultures: "the protection of non-dominant groups which, while wishing in general for equality of treatment with the majority, wish for a measure of differential treatment in order to preserve basic characteristics which they possess and which distinguish them from the majority of the population."[16]

A subcommission focusing on minority rights was not approved by the Human Rights Commission because, according to Humphrey,

"The national states which control the United Nations are more interested in assimilating their minorities—sometimes called nation-building—than in helping them retain their identities."[17] Consequently, the Human Rights Commission neglected cultural and linguistic rights by rationalizing that if all people are treated equally there is no need for special protection of minorities except against discrimination.

"IS THERE ANYTHING SURPRISING IN SYSTEMS ANTAGONISTIC IN THEORY CONVERGING IN THE PRACTICAL CONCLUSIONS?"

The question about antagonistic systems converging, posed by the French philosopher Jacques Maritain, provided a pragmatic solution to ideological differences over universal rights.[18] While justification of human rights might differ, Maritain argued, all belief systems ultimately support human rights, including the right to an education. The major drawback to this pragmatic solution was that it left unanswered basic questions that would plague attempts to implement human rights doctrines. Maritain's argument was presented in the introduction to a collection of symposium papers written in 1947 for UNESCO. The leaders of UNESCO requested the essays as a means of resolving philosophical differences on human rights for the drafters of the Universal Declaration of Human Rights. The general purpose of the symposium was to find a common philosophical basis for protection of human rights.

Maritain's introductory essay stressed that all religious and philosophical systems result in a similar set of moral standards. He believed that all world cultures were evolving in the same direction and that they would inevitably all accept common ethical beliefs. Consequently, one could ignore, he maintained, current philosophical differences and focus on universal human rights. Using an appropriately organic metaphor to illustrate the evolution of religions and cultures, Maritain wrote, "There is a kind of plant-like formation and growth of moral knowledge and moral feeling, it itself independent of philosophic systems and the rational justifications they propound ... while all these systems quarrel over the why and wherefore, yet in their practical conclusions they prescribe rules of behavior which are in the main and for all practical purposes identical for a given age and culture."[19]

Maritain's claim that, despite philosophical differences, all cultures will eventually agree on basic rules of behavior is reiterated in the summary statement of the volume's essays and is echoed in the final draft of 1948 Universal Declaration of Universal Human Rights. Even today, the same argument continues to be made. In his 1998 history of human rights, Paul Gorden Lauren wrote, "Despite their [the world's religions] vast differences, complex contradictions ... cultural variations ... all of the great religious traditions share a universal interest in addressing the integrity, worth, and dignity of all persons, and, consequently, the duty toward other people who suffer without distinction."[20] Lauren suggested that common ideas about human rights exist in such disparate philosophical traditions as China's Mohist and Confucian schools of moral philosophy, the laws of King Hammurabi of ancient Babylon, Islamic doctrines, and the civilizations of pre-Columbian America.

Reflecting this belief in the inevitable evolution of civilizations to a universal acceptance of a common human rights doctrine, the summary statement to UNESCO's 1947 collection of symposium essays ignored ideological differences and skipped over definitions of key words, such as *right* and *liberty*. With the hopeful title, "The Grounds of an International Declaration of Human Rights," the summary statement admitted, "For the purposes of present inquiry, the Committee did not explore the subtleties of interpretations of right, liberty and democracy ... reserving for later examination the fashion in which their differences of interpretation will diversify their further definitions."[21]

Disregarding the possible objections of advocates of laissez-faire government who would not want government entangled in social and economic issues, the summary statement maintained that economic and social rights, which include the right to an education, are necessary for the exercise of political and religious rights. "By liberty they [the essayists] mean ... the positive organization of the social and economic conditions within which men can participate to a maximum as active members of the community and contribute to the welfare of the community ... this liberty can have meaning only under democratic conditions."[22]

However, despite attempts to gloss over differences, a close reading of the 31 collected essays reveals important divisions over the meaning of human rights. Even UNESCO's original questionnaire inviting essays from scholars and political leaders of member nations of the UN acknowledged potential conflicts. Reflecting the growing tensions of the Cold War, UNESCO's questionnaire emphasized the split between "the premise of inherent individual rights ... with a bias against strong central authority and against government interference" and "the other ... based upon Marxist principles and the premise of a powerful central government ... wedded to total planning."[23] Recognizing that the Soviet Union restricted individual freedoms, the questionnaire adopted the hopeful attitude that Communism when "properly applied will eventually permit the fullest degree of individual development and variety."[24] In addition, the questionnaire recognized the possible evolution of differing rights theories in India and

Africa. Despite these qualifications, the questionnaire expressed the hope that respondents would find a "common formulation of the rights of man [/woman] ... [that will] reconcile the various divergent or opposing formulations now in existence."[25]

THE SOCIALIST STATE AND THE UNIVERSAL RIGHT
TO EDUCATION

Serious ideological differences between communist and liberal essayists cast doubt on the belief that human societies are evolving to common concepts of human rights. The essayists Boris Tchechko and Sergius Hessen presented a different view of the ultimate goal of history from that of Maritain. They saw an evolution to communism and the eventual withering away of the state. Their essays underscored differences in concepts of liberty rights and the right to an education.

While analyzing the human rights content of the 1936 Constitution of the Soviet Union, Boris Tchechko justified the authoritarian state and the limitation of political and intellectual freedom in the granting of the right to an education. The 1936 Soviet Constitution provided the right to free universal education to all citizens. However, as Tchechko noted, individual liberties, particularly "liberty of conscience, publication, association, and ultimately, the formation of political parties," were not necessary rights in the Soviet Union.[26] The reason, according to Tchechko, was that these liberties were no longer necessary in a socialist state. He quoted Stalin: "Several [political] parties and, by deduction, party freedom, can only exist in a society in which there are antagonistic classes, with mutually conflicting interests, side by side. In the U.S.S.R., however, there are no such classes."[27] Therefore, in a classless society, there was no need for individual liberty; in fact, individual liberty could result in revolt against the classless society and a regression to capitalism. "Maxim Gorki," Tchechko wrote, "defines individualism as a fruitless attempt by man to protect himself from the violence and oppression of the capitalist State."[28]

Consequently, the right to an education in the Soviet Union meant preparation for a classless society. Because there were no conflicting social classes, there was no reason to support freedom of thought. Everybody was free to believe in communism. Any other point of view was against the interests of the dictatorship of the proletariat and worked against the inevitable direction of history. With the twisted logic that was the hallmark of Soviet Communism, Tchechko wrote that intellectual freedom exists because "intellectuals have equal rights and freedom in a Soviet country, on exactly the same footing as the working classes and the peasants."[29] In other words, intellectuals had the freedom to believe in communism, and there was no reason for intellectuals to hold opposing political ideas because there were no conflicting social classes.

Consequently, in Tchechko's argument, the general protection of human rights and the right to an education were protected by an authoritarian socialist state that screened out any infection from capitalist ideas. The right to an education that supports communism was necessary for the existence of a socialist society. In turn, the socialist state provided the means to exercise human rights and the right to an education.

Sergius Hessen, a professor of History of Education at the University of Lodz, Poland, provided an important variation on Tchechko's argument. In a similar manner, Hessen argued that the evolution of socialist societies made possible the exercise of the right to an education. Historical determinism ensured the inevitable triumph of socialism. Hessen's argument focused on the historical evolution of human rights and the achievement of claims rights.[30]

Writing from a Eurocentric perspective, Hessen traced the evolution of human rights from the absolutist state of the European Middle Ages through liberal, democratic, and socialist states. According to Hessen, in the absolutist state, human rights were defined by the rule of law. In the absolutist state, laws protected citizens from the arbitrary exercise of power by rulers. Of course, laws could be tyrannical. To counter the tyranny of law, the liberal state placed an emphasis on freedom from government control. In the liberal state, human rights were liberty rights, such as freedom of speech, religion, and enterprise. However, the liberal state did not guarantee the ability of citizens to exercise these rights. Poverty, illness, and lack of education could hinder the ability to exercise liberty rights.

The next evolutionary stage, according to Hessen, was the democratic state, which turned liberty rights into claim rights. Claim rights required the state to provide the conditions that made possible the exercise of liberty rights. For instance, the state must ensure social conditions that made it possible to meaningfully exercise free speech rights. In the democratic state, economic and social rights were added to liberty rights. Now human rights included, for example, the right to education, health care, an adequate wage, and decent living conditions. According to Hessen, the democratic state, however, could not provide all these rights equally to all citizens because of the existence of capitalism and social classes. Therefore, according to Hessen, the evolution of the socialist state was necessary to guarantee claim rights.

The socialist state, Hessen argued, added economic rights or the rights of humans as producer and consumer to the list of human rights. The object of economic rights was to ensure freedom from exploitation and the right to the full value of a worker's labor. Consequently, the socialist state embodied the whole history of human rights, including the principle of the rule of law, liberty rights, claim rights, and the new economic rights.

"Communism," Hessen wrote, "is ... not the alternative to liberal Socialism, but rather its constituent. It is not a higher and more distant ideal ... but only a technique of the realization of the rights of man [/woman]."[31] The important principle that communism introduced was "to everyone according to his [/her] need."[32] Socialism, Hessen argued, guarantees only a fairly paid job or "to everyone according to his [/her] work."[33] Therefore, following Hessen's logic, by meeting all human needs, communism ensured the true exercise of human rights. Of course, many of the previous liberty rights, such as the right to free enterprise and speech, became unnecessary in a communist society.

The right to education, considered as part of the inevitable evolution to a communist society, has a variety of meanings. In the absolutist state, education served the purpose of creating obedient citizens who agreed to the rule of law. In a liberal state, people had the freedom to choose an education that reflected their religious, political, and economic beliefs. In a democratic state, education was a claim right, and government was obligated to provide free universal education. In a socialist society, a fair wage ensured that all people had an equal chance to use free universal education. Finally, in a communist society, education ensured equal educational opportunity by teaching an ideology that maintains a communist society.

According to this reasoning, the right to an education in a communist society had the same meaning as it did in the absolutist state. The primary purpose was maintaining obedience to communist laws or the rule of law. Hessen recognized that the communist state returned to an emphasis on the rule of law as opposed to the liberty rights of the liberal state. Hessen wrote, "Indeed, according to Stalin, there can be no real building up of Socialism without the 'atmospheres of security.' 'We need the security of Law now more than ever,' declared Stalin in his speech on the Constitution."[34]

CULTURAL DIFFERENCES AND UNIVERSAL RIGHTS

The essays by Tchechko and Hessen contrast starkly with the ideas of other Western scholars interested in protecting liberty rights in the context of the liberal state. In addition, there are differences between these Western thinkers and Eastern scholars as revealed in essays by the Chinese philosopher Chung-Shu Lo and the Indian political scientist S. V. Puntambekar. Chung-Shu Lo observed that "the problems of human rights were seldom discussed by Chinese thinkers.... There was no open declaration of human rights in China ... until this conception was introduced from the West."[35] In fact, according to Lo, when the concept was introduced, there was no Chinese equivalent word for the term "rights." The Chinese translation of "rights" included two words: *Chuan Li*, meaning "power and interest." Lo claimed this translation was made by an unnamed Japanese writer on Western public law in 1868 because Japan also lacked any equivalent words for human rights.

Although Lo recognized the lack of any human rights tradition in China, he tried to squeeze traditional authoritarian and Confucian concepts of government into a human rights mold. Lo quoted from what he referred to as an old Chinese classic, *Book of History*: "Heaven sees as our people see; Heaven hears as our people hear. Heaven is compassionate towards the people.... Heaven loves the people; and the Sovereign must obey Heaven."[36] Based on this tradition, Lo argued, the Chinese people had the right to revolt against rulers who did not serve the welfare of the people.

However, this right to revolt was not related to any other rights. Traditional Chinese political philosophy supported an authoritarian state as long as the sovereign ruled in the interest of the people. For instance, there was little room in traditional Confucian philosophy for concepts of human rights. As a code of conduct, Confucianism envisioned an authoritarian government managed by enlightened and wise rulers who ensured the moral conduct of the masses. Led by benevolent rulers, government was to protect the welfare of the people.

Overall, Confucius believed that the masses were incapable of learning and following a moral code. In his words, "The common people can be made to follow a path but not to understand it."[37] Confucius ranked members of society according to their level of knowledge. Confucius said, "Those who are born with knowledge are the highest. Next come those who attain knowledge through study.... The common people ... are the lowest."[38]

Because they are incapable of attaining their own welfare, the benevolent ruler must work for the good of the people. In fact, the highest title, "Sage," is reserved for rulers who benefit the masses.

> Tzu-kung said, "If there was a man who gave extensively to the common people and brought help to the multitude, what would you think of him? Could he be called benevolent?"
>
> The Master said, "It is no longer a matter of benevolence with such a man. If you must describe him, 'sage' is, perhaps the right word."[39]

Despite Lo's claim of an ancient right to revolt, Confucius argued that filial piety was the key to avoiding revolution. Concerned with the education of noble men, Confucianism envisioned the good son becoming the good father who then became the good ruler. Learning obedience to the father was preparation for obedience to the ruler or state. According to Confucius, "It is rare for a man whose character is such that he is good as a son and obedient as a young man to have the inclination to *transgress his superiors*: It is unheard of for one who has no such inclination *to be inclined to start a rebellion*" [emphasis added].[40]

Twisting the Western concept of rights, Lo claimed that the Chinese relationship of the ruler to the ruled paralleled the European tradition. Lo observed, "The sovereign as well as the officials were taught to regard themselves as the parents or guardians of the people, and to protect their people as they would their own children."[41] The Chinese idea of the ruler's obligation to manage the masses for their own good was not comparable to the Western tradition of liberty rights.

In contrast to the authoritarian and absolutist concepts of human rights in Chinese tradition and Stalinist theory, S. V. Puntambekar presented a Hindu concept of human rights that focused on the spiritual nature of humans. He also disagreed with the emphasis on reason and science that marked the emergence of human rights doctrines during the European Enlightenment. In criticizing the Enlightenment tradition for suppressing the spiritual nature of life, Puntambekar wrote, "We shall have to give up some of the superstitions of material science and limited reason, which make man too much this-worldly, and introduce higher spiritual aims and values for [human]kind."[42]

For Puntambekar, the purpose of human rights was to free the spiritual side of humans. He argued, "The ordinary condition of man is not his ultimate being. He has in him a deeper self, call it soul or spirit. In each being dwells a light and inspiration which no power can extinguish, which is benign and tolerant, and which is the real man."[43] On the basis of the teachings of Buddha, Puntambekar identified five social freedoms and five individual possessions or virtues necessary for achieving the good spiritual life. Each social freedom was linked to an individual possession or virtue.

Again, it is important to emphasize, that in Buddhism these social freedoms and virtues help the person to escape from worldly desires to a spiritual world or Nirvana. Conceptually, this attitude is quite different from the beliefs of the Enlightenment, Stalinism, Confucianism, or the ideologies of capitalism and democracy. Puntambekar provided the list of social freedoms and individual virtues, shown in Table 1.1.

Puntambekar's list of Hindu human rights casts doubt on the wisdom of simply ignoring justifications for the practice of human rights. For instance, Jacques Maritain might have argued, "The Hindu list of human rights corresponds to a European list. Therefore, there is universal agreement on human rights." There is a problem with this approach, however, when one begins to pin down the meaning of human rights, such as the right to an education. Maritain claimed that disre-

TABLE 1.1
Hindu Concept of Human Rights

Social Freedoms	Individual Possessions or Virtues
1. Freedom from violence	1. Absence of intolerance
2. Freedom from want	2. Compassion or fellow freedom
3. Freedom from exploitation	3. Knowledge
4. Freedom from violation or dishonor	4. Freedom of thought and conscience
5. Freedom from early death and disease	5. Freedom from fear and frustration or despair

Note. From "The Hindu Concept of Human Rights0 by Maritain, *Human Rights: Comments and Interpretations* (Westport, CT: Greenwood Press, 1973), p. 12.

garding justifications and meanings provides a pragmatic method for achieving a statement of human rights. Ironically, this so-called practical approach fails when attempting to practice human rights. For instance, consider from a Hindu perspective Article 26's declaration of the right to education. Puntambekar might argue that the content of education should lead the individual to an escape from worldly desires to spirituality. There is a striking difference between Buddhist educational traditions and Western traditions of educating good citizens and workers. The educational philosopher Timothy Reagan explained Buddhist educational ideals:

> The core of Buddhism is expressed in what is called the *Triple Refuge* (*trisharana*), which is the basic profession of faith for the Buddhist. Every Buddhist recites the Triple Refuge ... "I go to refuge to the Buddha; I go for refuge to the Doctrine (Dharma); I go for refuge to the community (Sangha)".... Buddhism is, at its core, arguably less concerned with metaphysical and theological matters than with psychological ones ... the teachings of Buddha include ... 1. Human life inevitably involves suffering, 2. Suffering arises from our desires, 3. There is a state of being in which there is no suffering, 4. There is a way to achieve this state of being.[44]

CONCLUSION: SEARCHING FOR THE MEANING OF EDUCATION AS A HUMAN RIGHT

A careful reading of UNESCO's 1947 symposium essays reveals unresolved political and philosophical differences. Consequently, Article 26's provision of a "right to education" lacked any agreed-on justification or definition that cut across ideological and cultural boundaries. Obviously, education meant different things to a Buddhist and to a Stalinist.

Two essays in UNESCO's collection attempted to flesh out the meaning of education in relation to human rights and to resolve the problem of cultural differences. The essays by I. L. Kandel on education and A. P. Elkin on indigenous cultures provided a starting point for justifying a universal concept of the right to education and a definition of education that accounts for cultural diversity.

Kandel's presentation—at the time he was professor emeritus of education at Columbia University—outlined the type of education he believed would protect human rights. Arguing from a Eurocentric perspective, he contended that traditional education *did not* protect human rights. The history of education, he maintained, revealed that government schools are primarily used for "indoctrinating the younger generation in ... religious beliefs" and by the "national state ... to develop a sense of loyalty to the political group or nation."[45]

In addition, the indoctrinating function of education was accompanied by unequal educational opportunities which contributed to the separation of social classes. Inequality of educational opportunity, he contended, was reinforced by a lack of awareness by the poor of the possibilities of using education to advance in the social system. Kandel stated, "One of the tragic results of the traditional organization of education into two systems—one for the masses and the other for a select group—is that, even when equality of educational opportunity is provided, certain social and economic classes feel that the opportunities are not intended for them."

Therefore, according to Kandel's argument, providing the right to an education did not necessarily result in protection of human rights. As authoritarian systems of indoctrination, schools could actually undermine human rights. In reference to the free access to primary and secondary education in France, Kandel observed that in "neither case was there, except by indirection, any deep-rooted training for the use and enjoyment of those freedoms which are included in the list of human rights."[46] In fact, Kandel argued, just the opposite occurred because of an authoritarian system of education dominated by examinations.

In addition, Kandel linked human rights education to teacher education. Similar to the examination system creating authoritarian education in the schools, teacher exams and authoritarian training produced authoritarian educators. "If the teacher is to be more than a purveyor of knowledge to be tested by examinations, then the traditional limitations placed upon him by prescribed methods of instruction, and by control through inspection and examinations must be replaced."[47] If students are to be educated in the freedoms given by human rights doctrines, then, according to Kandel, they must have professional freedom which includes "freedom of speech, expression, communication, information and inquiry."[48]

Attacking existing racial segregation in places such as the United States and South Africa, Kandel criticized the use of education "as an instrument of nationalistic policy, which too frequently mean[s] indoctrination in either national or racial separatism and superiority."[49] An education devoted to human rights, he contended, depended on recognition of racial and cultural equality.

Although Kandel was clear about the types of education that *do not* contribute to maintenance of human rights—schools that were indoctrinating, nationalistic, unequal, authoritarian, examination controlled, and with prescribed methods of instruction and curricula—he was somewhat vague about the type of schooling that supported human rights. His ideal school system for protecting human rights included

- training in the methods of free inquiry
- recognition of the contribution of all cultures
- the discipline required to exercise freedom.[50]

Kandel never clearly explained the meaning of discipline in this sense. He simply stated, "Education for the various freedoms demands discipline. To paraphrase Rousseau, man must be disciplined to enjoy the freedoms which are his rights."[51]

Whereas Kandel was vague on the actual content and structure of an education that supported human rights, he did provide a clear outline of what education should not be. According to this outline, the right to an education meant the right to a schooling that:

1. Was *not* unequal.
2. Did *not* practice racial and cultural segregation.
3. Was *not* nationalistic.
4. Did *not* indoctrinate.
5. Did *not* control teacher and student learning through a system of national examinations.
6. Did *not* prescribe methods of instruction.
7. Did *not* deny teachers freedom of speech and inquiry.

I believe that Kandel's presentation provides an important starting point for defining a general concept of education as related to the right to education. The major shortcomings of his presentation were the neglect of cultural differences and the failure to establish education as a universal right. I deal with these issues in the next chapter.

ᕙ 2 ᕗ

Justifying a Universal Right to Education
for Indigenous and Minority Cultures

A universal justification for the right to education must be acceptable to all cultures. Consequently, I examine the meaning of the right to education for minority and indigenous cultures. My general justification is that all people have the right to an education that provides them with the ability and understanding to determine the advantages and disadvantages of the global economy and culture. In other words, all people should have the power to mediate the relation between their own cultures and the current world system.

This justification, as I discuss in this chapter, raises a number of important issues. One issue is the relation of minority and indigenous cultures to the global economy and culture. This issue requires a definition of minority and indigenous cultures and a definition and description of the global economy and culture. The second issue is the seemingly irresolvable conflicts between some cultural practices and human rights doctrines. Should people have the right to cultural practices that violate the Universal Declaration of Human Rights?

The suggestion that a universal justification for the right to education involved determination of the advantages and disadvantages of the global culture and economy was made by the Australian anthropologist A. P. Elkin at UNESCO's 1947 symposium. Unlike other participants, he dealt directly with the issue of cultural rights. A long-time student of Australian Aboriginal culture and advocate of cultural rights for indigenous people, Elkin's essay contained a manifesto, reflecting the language of the time, called "Rights of Primitive Man." A key part of the manifesto was "The Right to Education in Civilization." Unfortunately, from the hindsight of later years, Elkin's manifesto was marred by the use of terms such as "Primitive Man" and "Education in Civilization. However, the manifesto did provide an important step in reconciling human rights education with cultural differences.

COLONIALISM AND THE DEVELOPMENT OF A WORLD SYSTEM

The basic premise of Elkin's justification for the right to education is that all indigenous people were affected by the system of colonialism that developed during and after the 15th century. Elkin's essay was written just as colonialism was being replaced by the current global system. While Elkin's essay was primarily concerned with indigenous cultures, it also had implications for minority cultures.

Understanding the fruits of colonialism and the issues surrounding minority and indigenous cultures is essential for appreciating Elkin's manifesto. In discussing colonialism and the present global system, I use as interchangeable terms "world system," "global system," and "global culture and economics." The terms "colonialism" and "postcolonialism" refer to different stages in the evolution of a world system. The colonial period began in the 15th century and disintegrated in the 1940s and 1950s. Postcolonialism emerged with the creation of new forms of international political and economic organizations and the expansion of transnational corporations. In fact, the creation of the UN and the writing of the Universal Declaration of Human Rights in the 1940s symbolized the transition from colonialism to postcolonialism.

Why is the emergence of the current world system associated with European colonialism? Certainly, international trade routes existed long before Columbus sailed west from Spain in 1492. However, the spread of the Spanish Empire brought the Americas into the arena of world trade and created a true world system. Why Spain? Enrique Dussel argued that Spain, at the time of Columbus's sailing, was on the periphery of an inter-regional system whose center was Bagdad. Portugal had already claimed the trade routes to India by sailing along the coast of South Africa. China was more interested in trade in an inter-regional system that involved traveling west to India. In the 15th century, before Columbus, Chinese traders did travel east to Alaska and possibly to California but found nothing of interest.

"Spain had only one opportunity left," Dussel wrote: "to go toward the center, to India, through *the Occident*, through the West, by crossing the Atlantic. Because Spain bumps into, finds without looking, Amerindia ... and thus inaugurates, slowly but irreversibly, the first *world* hegemony."[1] Seville became the first modern port of the colonial period, followed later by Amsterdam and London. By 1550, Spain had colonized more than 2 million square kilometers, larger than the whole of Europe, along with 25 million indigenous peoples.[2] During that period, European nations moved east, colonizing India, Indonesia, and Southeast Asia, and south through Africa. By 1800, Europeans dominated 35% of the earth's land surface; this figure increased to 67% by 1878 and to 84% by 1914. British dominions, colonies, and protectorates alone extended from Canada through the Caribbean, Central America, the South Pacific islands, Australia and New Zealand, Hong Kong, Southeast Asia, India, and south through the African continent from Egypt to South Africa. The sun never set on the British Empire.[3]

European colonialization was driven by a belief that Europeans were spreading "civilization" and the "true" religion. Memories of the Roman Empire infused Westerners with a bold and grandiose vision of their role in creating a global culture and economy. Arrogantly, Romans, and later Europeans and Americans, justified Western expansionism as necessary for civilizing the world. For the early Romans, the goal of *Imperium romanum*, the geographical authority of the Roman people, was the entire world. The ultimate destiny of the Roman Empire, its leaders believed, was "to civilize" the world's peoples. The Roman *Imperium* was viewed as both a political expression and a source of knowledge. The *Imperium* gave knowledge to the world. The center of knowledge and culture was Rome. Rome contained the perfect *civitas* or civilized political order. The collective ethical life of Rome was *mores*. *Civitas* and *mores* could be exported to the empire. Thus, the city of Rome was the model for the culture and morals of the empire. In this context, those living outside the Roman Empire were without culture and morals. Those outside the empire were considered irrational barbarians or natural slaves. Cicero, as quoted by Anthony Pagden, wrote that Roman conquest of barbarians "is justified precisely because servitude in such men is established for their welfare."[4] Christianity combined with the legacy of Rome to convince Westerners that it was their destiny to civilize and convert the world. For early Christians, barbarian was synonymous with *paganus*. Pagans were both non-Christian and without civilization. *Imperium romanum* and Christianity were considered geographically the same. Consequently, pagans or non-Christians were considered less than human.[5] In this context, it was the duty of the Christian world to convert and civilize all people and to make them pious and virtuous. Among early Christians, *pietas* or pious meant being in compliance with religious laws and loyalty to the family. *Virtus* or virtuous meant a willingness to sacrifice oneself for the good of the Christian community.[6] In *Culture and Imperialism*, Edward Said argued, "There was a commitment which ... allowed decent men and women to accept the notion that distant territories and their native peoples should be subjugated, and ... these decent people could think of the *imperium* as a protracted, almost metaphysical obligation to rule subordinate, inferior, or less advanced people."[7]

As Edward Said demonstrated, colonialism and postcolonialism affected both the colonist and the colonized.[8] Everyone was touched by the spread of European power from the 15th to the 20th centuries. European colonialism brought the world together as Europeans sailed up Chinese rivers or terrorized and subjugated local populations in Southeast Asia, the South Pacific, North and South America, and Africa. World cultures were fundamentally changed as European missionaries, priests, and educators followed military and political power. Civilizations and languages changed, or in some cases disappeared, as colonial trade routes tied the world together. In turn, the traders and colonizers brought home artifacts and ideas from the nations they plundered. The current populations of Europe, particularly those of England and France, are a mixture of previously colonized peoples from India, Pakistan, Africa, Southeast Asia, Africa, and the Caribbean.

In some situations, colonialism dispersed populations around the world and forced them into new relationships. From 1520 to the 19th century, about 14 million enslaved Africans were transported to the Americas.[9] The British, in a constant search to supply their plantations and other enterprises with low-paid workers, often imported and exported laborers from their colonies. The British transported workers from India to Africa and the Caribbean. In the Caribbean, the former British colonies of Trinidad, Tobago, and Guyana share a mixed population of descendants of Africans, East Indians, English, and Portuguese. British establishment and development of Singapore resulted in a mixed cultural population of Tamils, Chinese, Malaysians, and Eurasians. The British used Chinese workers in tin mines and Tamil workers on rubber plantations. After World War II, the British departure from these areas left societies on the brink of racial conflict. In 1964, on a day now celebrated as Racial Harmony Day, Singapore erupted in a violent race riot. One result was the creation of an educational system based on the recognition of the right to education in the mother tongues—Tamil, Malay, and Chinese—and in English.[10]

A good example of colonialism's ethnic mixing is Mauritius in the southwestern Indian Ocean. In 1715, it was settled by French planters who imported African and Malagasy (from Madagascar) slaves. In 1814, the French surrendered the island to the British during the Napoleonic wars. In turn, the British brought in Hindu, Tamil, and Chinese workers. Today, the island is ethnically divided with descendants from "North India (Hindi-speaking, 42%), 'Creoles' of largely African descent (27%), Muslims of Indian origin (16%), Tamils and Telugus of South Indian descent (9%), Chinese (3%), *gens de couleur* (2%) and Mauritians of French descent (2%)."[11]

In the postcolonial world, as the Norwegian anthropologist Thomas Hylland Eriksen indicated, very few ethnic groups have their own territory. Today, most nations are polyethnic. In Eriksen's words, "The current processes of cultural globalisation break down cultural boundaries and make it difficult to defend the idea that a 'people' is culturally homogeneous and unique."[12]

In fact, colonialism contributed to the undermining of the 19th-century European concept of culture. In the romantic vision of Europeans, nations had homogeneous cultural traditions that needed to be protected. Nationalism was linked to the idea of cultural purity. French, English, German, and other European romanticists sang the praises of their countries' cultural legacies. In its most extreme form, the combination of cultural romanticism and nationalism produced Nazism and Italian fascism. Even today, groups, such as the Aryan Nation in the United States link cultural and racial purity with extreme nationalistic proclamations. Today, faced with the fruits of colonialism and current globalization, anthropologists dismiss the idea of cultural homogeneity as a myth created by 19th-century nationalists. Even cultures that were at one time considered "pure" were in fact divided by social class, gender, regionalism, and language diversity.

MINORITY AND INDIGENOUS CULTURES IN MULTICULTURAL SOCIETIES

As a result of colonialism, the place of minority and indigenous cultures in national school systems has become a major issue. This educational issue is reflected in Elkin's manifesto. A minority culture is one that exists in a nation dominated by another culture. Today, all indigenous cultures are minority cultures. On the other hand, not all minority cultures are indigenous cultures. The status of minority culture is often the result of immigration or the forced inclusion of that culture into a larger nation. For instance, the 1990 *World Directory of Minorities* identified Mexican Americans as a minority culture in the United States. This minority status is a product of both U.S. conquest, or colonization, of northern Mexico in the 1840s and later immigration from Mexico.

Currently, the growth of cultural minorities results primarily from immigration from developing countries to high-income countries. According to the World Commission on Culture and Development, the net immigration in recent years is approximately 1.4 million annually, with two thirds of the immigrants originating in developing countries. For instance, in Great Britain and France, over 5% of the population is composed of cultural minorities who have immigrated from former colonies in Asia, West India, and Africa.[13] The United States is host country to immigrants from developing countries around the world, including nations of the former Soviet Union.

In contrast to the role of immigration in creating cultural minorities, some cultures gain minority status by the conquest or creation of new nations. Mayans are a cultural and indigenous minority in Guatemala as a result of the Guatemalan nations being controlled by those sharing a Spanish or Hispanic culture. Table 2.1 provides examples of a few of the world's cultural minorities. In the table , Indians form a cultural minority in South Africa because the British transported workers from India in the 19th century. The Hmong were forced out of China into the mountains of Laos. The Welsh and Burakunin gained minority status by the expansion and consolidation of Great Britain and Japan, respectively.

The distinction between minority cultures and indigenous peoples is, at times, a little fuzzy because all indigenous peoples are now minority cultures. The UN's International Labor Office defined indigenous peoples as "tribal peoples in independent countries whose social, cultural and economic conditions distinguish them from other sections of the national community, and whose status is regulated wholly or partially by their own customs or traditions."[14] In the framework of colonialism, the International Labor Office expanded on the definition to include

TABLE 2.1
A World of Minorities: Selected Groups and Countries, 1989

Country	Minority	Number (in millions)	Percentage of Total Population
Canada	Indians and Metis	0.6–1.2	2.5–4.75
England	Welsh	2.64	4.5
Bulgaria	Turks	0.9	10
Egypt	Copts	6	40
South Africa	Indian	.87	3
India	Adivasis	5.2	7.5
Sri Lanka	Tamils	27	18.2
Japan	Burakunin	2.3	1.6–2.5
Laos	Hmong	.4	10
Malaysia	Chinese	3.9	34

Note. Adapted from "World Directory of Minorities, 1990," by Minority Rights Group, 1995, in Javier Perez de Cuellar, Our Creative Diversity: Report of the World Commission on Culture and Development (Paris: UNESCO, 1995), p. 58.

"populations which inhabited the country, or a geographical region to which the country belongs, at the time of conquest or colonization."[15] In addition, the definition included those groups that identify themselves as indigenous. This definition of indigenous includes, for example, Native Americans and Hawaiians in the United States, Aborigines in Australia, Mayans in Guatemala, Maoris in New Zealand, and Hmongs in Laos. The World Commission on Culture and Development estimated that in 1995 indigenous peoples composed 7% of the population of China and India (80 and 65 million respectively). In the Americas, the largest numbers of indigenous peoples are in Peru (8.6 million) and Mexico (8 million). In Africa, the number is 25 million.[16] The international group Worldwatch estimated that there are at least 300 million indigenous people worldwide and that between 4,000 and 5,000 of the 6,000 world languages are spoken by indigenous peoples.[17]

ELKIN'S MANIFESTO ON CULTURAL AND EDUCATIONAL RIGHTS

Both minority and indigenous cultures face similar education problems about language and culture. An important assumption of Elkin's manifesto is that indigenous cultures, and I include minority cultures, cannot be isolated from outside cultures and that protection of cultural rights must be based on a realistic understanding of their changing nature as a result of contact with the larger global community. Already, Elkin argued, indigenous cultures have been fundamentally changed by the domination of outside cultures. In 1947, Elkin wrote: "'Civilized' power and peoples have disturbed and confused native peoples' ways of life, upset their adjustment to their environments, and indeed, changed the very environments."[18]

In addition, some indigenous and minority cultures have been affected by policies of "cultural ethnocide." For instance, the United States government consciously practiced cultural ethnocide toward Native Americans and Hawaiians. In some cases, cultural ethnocide has been the unconscious result of economic development. The World Commission on Culture and Development defined cultural ethnocide as

> the process whereby a culturally distinct people loses its identity as its land and resource base is eroded, and as the use of its language and social and political institutions, as well as its traditions, art form, religious practices and cultural values are restricted. This may be the result of systematic government policy: but even when due to the impersonal forces of economic development it is still ethnocidal in its effects.[19]

As a result of the exploitation of indigenous peoples, Elkin contended, so-called civilized nations have a responsibility to help these people adjust to cultural change and to protect them from further exploitation. Providing the right to education is a key responsibility of formerly exploiting cultures. The right to education is stated in Item 3 of Elkin's manifesto, which, I recognize, is marred by use of the words "primitive" and "civilized." Elkin's 1947 Rights of Primitive Man:

1. A basic right of primitive man today is the right to be considered a human being in the same manner and degree as civilized man.

2. The right to his own pattern of civilization and personality.

3. The right to education in civilization.

4. The right to community land.

5. The right to economic development.

6. The right to the disposal of one's own labor.

7. Primitive woman's right to a secure sexual and related social and economic position.

8. The mixed-blood minority group's right to the rights of the society of which it forms part.

9. The right of justice.

10. The right to political self-determination.

11. The community's right to freedom of religious beliefs and practices.

12. The right to health of body, mind and spirit.[20]

Most rights in Elkin's manifesto are liberty rights intended to protect indigenous peoples from economic, political, religious, and sexual domination and exploitation by other cultures, particularly European cultures. Even the 12th article, "The Right to Health," is presented as protection from foreign infections and labor practices. In explaining the 12th article, Elkin wrote, "The contact of Europeans with peoples of primitive culture ... has had several disastrous effects. New diseases have been introduced against which no immunity existed. The taking of native from their own environment to work in another quite different one, has taken its toll."[21]

The third article, "The Right to Education in Civilization," is given as both a liberty right and a claim right. As a liberty right, it guarantees that education will *not* be used as a method of imposing a foreign culture and destroying indigenous cultures. In Elkin's words, "The instruments and methods of education introduced and used amongst primitive people must not be instruments of imposed propaganda."[22] Also, as a liberty right, the article provides "the basic right of free personality development within a people's own pattern of civilization."[23]

Elkin specified three claim rights as part of the right to education. These three educational claim rights provide an important guide for reconciling the right to education with cultural rights. Elkin's educational claim rights for indigenous cultures:

1. The development of an appreciation by a people of its own cultural background and of ... an awareness of the cultural changes resulting from contact with [so-called] civilization.

2. The opening of the door, on approved educational principles, to world thought, science, technical achievement, literature and religion, to be used and built into their own changing culture as they find possible.

3. Primitive peoples have a right to benefit from the [so-called] civilized world's advances in both the method and content of education, conceived of in the widest sense. This right derives from, and must be subservient to, their second basic right ["2. The right to his own pattern of civilization and personality"].[24]

HUMAN RIGHTS AND THE END
OF THE COLONIAL SYSTEM

At the time, Elkin's attempts to promote the universality of human rights through recognition of cultural rights were largely ignored. In addition, the pragmatic approach of Maritain and other participants in drafting the Universal Declaration of Human Rights failed. Philosophical differences undermined attempts to implement the Universal Declaration of Human Rights and exposed the flaws caused by ignoring the difficult questions of political and cultural differences. The Cold War took a heavy toll on those trying to defend the universality of the document. In the United States, the Declaration's economic and social rights clashed with the values held by Americans wedded to principles of free enterprise and laissez-faire government. Advocates of the free market did not believe that claim rights should obligate governments to ensure, as provided in Article 23, "Everyone has the right to work ... to protection against unemployment ... to equal pay for equal work ... [and] to form and to join trade unions for the protection of his interests."[25] Many segregationists objected to equal rights "without distinction of any kind, such as race, color."[26] Swept up in the anticommunist hysteria of the 1950s, the extreme right wing in the United States declared the Universal Declaration of Human Rights a Communist plot designed to undermine the U.S. government and the so-called American way of life. In 1952, Republican Senator John Bricker declared on the floor of the U.S. Senate that the document was a "U.N. Blueprint for Tyranny." The result was the refusal by the U.S. Congress to ratify the Universal Declaration of Human Rights.[27]

Cold-War paranoia swept through the Soviet Union as leaders feared that freedom of press and speech would undermine the dictatorship of the proletariat by spreading bourgeois ideas and values. Parts of the Universal Declaration of Human Rights conflicted with the Soviet argument that certain rights were necessary only as protection against capitalist-controlled governments. In communist societies, it was argued, these rights were counter-revolutionary because they undermined the dictatorship of the proletariat as exercised through the Communist Party. A multiple political party system threatened the true interests of the working class. Consequently, the Soviet government objected to Articles 17, 18, 19, and 20, which provided, "Everyone has the right to own property alone as well as in association with others ... to freedom of thought, conscience and religion ... to freedom opinion and expression ... [and] to freedom of peaceful assembly and association."[28]

During the 1950s, while the Cold War's two superpowers remained divided over political and economic issues, the crumbling of European colonial empires created a demand for recognition of cultural rights, which, in turn, highlighted the question of cultural and language rights in education. Demands for civil rights and protection against racism and sexism accompanied the independence of India from Great Britain, the ouster of the French, Dutch, and English from Southeast Asia, and the independence of African nations and Caribbean colonies.

The breakdown of colonialism in the 1940s and 1950s increased the number of independent world nations and their representatives in the United Nations. These new members demanded a specific UN declaration on the independence of colonial people, the right to racial equality, and the rights of indigenous peoples.[29] On December 14, 1960, the UN adopted the Declaration on the Granting of Independence to Colonial Countries and Peoples with nine major colonial powers abstaining during the voting. The nine abstaining nations—United States, England, the Union of South Africa, Portugal, Spain, Australia, Belgium, France, and the Dominican Republic—continued to resist the recognition of cultural and language rights.

Of particular importance for the meaning of the "right to education" is the Declaration on the Granting of Independence to Colonial Countries and Peoples. This document recognizes cultural and language rights. The Declaration grants equal rights without distinction "as to ... language." In addition, the Declaration states: "All peoples have the right to self-determination; by virtue of that right they freely ... pursue their economic, social and cultural development."[30] Similar to Elkin's propositions about indigenous peoples, this declaration supports cultural rights as part of the right to education.

THE 1960 CONVENTION AGAINST DISCRIMINATION
IN EDUCATION

The meaning of the "right to an education" was indirectly clarified by the continuing pressure on the UN to issue a declaration on racial discrimination. During the 1950s, the job of developing a declaration supporting racial equality was given to the subcommission on the Prevention of Discrimination and Protection of Minorities. In turn, the subcommission, after initiating a study in the 1950s on discrimination in education, asked UNESCO to draft a convention prohibiting discrimination in education. As a result of UNESCO's more energetic efforts, the 1960 Convention Against Discrimination in Education was issued six years earlier than the adoption by the UN General Assembly of the International Convention on the Elimination of All Forms of Racial Discrimination.

Consequently, the 1960 Convention Against Discrimination in Education is a pioneering document that helps clarify the meaning of the right to an education and gives recognition to language rights. This Convention is a guide for ensuring that everyone has a right to an education. The Convention defined "discrimination" as "any distinction, exclusion, limitation or preference."[31] Identified as objects of discrimination in education are:

1. Race

2. Color

3. Sex

4. Language

5. Social class

6. Religion

7. Political opinion

8. National origin.[32]

The exercise of language rights is recognized as one possible exception in allowing distinctions in school systems. Although unequal educational opportunity based on language and religion differences was forbidden by the Convention, the document did stipulate that "the following situations shall not be deemed to constitute discrimination: ... The establishment or maintenance, for religious or linguistic reasons, of separate educational systems or institutions offering an education which is in keeping with the wishes of the pupil's parents or legal guardians." By stating that "participation ... is optional," the Convention tried to limit the possibility that separate religious and language schools would result in discrimination.

Also, the Convention Against Discrimination in Education introduced the ideas of biculturalism and bilingualism. In Article 5 of the Convention, the right to "the use or the teaching of their [national minorities] own language" was qualified by the important statement that "this right is not [to be] exercised in a manner which *prevents the members of these minorities from understanding the culture and language of the community as a whole and from participating in its activities.*"[33]

Article 5 paralleled Elkin's concerns that indigenous cultures have access to the benefits—which they determine—of global culture. In other words, protecting indigenous or minority cultures and languages should not result in exclusion from the dominant culture and language of a nation. Exclusion could cause further exploitation and control by the dominant culture and could deny children of minority or indigenous cultures the opportunity to participate in or reap whatever benefits they believe are available from the dominant culture.

Therefore, the right to an education that is free of discrimination is bilingual and bicultural for language and cultural minorities. People have a right to an education in their own language and culture. They also have a right to an education in the language and culture of the dominant group so that they can have equal economic and social opportunities and access to whatever benefits that they might want from the dominant culture.

A UNIVERSAL COVENANT OF LINGUISTIC HUMAN RIGHTS

The Convention Against Discrimination in Education and the concerns of indigenous peoples highlighted the importance of language rights. As exemplified by Singapore, Mauritius, the United States, and other postcolonial nations, language rights are a potential source of conflict in multicultural societies. It is generally recognized that there is an inseparable relation between language and culture. Particular words often embody cognitive and affective meanings that defy translation into other languages. In addition, literary and oral traditions depend on the preservation of language. In other words, the right to one's culture requires the right to one's language.

A long-time champion of linguistic and cultural rights, Tove Skutnabb-Kangas, proposed a universal covenant protecting linguistic human rights as part of the protection of cultural rights. These linguistic rights add an important dimension to the concept of a right to an education. Key to her proposal was the definition of a mother tongue. A mother tongue, she wrote, can be distinguished as "the language one learned first (the language one has established the first long-lasting verbal contacts in)" or "the language one identifies with/as a native speaker of; and/or the language one knows best."[34]

According to her proposed Universal Covenant of Linguistic Human Rights, which must be considered in relating a universal concept of education with the protection of cultural rights, everybody has the right:

- To identify with their mother tongue(s) and have this identification accepted and respected by others.

- To learn the mother tongue(s) fully, orally (when physiologically possible) and in writing.

- To education mainly through the medium of their mother tongue(s), and within the state-financed educational system.

- To use the mother tongue in most official situations (including schools).

- For other languages whose mother tongue is not an official language in the country where the person is resident, to become bilingual (or trilingual, if s/he has two mother tongues) in the mother tongue(s) and (one of) the official language(s) (according to her own choice).

- The relation between languages to any change ... [in] mother tongue.... [being] voluntary (includes knowledge of long-term consequences) ... [and] not imposed.

- To profit from education, regardless of what her mother tongue is.[35]

Of fundamental importance to Tove Skutnabb-Kangas's Universal Covenant of Linguistic Human Rights is the stress on bilingual education if the student's language is not the official national language or the language of global culture and economics, which at this time is English. Bilingualism resolves the problem of maintaining the mother tongue and associated culture while ensuring that students have access to the world's knowledge.

This Covenant reflects the rights provided by the UN 1991 Declaration on the Rights of Persons Belonging to National or Ethnic, Religious and Linguistic Minorities and the International Labour Organisation's Convention No. 169 on the rights of indigenous peoples. The 1991 Declaration specifically recognized the right to learn one's mother tongue. Article 4 stated, "States should take appropriate measures so that, wherever possible, persons belonging to minorities may have adequate opportunities to learn their mother tongue or to have instruction in their mother tongue."[36]

Convention No. 169 took a broader approach by insisting on education in the mother tongue and the dominant or official language of the nation. This approach supports the idea of bilingual education for minority language groups. In reference to education in the mother tongue, Article 28 of the Convention stated, "Children belonging to the peoples concerned shall, wherever practicable, be taught to read and write in their own indigenous language or in the language commonly used by the group to which they belong.... Measures shall be taken to preserve and promote the development and practice of the indigenous languages of the peoples concerned."[37] Learning the dominant or official language is also stressed in the same article of the Convention: "Adequate measures shall be taken to ensure that these peoples have the opportunity to attain fluency in the national language or in one of the official languages of the country."[38]

ARE CULTURAL AND LINGUISTIC RIGHTS IN CONFLICT WITH UNIVERSAL HUMAN RIGHTS?

Is a universal concept of human rights in conflict with cultural rights? There is only a conflict, anthropologists now argue, if you cling to the 19th-century concept of nationalism and cultural purity. Given the multicultural nature of most of the world societies, protection of cultural rights is possible only if all cultures recognize the rights of other cultures.

During the postcolonial period, the strongest voices heard against universal rights have been cultural relativists. Cultural relativists have argued that there are no universal concepts that can be adopted by all cultures. Universal rights represent a form of cultural invasion. In response to cultural relativists, the University of Sussex anthropologist Richard Wilson wrote, "Cultural relativism provides an inaccurate set of descriptions ... since it wields a misguided conception of culture.... The various relativisms totalise and reify 'culture,' constructing it as internally uniform and hermetically bounded."[39] Similar to 19th-century anthropologists, Wilson argued, current cultural relativists neglect the legacy of colonialism.

For instance, in colonized countries such as Mauritius, Singapore, and the United States, there must be some commonly accepted agreement among all cultural groups if cultural rights are to be protected. This has meant some form of compromise. These compromises, of course, have not completely ended intercultural rivalry. Squabbles still continue over issues of language and schooling.

In fact, education is often the most contentious area in postcolonial societies, followed by language and religion. What should be the language used in schools? What culture should be reflected in the curriculum? In the United States, questions about bilingual schooling and multicultural curricula have divided communities. In 1998, Californians voted on a bilingual referendum that resulted in significantly reducing access to bilingual programs by the Spanish-speaking community. English-only groups have used their political power to make English the official language of many states while ignoring the concerns of minority language communities.

In Mauritius, the school system offers optional classes in "ancestral tongues." However, determining the official language of the schools required a compromise over the 15 different languages spoken in the nation. The most common language, Kreol, a form of French Creole, is seldom written. The result was English as the official language. Interestingly, English is no one's ancestral language because most of the English colonists returned to England. Erickson concluded, "By choosing English, an ethnically neutral language, as the language of the state, Mauritians avoided turning nation-building into a particularistic ethnic project at the beginning."[40]

The cultural compromises required by the reality of multicultural nations provide a justification for human rights doctrines that protect cultural rights. Human rights doctrines do require that cultural and religious practices do not violate human rights. Article 2 of the 1992 UN Declaration on the Rights of Persons Belonging to National or Ethnic, Religious and Linguistic Minorities proclaimed, "Persons belonging to national or ethnic, religious and linguistic minorities have the right to enjoy their own culture, to profess and practice their own religion, and to use their own language, in private and in public, freely and without interference or any form of discrimination."[41]

Cultural relativists might consider human rights doctrines a form of cultural imperialism. On the other hand, in recent centuries the problem is to protect cultures from eradication by outside forces. Human rights doctrines provide protection against these destructive forces. However, this protection does require conformity to human rights. Similar to Mauritius's compromise over language, cultural survival requires a compromise that accepts human rights doctrines, including the right to education.

The legal scholar Michael Perry approached cultural relativism from the perspective that there are universal human needs. These human needs take precedence over other issues arising in a multicultural society. These needs include biological needs, such as food, shelter, and protection from physical harm and diseases, and social needs, such as affection and community. Perry wrote, "Some significant needs, some social needs as well as biological, are shared across the human species: the needs that are the correlates of the shared appetites and sense. Some needs are universal and not merely local in character. Some needs are *human*."[42]

Of course, different cultures have their own distinct means of fulfilling needs, such as differing diets and food preferences, methods for preventing and curing diseases, forms of family organization, religious practices, and other social practices. However, cultural protection requires that some limitations be placed on social practices so that one group does not infringe on the cultural practices of others. In a multi-cultural society, this requires a delicate balance between cultural practices and cultural rights. Sometimes it is impossible to achieve a satisfactory resolution of cultural conflicts.

Consider the issue of abortion rights in the United States. Some religious groups, such as Catholics and fundamentalist Protestants, have considered abortion to be murder. In their religious traditions, the fetus is a human. In fact, antiabortion groups can claim that abortion is a violation of the Universal Declaration of Human Rights, which protects human life. On the other hand, proabortion groups have argued that abortion is a woman's right whose exercise is necessary for protecting society and mothers from unwanted births. By increasing the population, placing a drain on family budgets, and increasing the numbers of neglected and homeless children, unwanted children, proabortion groups argue, create an economic, social, and emotional strain on the family and society. Although the U.S. government recognizes the right to abortion, antiabortion groups have justified the use of violence against abortion clinics as necessary for protecting the human right to life.

Consider the cultural conflict over the contentious practice of female circumcision. In some African societies, female circumcision is considered morally proper and, for some, ennobling. It is also believed that removing the clitoris enhances the girls' well-being. Often, mothers submit their willing daughters to this practice. Is it a matter of "cultural preference" if I find the practice abhorrent, or is it a matter of human rights? Is it a violation of women's rights? Both the UN Declaration on the Elimination of Violence Against Women and the Sub-Commission for the Prevention of Discrimination and Protection of Minorities have adopted resolutions that female circumcision violates the rights of children and women. Does it violate human rights if mothers and daughters willingly participate? Is it a violation only if mothers and daughters object and are forced to participate?

Therefore, it is possible that human rights doctrines alone do not in all cases provide a means for reconciling cultural differences. Abortion and female circumcision involve human rights issues that are difficult to resolve and can, particularly in the case of abortion, result in violence and social instability. These situations require, according to Michael Perry a "productive moral discourse" across cultural boundaries.[43] These productive moral discourses assume that cultures divided over moral issues, such as abortion, can achieve some form of compromise through a critical dialogue.

The right to education could play an important role in fostering "productive moral discourses." In schools, dialogues over cultural differences could resolve some of these contentious cultural differences.

However, a productive moral discourse requires that schools are not used, in Kandel's words, as nationalistic institutions for indoctrination into the culture of the dominant group and into beliefs that support racial separatism and superiority. For a productive moral discourse, schools must recognize freedom of speech and access to information for teachers and students and must teach about human rights. Schools could become centers for discussion of dissenting cultural discourses.

THE EDUCATIONAL RIGHTS OF INDIGENOUS PEOPLES

In the 1990s, the Draft Declaration of Indigenous Peoples Rights was an attempt to resolve potential conflicts between cultural rights and the more general aspects of human rights. In addition, it represented an expansion of Elkin's original concerns. The Draft Declaration is an early product of the Working Group on Indigenous Populations of the United Nations Sub-Commission on Prevention of Discrimination and Protection of Minorities. The ultimate goal of the Sub-Commission is UN acceptance of a Declaration of Indigenous Peoples Rights by the end of the International Decade of Indigenous Peoples. In drafting the Declaration, numerous indigenous peoples from all over the world have sent representatives.[44]

The Draft Declaration resolved the potential conflict between human rights and cultural rights by extending cultural rights to all people as long as they do not violate the Universal Declaration of Human Rights. In this context, universal acceptance of human rights becomes the glue that holds together multicultural societies and protects indigenous cultures.

The acceptance of universal human rights is basic for maintaining an argument for the protection of cultural rights. The Draft Declaration of Indigenous Peoples Rights asserted that the violation of cultural rights is a violation of human rights. The violation of human rights results, according to the Declaration, in indigenous peoples losing control over their own destiny. Similar to Elkin's manifesto, the Declaration emphasized the importance of indigenous peoples controlling the impact of outside forces and internal social and economic growth. The Declaration asserted, with regard to human rights and development:

> That the indigenous peoples have been deprived of their *human rights and fundamental freedoms*, resulting ... in their colonization and dispossession of their lands, territories, and resources, thus preventing them from exercising, in particular, *their right to development in accordance with their own needs and interests* [emphasis added].[45]

The Declaration also made the connection between the self-interest of indigenous peoples in ending cultural discrimination and the modification of indigenous cultures to include antidiscrimination rights. The Declaration stated:

> Welcoming the fact that indigenous peoples are organizing themselves for political, economic, social and cultural enhancement and to bring about an end to all forms of discrimination and oppression wherever they occur.[46]

In other sections of the Declaration, human rights doctrines were used to protect cultural rights. For instance, Article 1 stated:

> Indigenous peoples have the right to the full and effective enjoyment of all human rights and fundamental freedoms recognized in the Charter of the United Nations, the Universal Declaration of Human rights and international human rights law.[47]

In Article 1, human rights were used to protect cultural differences, while requiring that cultural and religious practices do not violate human rights. Therefore, the protection of cultural rights requires weaving human rights into the modification and development of indigenous cultures.

On the right to education, the Declaration asserted that indigenous children have a right to education in their own language and according to cultural practices. Article 15 stated:

> Indigenous children have the right to all levels and forms of education of the State. All indigenous peoples also have this right and the right to establish and control their educational systems and institutions providing education in their own languages, in a manner appropriate to their cultural methods of teaching and learning.[48]

Therefore, the Draft Declaration of Indigenous Peoples Rights supported arguments that acceptance of human rights is the main hope for protection of cultures, particularly indigenous and minority cultures. This argument provides a justification for both universal human rights and the right to education. In regard to universal rights and the legacy of colonialism, this justification can be summarized thus: The multicultural legacy of colonialism requires recognition of:

1. Universal rights as necessary for protecting cultural rights in multicultural societies.
2. Universal rights as necessary for ensuring the social stability of multicultural societies that recognize cultural rights.
3. The right to education as a means of promoting moral discourses about cultural conflicts.

CONCLUSION: JUSTIFYING THE RIGHT TO EDUCATION IN THE CONTEXT OF THE GENOCIDE OF INDIGENOUS PEOPLES AND COLONIALISM

The rape of indigenous peoples, the legacy of colonialism, and the existence of minority cultures provide a basic justification for the right to education. The key element in this justification is the protection of cultural rights in multicultural societies. In this context, the justification for the right to education reflects Elkin's educational claim rights for indigenous cultures and the needs of postcolonial multicultural societies. In the following list of educational rights, I have included the right to education in one's mother tongue and right to instruction that is appropriate for one's culture. In regard to the right to education for indigenous and minority cultures in multicultural societies, all people have the right to an education that teaches:

1. An understanding of their own cultural and their relation to it.

2. Their mother tongue.

3. The dominant or official language of the nation.

4. An understanding of the effect of the world culture and economy on their own culture and economy.

5. How to control the effects of the world's culture and economy on their own culture and economy.

6. How to conduct moral discourses about cultural conflicts.

7. Human rights.

This list of rights preserves cultural differences and cultural self-determination, while recognizing the existence of a universal body of knowledge that might be of value to all people. It also recognizes the importance of human rights doctrines in protecting cultures in multicultural societies. It is similar to the general principles established for indigenous education at a gathering of native educators from around the world in Santa Fe, New Mexico, in 1997. At the gathering, 14 different models of indigenous education were linked by several overall themes. One of these themes expressed the importance of learning to negotiate the boundaries between local and international cultures. Summarizing this theme, Maenette Kape'ahiokalani Padeken Ah Nee-Benham and Joanne Elizabeth Cooper wrote:

> We want our children to articulate a Native self-identity, to be centered in their unique Native ways of knowing, and to live as proud Native people. Pride and knowledge of one's culture, history and language meant that

our children would respect their ancestors and take care of their home-
land. Finally, we want our children to confidently negotiate the boundaries between their Native and non-Native worlds and make choices that
maintained self and cultural integrity.[49]

Recognizing the legacy of colonialism and growing global hybridization, "The Right to Education for Indigenous and Minority Cultures in
Multicultural Societies" would prepare people for the determination of
the benefits and detriments of world culture and economics. The determination of what aspects of world culture are beneficial, according
to Elkin, should be made by the members of particular cultures. As
Elkin argued, world knowledge should be "used and built into their
[indigenous peoples] own culture as they find possible."[50]

Translated into a global framework, this means that people would
retain the right to determine the benefits of world knowledge and the
right, if they choose, to integrate that knowledge into their own culture.
The exercise of the right to determine the benefits of global culture,
without its being imposed by a dominating economic or political
power, stops the cultural imposition practiced by colonial powers and
modern global economics. In addition, human rights and education
protect cultural differences and mother tongues, while ensuring a productive moral discourse about cultural conflicts.

In the next chapter I justify the right to education in the context of
global culture and economics. Cultural and language rights remain important considerations in evaluating the effects of globalization on the
right to education.

⋙ 3 ⋘

The Right to Education
in a Global Culture and Economy

The previously stated "Right to Education for Indigenous and Minority Cultures in Multicultural Societies" is applicable, with modifications and elaboration, to all people in the present global culture and economy. I believe the fundamental justification for the right to education is the undeniable effect on all humans of recent colonialism and of the current global economy and culture. Based on this justification, the goal of education is to provide all people with the ability to determine the personal and group benefits from the ongoing process of the hybridization of the world's cultures and the economic impact of global financial structures. This justification and goal provide the guiding principle for determining the minimum content for fulfilling the right to education for all people. Establishing a universal justification for the right to education based on these principles resolves many of the cultural issues raised by the original Universal Declaration of Human Rights.

THE EVOLUTION OF A WORLD SYSTEM

The current global system emerged from past colonial empires. Postcolonialism is an extension of the colonial system. To manage its colonials in the 16th century, Spain was required to simplify the processes involved in expropriation of land, cultural domination, military occupation, and political control. The result was the growth of government bureaucracy and international financial management. In differing degrees, other European governments organized international systems of financial and political control. In this process were the seeds of the current world system. Europeans justified capitalist and free-trade economics as beneficial for all the world's peoples in a manner similar to arguments about spreading "civilization" and the "true" religion. Consider the argument made by the great 19th-century capitalist theorist Adam Smith. On the negative and positive aspects of colonialism, Smith wrote, "By uniting, in some measure, the most distant parts of the world, by enabling them to relieve one another's wants, to increase one another's enjoyments, and to encourage one another's industry, their general tendency would seem to be beneficial."[1] The major negative factors, according to Smith, were the result of the imbalance of power between nations. This could be rectified by creating a true world market based on free trade. Smith argued: "But nothing seems more likely to establish this equality of force than that mutual communication of knowledge and of all sorts of improvements which an extensive commerce from all countries to all countries naturally, or rather necessarily, carries along with it."[2]

Also in the 19th century, Karl Marx and Friedrich Engels recognized the role of colonialism in building a world system. They wrote: "Modern industry has established the world market, for which the discovery of America paved the way.... [The] need of a constantly expanding market for its products chases the bourgeoisie over the whole surface of the globe.... The bourgeoisie, by the rapid improvement of all instruments of production, by the immensely facilitated means of communication, draws all, even the most barbarian nations into civilizations."[3]

Most writers have neglected the importance of Japan in building a world system in the 19th and early 20th centuries. As I argued in *Education and the Rise of the Global Economy*, 19th-century Japan strengthened its government and military system and imported European forms of schooling as preparation for challenging the expansion of European countries into Asia. The Japanese government's colonial expansion in the early 20th century and its participation in World War II were justified by claims of protecting Asia from European and American exploitation. After World War II, Japan would continue its role in the global system.[4]

The organization of the UN and the Universal Declaration of Human Rights symbolized the world system that emerged after World War II. Rather than single nations controlling particular land masses, the postcolonial system was organized around international organizations and financial systems and transnational corporations. Of course, these new organizations did not reduce the power of former colonial nations, such as the United States, Japan, and the nations of Europe (or, as presently organized, the European Union). During the postcolonial period, economists and political analysts argued that the power of transnational corporations was replacing the power of the nation state. By the 1980s and 1990s, new information technology, by speeding up communication, tightened the linkages in world financial markets and in and between transnational corporations. The development of recent globalization has been well documented in many books and articles.[5]

Walter Mignolo identified four stages of globalization leading to the increasing influence of transnational corporations. The first two stages are phases in colonialism, and the third stage represents the rise of the United States as a superpower after World War II. The final stage focuses on transnational corporations.

Four Stages of Globalization

1. Christianization (Spanish Empire).

2. Civilizing mission (British Empire and French colonization).

3. Development and modernization (United States imperialism).

4. Transnational corporations.[6]

Currently, globalization is taking place against a background of concern about protecting local cultures and languages. This is a logical outgrowth of the revolt against colonialism that occurred after World War II. Part of that revolt, as I described previously, was an increasing interest in protecting indigenous and minority cultures. Now threats to local cultures and languages are resulting from the influence of transnational corporations with their use of advertising, control of media, and promise of high-paying jobs.

Under colonialism, the English enforced English-only policies in colonial schools and governments. Now, rather than being forced to learn English, non-English speakers voluntarily rush to learn English because it is the language of international business and scholarship. As a result of colonialism and current globalism, 75% of the world speaks only 12 languages. Because of China's large population, Chinese is the most frequently spoken language. However, the other rankings according to numbers of speakers reflect the influence of colonialism and transnational corporations: Chinese, English, Spanish, Russian, Hindi, German, Japanese, Arabic, Bengali, Portuguese, French, and Italian.[7]

As I discussed previously, language is directly related to culture, but it is a mistake to assume that because large numbers of people speak English they have adopted English and American cultures. Many of the world "Englishes" are hybridizations of local languages and English. In India and Nigeria English usage reflects the grammar and syntax of local languages.[8] In the same manner, it is a mistake to assume that global culture and economics directly control local cultures and economies. Similar to language, a process of cultural hybridization occurs in the interaction between the global and the local.

McCULTURE AND THE HYBRIDIZATION OF WORLD CULTURES

Without a doubt, the major factors in the current hybridization of cultures are media, advertising, and brand names. Consider the effect of media on the interconnectedness of today's world. A *New York Times* story about the 1999 NATO bombings of Serbia opened, "Even after the air raid sirens wailed, Sara, nearly 5, refused to go down to the basement shelter until the 'Ninja Turtles' [television] program was over. Then the night sky turned orange ... and on a hill ... a bomb exploded.... 'There was a big cloud of dust and a huge pressure of the air,' he [Sara's father] said. 'I told Sara, Where are our Ninja turtles to help us now? and then we went to the shelter.'"[9]

Consider Nelson Mandela's amazement after landing at Goose Bay in the Arctic Circle and being greeted by young Inuit chanting, "Viva ANC [African National Congress]!" The Inuit had watched Mandela's release from a South African prison on television. In his autobiography, *Long Walk to Freedom*, Mandela recalled, "What struck me so forcefully was how small the planet had become during my decades in prison; it was amazing to me that a teenage Inuit living at the roof of the world could watch the release of a political prisoner on the southern tip of Africa. Television had shrunk the world, and had in the process become a great weapon for eradicating ignorance and promoting democracy."[10]

Euphemistically called McCulture, an expanding culture and economics of fast food franchises, clothing chains, shopping malls, world music and media, and international corporations encircle the earth. In almost every population center, there are malls and international franchises, including Taco Bell restaurants in Mexico City, McDonalds in Beijing, The Gap in Venezuela, Disney theme parks in France and Japan, the pounding beats of rock music on the streets of Manila, Toyotas rambling through the jungles of Africa and South America, T-shirts advertising the Hard Rock Cafe in New York on peasant youth in Ecuador, and cinema signs blazing with the titles of U.S. films in the major world's languages.

Touring the small Caribbean island of Saint Lucia, the only restaurant I could find open on Sunday in a small town was a Kentucky Fried Chicken (KFC) in a strip mall. As I discovered at the local KFC, McCulture is not a simple case of Western or Japanese domination.

Sitting next to me in the KFC was a young male descendent of Arawak Indians and Africans who asked me, "How do you like the United States?"

"I was born there," was my simple reply. In turn, I asked, "What do you think of the United States?"

Indicating that he wanted to finish my half-filled container of french fries, he answered, "It's the land of death. It kills the world."

Cultures are a hybridization of the local and global. Allan and Carmen Luke have documented the blending of global and local cultures in Thailand along with the international effects of educational policies. Teaching at the University of Queensland in Australia, the Lukes went to Thailand as part of what they described as an attempt to increase university revenues through a "burgeoning educational export industry focused principally on Asia."[11] In their words, "The educational export industry is one of the fastest growing sectors of the Australian economy."[12]

Their purpose in Thailand was to assist educational development in the Chiang Mai and Chiang Rai provinces where government schools were having difficulty educating indigenous people, such as the Hmong, Karen, and Ha. On arriving, the Lukes found a world of middle-class youths seemingly preoccupied with "MTV, video games, Michael Jordan, the Spice Girls and hanging out in shopping malls."[13]

In contrast, at the bottom of the social scale were refugees and guest workers living in extreme poverty. In addition, European and North American ecotourists roamed the markets and the countrysides in the search of a "real" nature experience. "On the Myanmar-Thai borders," the Lukes wrote, "kids wear Chicago Bulls hats back to front, pirated copies of Hong Kong videos are offered, and Thai made Toyota pick-up trucks rule the road."[14] Their cell-phone–toting Thai educational colleagues, many of them educated in the United States, spoke the language of global school reform by using terms such as school-based management, performance indicators, and quality assurance.

What the Lukes soon discovered was that global culture was being transformed to fit local needs and power structures. Thai educators altered global educational policies to meet local conditions. Local counterculture youth dressed like North American bikers, and hippies blended Thai folk songs and Chinese music with U.S. folk/rock traditions. Symbolically, the rock bands used Western instruments and traditional Thai instruments. The actual result of global culture, according to the Lukes, is "hybridization."[15] As the Norwegian anthropologist Thomas Hylland Eriksen argued, the key words of cultural globalization resulting from migration and transnational communication are creolization and hybridization.[16]

Hybridization is also caused by the worldwide movement of people. Cvetkovich and Kellner wrote: "A transnational diaspora from every continent involving vast migrations of peoples and individuals produces the conditions for new transnational hybridized cultures and identities."[17] They used a quote from Salman Rushdie's short stories *East, West* to illustrate their point about the growing hybridization of personal identity. An Indian character reflected, after obtaining an English passport, on the problems presented by his increased cultural choices:

> But I, too, have ropes around my neck, I have them to this day, pulling me this way and that, East and West, the nooses tightening, commanding, *choose, choose.*
>
> I buck, I snort, I whinny, I rear, I kick. Ropes, I do not choose between you. Lassoes, lariats, I choose neither of you, and both. Do you hear? I refuse to choose?[18]

The Report of the World Commission on Culture and Development came to a similar conclusion about the hybridization of world culture. Sponsored by UNESCO and written by Javier Perez de Cuellar of Peru and other members from around the world, the Report recognized that developed countries play the primary role in shaping global culture. However, this influence has been declining slightly since the 1970s. Using statistics on the export of cultural goods, such as printed matter and literature, music, visual arts, cinema, and photography, the Commission estimated that in 1975 developed nations exported about 96% of the world's cultural goods, but by 1991, this percentage declined to about 68.2%. Comparing population with cultural exports, the Commission estimated that countries with a combined population of 31.8% of the world's people exported 68.2% of the world's cultural goods.[19]

Therefore, although developed nations dominate cultural exports, other nations are having an increased impact on world culture. As the World Commission reported, "It is not just American television that has a worldwide following, but also English pop groups, Japanese cartoons, Venezuelan and Brazilian soap operas, Hong Kong kung fu films, and Indian films in the Arab world."[20]

In addition, the globalization of culture is uneven, with poorer population having less access to media. In 1995, UNESCO estimated there were about 50 televisions per 1,000 inhabitants in developing nations, while there was almost 1 television for every inhabitant in developed nations.[21] Usage of the Internet fits a similar economic profile, with North America having six times more users than do Eastern Europe, Africa, Central and South America, and the Middle East.[22]

Outside cultural influence also varies among nations. For instance, less than 5% of the televisions programs watched in India are foreign, whereas almost 40% of the television programs watched in Australia and the Philippines are foreign, and in Korea the figure is roughly 15%.[23]

In summary, the hybridization of the world's cultures is advancing at a rapid pace, but, the results are uneven and unpredictable. Developed nations have dominant influence over world culture, but their influence is mediated by local cultures. The ability of mass media to influence local cultures is a function of economics. Although the populations of rich nations are more attuned to changes in world culture, with poorer nations following in the wake, no one can escape its influence. It is important, particularly for poorer nations that primarily import cultural goods, that education prepare people to make judgments about advantages and disadvantages of outside cultural influence.

ECONOMIC DEVELOPMENT AND THE INSTRUMENTAL USE OF CULTURE

The hybridization of world culture represents only one dimension of the evolution of global culture. Another facet is the conscious attempt to change culture as part of economic development. Organizations such as the World Bank and the Organization for Economic Cooperation and Development consider cultural changes an important part of their development work. A primary funding source for development projects, the World Bank treats culture as something to be manipulated or changed for the purpose of fulfilling economic policies. The World Bank's 1995 Policy Statement, *Priorities and Strategies for Education: A World Bank Review*, defined basic education as "language, science and mathematics, and communication that provide the foundation for further education and training. It also includes *the development of attitudes necessary for the workplace*" [emphasis added].[24]

In response to the troublesome use of culture as an instrument for economic development, the General Conference of UNESCO passed a resolution in 1991 requesting the UN Secretary-General to "establish an independent World Commission on Culture and Development ... to prepare a World Report ... for both urgent and long-term action to meet cultural needs in the context of development."[25] The 1994 report of the World Commission report, *Our Creative Diversity*, warned: "In the view that emphasizes economic growth, culture does not play a fundamental role but is purely instrumental: It can help to promote or hinder economic growth.... Culture enters into this analysis not as something valuable in itself, but as a means to the ends of promoting and sustaining economic progress."[26] "Thus," the World Commission report stated:

> Protestantism and Confucianism has been thought to encourage saving, capital accumulation, hard work, hygiene and healthy living habits, and entrepreneurial attitudes. More recently, evangelical fundamentalism that has spread in East Asia , Latin America and Africa has been regarded as the religion of micro-entrepreneurs who constitute the germ of capitalist economic growth. When *cultural attitudes and institutions hamper economic growth, they are to be eradicated*.[27]

One of the failures of the 1990 World Conference on Education for All was its treatment of culture as instrumental for education rather than as a determining factor in the type of education to be received. Although conference delegates concurred that"traditional knowledge and indigenous cultural heritage have a value and validity in their own right and a capacity to both define and promote development,"[28] roundtable discussions about achieving Education for All treated culture as instrumental.

The Conference's roundtable discussion of education and indigenous cultures, "Understanding Culture: A Precondition for Effective Learning," reflected a conservative and ambiguous approach to the topic.[29] The roundtable never considered the possibility of indigenous cultures as real alternatives to the dominant cultures of the global economy. The roundtable did pay homage to "affirming and enriching cultural identities."[30] However, the word "enriching" referred to changing indigenous cultures to meet the requirements of economic development. Participants agreed that culture can be used to impose the benefits of development and that it should be considered a means to achieving a basic education. The written summary of the roundtable discussion quoted the work of R. Kidd and N. Colleta: "The central ... thesis is that a culture-based non-formal education development strategy enables new knowledge, skills and attitudes to be introduced within the framework of existing knowledge, cultural patterns, institutions, values and human resources."[31] What really captures the emphasis on the instrumental concept of indigenous culture, as opposed to preservation of indigenous culture, is the comment, "Indigenous culture is the fabric within which development can best be woven."[32]

The World Commission on Culture and Development's report distinguished between the instrumental use of culture and what Commission members called "human development." In contrast to economic development, human development makes culture its end rather than a means to an end. The purpose of development is cultural enrichment and the enjoyment of life. In the context of human development, poverty has a dual meaning: poverty caused by a lack of material goods and poverty caused by a low quality of emotional existence. In the words of the report, "This view of *human* development ... is a culturally conditioned view of economic and social progress. Poverty of a life, in this view, implies, not only lack of essential goods and services, but also a lack of opportunities to choose a fuller, more satisfying, more valuable and valued existence.... Culture then is not a means to material progress: it is the end and aim of 'development' seen as the flourishing of human existence in all its forms and as a whole."[33]

DEVELOPMENT, CULTURAL FREEDOM, AND JUSTIFICATION
OF THE RIGHT TO EDUCATION

The World Commission report argued that economic development must be governed by the principles of "cultural freedom." Cultural freedom, according to the report, is a form of collective freedom as opposed to individual freedom. However, cultural freedom protects the individual right to choose a culture. Development, the report contended, must be guided by principles of cultural freedom. The World Commission's "Guiding Principles of Cultural Freedoms for Development" include:

1. All people have the right to follow or adopt a way of life of their choice.

2. Individual rights can exist independently of collective rights, but the existence of collective rights, of cultural freedom, provides additional protection for individual freedom, which includes the freedom of cultural choice.

3. Cultural freedom, by protecting alternative ways of living, encourages creativity, experimentation, and diversity, the very essentials of human development.[34]

Principle 3 echoes my justification of education as necessary for people to be able to determine the advantages and disadvantages of the global culture and economy. The ability to make these decisions depends on comparison based on differing cultural perspectives. The existence and protection of various cultures provide the opportunity to consider alternatives about the good life. Cultural diversity provides possible alternatives to the general drift of world culture. In the words of the World Commission report, "Indeed, it is the diversity of multicultural societies, and the creativity to which diversity gives rise, that makes such societies innovative, dynamic and enduring."[35]

GLOBAL ETHICS AND THE RIGHT TO EDUCATION

The World Commission on Culture and Development contended that the present close-knit world requires global acceptance of a common ethical system. Although I think that some aspects of its ethical recommendations warrant acceptance, some parts undermine the possibilities of achieving human rights and contradict its claims of supporting cultural diversity. The major articles of its ethical system are:

1. Human rights and responsibilities.

2. Democracy and the elements of civil society.

3. The protection of minorities.

4. Commitment to peaceful conflict resolution and fair negotiation.

I consider the first article, human rights, as an essential part of a global ethic and the actualization of the right to education. However, the World Commission's article is seriously limited by its interpretation of the meaning of "responsibilities." I shudder sometimes when I hear people linking rights to responsibilities, because it often signals a fear that a recognition of rights might lead to untrustworthy and irresponsible behavior. What advocates of duties and responsibilities often seek are other ways of controlling of human behavior. For instance, the World Commission expressed its uneasiness over a simple support of human rights with the following statement, "At the same time it should be recognized that rights have to be combined with duties, options with bonds, choices with allegiances, liberties with ligatures."[36]

I accept the language of responsibility if it is given a different meaning. I maintain that everyone should have a responsibility to ensure that the human rights of all people are protected. This statement shifts the emphasis from constraining behavior to requiring action. In this framework, a person has an obligation to actively pursue human rights doctrines and to protect the rights of others. The statement places the same commitment as the language of duties, bonds, allegiances, and ligatures on the individual not to interfere with the rights of others, but does not give a passive connotation to the word *responsibility*. I define responsibility as the *moral duty to actively ensure that human rights of all people are protected.*

With regard to Article 2, democracy does not guarantee protection of human rights or a just society. After many visits to Venezuela, which proclaims itself to be the oldest democracy in South America, I concluded that rule by the majority can be just as oppressive as any military dictatorship.[37] Despite a democratic government, Venezuela has been ruled by governments that ignore human rights. Rule by the majority has resulted in corrupt and dictatorial governments in Venezuela and other countries. Just as people voted for Hitler, a majority can vote away the rights of all.

However, I agree with the World Commission that "democracy provides an important basis for safeguarding the fundamental rights of citizens."[38] Democracy is important, but it does not guarantee protection of human rights. Without a civic culture that commits all people to exercising a moral duty to protect civil rights, democracy can quickly slip into a form of government that strips people of their rights. The U.S. government claimed to be democratic or to be a republic as it committed genocide and ethnocide against Native Americans in the 19th century. If all U.S. citizens had been committed to protecting human rights, including the rights of indigenous peoples, this might not have occurred. However, the majority of U.S. citizens did nothing to stop the genocide and ethnocide committed by their government. Therefore, key to a democratic system that protects human rights is a civic culture based on the moral commitment of all citizens to defend the rights of all.

Are other forms of government possible that also protect human rights? We should not discount the power of human imagination to conceive of new forms of government. The evolution of political systems should still continue. We cannot claim, at this point in history, to know what is best. Nor should we discount the role of cultural diversity in sparking the development of new political systems. Many indigenous cultures rely on the wisdom of elders for guidance and stability. Could this be a possible thought in the creative imagination of those wondering about alternatives to the good life?

Article 2, the protection of minorities, is an important part of human rights. I agree with Article 3, that global ethics should result in wars disappearing from the pages of history. Certainly, the greatest violation of human rights is war. Education should be committed to exploring peaceful resolutions of conflicts.

Therefore, I propose the following revision of the World Commission's proposal for a global ethics, and I add as an important aspect of global ethics a commitment to a continuous search for political, social, and economic systems that maximize the protection of human rights. This search will be made possible by a dedication to achieving a right to education for all people, including an education in human rights, the teaching of a moral duty to protect human rights, and an education that prepares people to explore alternative visions of political, economic, and social systems. Thus, my proposal for a global ethics includes:

1. Human rights and the moral duty of all to protect the rights of others.

2. Political systems and civic cultures that protect human rights.

3. The protection of minorities.

4. Commitment to peaceful conflict resolution and fair negotiation as an alternative to war.

5. A commitment to a continuous search for political, social, and economic systems that maximize the protection of human rights.

BIODIVERSITY, EDUCATION, AND HUMAN RIGHTS

As I explain, there is a connection among cultural rights, the protection of indigenous peoples' holistic knowledge of nature, environmental preservation of the planet, and the right to education. This argument surfaced in discussions over cultural rights after the 1995 publication of *Our Cultural Diversity*. Following the publication of its report, the World Commission on Culture and Development asked Halina Niec, adjunct professor of law at Poland's Jagiellon University and head of the Human Rights Clinic for refugees and asylum seekers in Poland, to bring together scholars from a variety of cultures to discuss the issues of human rights and cultural diversity. After submission of formal papers, UNESCO's Division of Cultural Heritage linked the participants together by video conference from nine different points around the globe to discuss their agreements and disagreements about rights and cultural diversity issues. Resulting from the papers and video conference was the 1998 UNESCO publication *Cultural Rights and Wrongs*.[39]

A unique development of this conference, which has important implications for the right to education, was linking cultural rights to environmental rights or biodiversity. The foremost advocate of this linkage was Darrell Addison Posey, coordinator of the Programme for Traditional Resource Rights of the Oxford Centre for the Environment, Ethics & Society at Oxford University. Posey argued that protection of the world's environment depends on the protection of indigenous cultures. Indigenous peoples are the last-remaining humans with a deep and close understanding of nature and the inter-relatedness of plants and animals. This inter-relatedness is a basic part of the belief systems of most indigenous peoples. In modern scientific terms, this inter-relatedness is called biodiversity; indigenous people refer to it with various concepts, such as "the family of life.", the "sacred hoop of life," and the "web of life."[40]

Posey did not romanticize indigenous people by claiming that their customs were always earth friendly, but he wanted to preserve their cultural knowledge. He wrote that the concept of the "'web of life' makes traditional human and cultural rights instruments quite inadequate and inappropriate for the protection of traditional ecological knowledge and the plants and animals (and their genetic materials) that share the web with human beings."[41] This traditional ecological knowledge extends far beyond the knowledge of the current scientific community because of its holistic understanding of nature.

As Posey explained, "One of the best ways [of saving the environment] is to relearn the ecological knowledge and sustainable principles that our society has lost.... This can come through listening to many peoples of the Planet who still know when birdnests, fish migrate, ants swarm, tadpoles develop legs, soils erode and rare plants seed—and whose cosmovisions manifest the ecologies and ethics of sustainability."[42]

The background for Posey's arguments can be traced to the Declaration of Belem issued by the First International Congress on Ethnobiology held in Belem, Brazil, in 1988. At the Congress, scientists and environmentalists met with representatives of indigenous peoples from around the world to develop a common strategy to stop the rapid loss of the earth's biological and cultural diversity.

The Declaration of Belem warned that fragile ecosystems and plant and animal species were being lost at the same rapid rate as were indigenous cultures. The Declaration linked cultural diversity and biodiversity with the statements: "Native peoples have been stewards of 99% of the world's genetic resources," and "There is an inextricable link between cultural and biological diversity." Besides calling for action to protect the environment, the Declaration called for "all other inalienable human rights to be recognized and guaranteed, including cultural and linguistic identity" and asked that "procedures be developed to compensate native peoples for the utilization of their knowledge and their biological resources."[43] The suggestion of compensating indigenous peoples for their knowledge is a unique part of the Declaration.

An important consideration for justifying and interpreting the right to education is the Declaration of Belem's statement on environmental instruction. The Declaration called for the implementation of "educational programs ... to alert the global community to the value of ethnobiological knowledge for human well-being."[44]

In 1993, the linking of indigenous peoples' intellectual property rights to environmental protection received support at the 1993 International Conference on the Cultural and Intellectual Property Rights of Indigenous Peoples held in commemoration of the UN International Year for the World's Indigenous Peoples. Convened by the Nine Tribes of Mataatua in New Zealand, the participants discussed the value of indigenous knowledge and biodiversity. Among the important recommendations of the conference were to:

- Prioritize the establishment of indigenous education, research, and training centers to promote their knowledge of customary environmental and cultural practices.

- Recognize that indigenous peoples are the guardians of their customary knowledge and have the right to protect and control dissemination of that knowledge.

- Recognize that indigenous peoples also have the right to create new knowledge based on cultural traditions.[45]

One of the unique features of the Mataatua Declaration is the appreciation of indigenous cultures as living cultures that have the right to evolve.

The inter-relation between cultural rights, the protection of indigenous peoples' holistic knowledge of nature, environmental preservation of the planet, and the right to education were acknowledged by the Convention on Biological Diversity, which was presented and signed at the 1992 UN Conference on Environment and Development (the Rio "Earth Summit"). Signed by representatives of 168 nations, the Convention went into force on December 29, 1993.[46] Recognizing the importance of indigenous cultures to environmental protection, Article 8, Section J, stated that each signatory shall,

> Subject to its national legislation, respect, preserve and maintain knowledge, innovations and practices of indigenous and local communities embodying traditional lifestyles relevant for the conservation and sustainable use of biological diversity and promote their wider application with the approval and involvement of the holders of such knowledge, innovations and practices and encourage the equitable sharing of the benefits arising from the utilization of such knowledge, innovations and practices.[47]

With regard to public education, the Convention mandated in Article 13 that all contracting parties shall:

> (a) Promote and encourage understanding of the importance of, and the measures required for, the conservation of biological diversity, as well as its propagation through media, and the inclusion of these topics in educational programmes; and

> (b) Cooperate, as appropriate, with other States and international organizations in developing educational and public awareness programmes, with respect to conservation and sustainable us of biological diversity.[48]

Environmental destruction and protection of biodiversity add other dimensions to the right to education. The right to education can be justified as necessary for the protection of individual and group life. An individual right to education includes environmental education that helps safeguard the planet and protects a person's basic right to life. The right to life is currently threatened by the destruction of the earth. In addition, the preservation and expansion of holistic knowledge about nature, which is key to maintaining the ecosystem, require that indigenous peoples have the right to education according to their own cultural practices, in their mother tongue and in the official or dominant language of their nation.

Therefore, the necessity of protecting the planet from environmental destruction provides another justification for the right to education as necessary for maintaining human rights because the right to life is the most fundamental right. This view interlaces concerns about biodiversity, cultural rights, the environmental destruction of the planet, human rights, and the right to education. These propositions are enumerated in the following summary.

Environmental Destruction and the Right to Education

1. Environmental destruction threatens the basic human right of the right to life.

2. The right to education, which includes environmental education, might safeguard the planet.

3. The preservation and growth of the holistic knowledge of nature of indigenous peoples could be safeguards against planetary devastation.

4. To protect the earth, indigenous peoples' education should include their cultural and scientific traditions and should be according to their cultural practices with instruction in their mother tongues and in the official or dominant languages of their nations.

5. Therefore, the right to education, which includes environmental education and respect for the holistic knowledge of indigenous peoples, is necessary for protection of the basic human right of right to life.

CONCLUSION: THE RIGHT TO EDUCATION FOR THE PRIVILEGED

So far, my discussion of the right to education has tended to focus on cultural and linguistic minorities and indigenous peoples. Up to this point, I have conveyed to readers a primary concern about the victims of colonialization and globalization.

However, what does the right to education mean for the world's privileged, whose children are almost certain to be well educated? Does the right to education have any meaning for these children? My answer is Yes. I have already discussed certain concerns related to the right to education that cuts across all social classes and cultural boundaries. One concern is that the right to education *does not include* nationalistic forms of schooling used to used to maintain beliefs in racial separatism and racial superiority. These forms of education are clear violations of human rights doctrines and, therefore, should not be part of the education of any members of society. In addition, all students, including students of the privileged, are entitled to an education that practices freedom of ideas and expression. Another concern is the environment. Planetary destruction affects all people. The right to education of the world's privileged should include environmental education.

The permanent results of colonialism, the inescapable impact of the global economy and culture, and environmental destruction have exposed all people to a world culture and economy. As Elkin suggested, all people, the advantaged and disadvantaged, should have the right to know how this world culture and economy are affecting them, and they should have the right to determine what benefits might be derived from the global culture and economics. Therefore, a universal right to education can be justified by the existence of a global culture and economy that affects, both positively and negatively, all the world's peoples.

In the next chapter, I discuss children's rights. Children's rights protect both the privileged and underprivileged. In addition, children's liberty rights provide a basic framework for schooling that supports the human rights of the victims and current beneficiaries of globalization.

◈4◈

Universal Justification for Education and Children's Rights

Children's rights, as provided for in the 1989 UN Convention on the Rights of the Child, can be justified by the right to education. For children to be able to exercise their right to education, they must have adequate medical care, nutrition, and housing. Also, children's rights guarantee nonauthoritarian forms of education by providing the right to free access to information and freedom of thought. Kandel's 1947 arguments against nationalistic and authoritarian forms of education are embodied in the Convention on the Rights of the Child.

Therefore, understanding and having the ability to mediate the effects of the global economy and culture justify the right to education, which, in turn, justifies children's rights; and children's rights provide the right to freedom of thought and access to information. In turn, freedom of thought and access to information help unlock the social imagination of students so that they can consider alternatives to the good life. The application of social imagination to the process of mediating the effect of world culture and economics could result in improved forms of political, economic, and social relationships.

In this chapter, I first consider the problems facing the world's children and the necessity for children's rights. Second, I discuss the role of children's protection and assistance rights in creating the necessary physical conditions for children to exercise their right to education. Last, I describe how children's liberty rights contribute to the formulation of a universal concept of education.

THE CONDITION OF THE WORLD'S CHILDREN

The almost unanimous ratification of the 1989 Convention on the Rights of the Child by all but two of the world's nations, Somalia and

55

the United States, reflected the concern about the conditions facing the world's children. UNICEF's 1999 "The State of the World's Children" reported that "96 percent of the world's children live in countries that are legally bound [by ratification of the Convention on the Rights of the Child] to grant the full spectrum of child rights: civil, political, social, cultural and economic."[1] This almost universal ratification of the Convention suggests that most nations recognize the current crisis in child care and accept the dependent state of childhood as justification for special rights. The "Preamble" to the Convention stated, "The child, by reason of his physical and mental immaturity, needs special safeguards and care, including appropriate legal protection, before as well as after birth."[2] Article 1 defined "a child ... [as] every human being below the age of eighteen years unless, under the law applicable to the child, majority is attained earlier."[3]

One source of the problems facing children is the legacy of colonialism and the dynamics of the global economy. These forces contributed to the disorganization of traditional family structures and left many children unprotected and neglected. In Asia, Africa, and the Americas, colonialists tried changing family and kinship structures to fit their concepts of child care and family. Today, global economics are having a similar effect. The whirlwind forces of the global labor market disperse families across national borders as workers move from country to country. Workers immigrate or illegally move across borders and leave their families or, in some cases, expose their families to the uncertainties of prosecution for illegal immigrant status and to the taunts of an unwelcoming and prejudiced host population. The brutalization of children has been a common theme of globalism. The great African diaspora left children maimed, dead, and enslaved. Dispersed by slavery to the Americas, children lost the protection of families and clans. Indigenous children witnessed the damage to their families and clans by the genocidal practices and diseases of foreign invaders. Often, children were the first to die in the indigenous peoples' holocaust. Children suffered the insecurities created by unstable family structures with the movements of workers from China, Japan, and Korea to other parts of Asia and from Europe to the Americas.

Children bear a tremendous burden in the rapid advance of globalism. Many of the world's children need protection and assistance because of malnutrition, exploitive child labor, and homelessness. These harmful conditions make it difficult for many children to exercise the right to education. Consider the effect of malnutrition. According to UNICEF's 1998 report *The State of the World's Children*, 200 million children under the age of 5 are malnourished. UNICEF estimated that malnutrition is responsible for more than one half of the annual 12 million under-5 deaths. One half of Asia's children are malnourished, while one third of African children are underweight. In Africa, where malaria is prevalent, one third of malnutrition cases are caused by the effects of malaria. Almost 2.2 million children die from diarrhoeal dehydration aggravated by malnutrition. Anemia is a major problem for both mothers and children. UNICEF estimated that the percentages of children's deaths from diseases where malnutrition is a factor are 19% for acute respiratory infections, 19% for diarrhea, 7% for measles, 5% for malaria, 18% for perinatal causes, and 32% for other diseases.[4]

In both developing and developed countries, malnutrition is a problem. In developed countries, widening disparities in income and the removal of government welfare benefits are resulting in malnourished children in low-income families. In the United States, over 20% of the children live in poverty. An estimated 13 million children in the United States, one quarter of the U.S. population under the age of 12, have a difficult time receiving adequate nourishment.

Besides death, malnutrition contributes to mental retardation, to disabilities caused by childhood diseases, and to adult health problems. The major problems are protein-energy malnutrition and deficiencies in iodine, iron, and vitamin A. Lacking adequate nutrients, malnourished children experience stunted growth. This stunted growth is reflected in mental retardation and learning problems. A collaborative study by the University of North Carolina (U.S.) and the University of San Carlos (Philippines) estimated that "226 million children under age five in developing countries, nearly 40 percent of this age group, suffer from moderate or severe stunting. High levels of stunting among children suggest that there will also be long-term deficits in mental and physical development that can leave children ill-prepared to maximum advantage of learning opportunities in school."[5]

Death rates for young people, as presented in Table 4.1, provide another indication of the regional distribution of health problems and violence affecting youth.

Wage labor often keeps children from attending school. Child labor in families and kinship groups often served an educative function and was considered preparation for adulthood. Now, child labor is tied to wage slavery outside the home and undercuts attempts to reduce poverty by raising education levels. The UN International Labor Office made a clear distinction between children who work a few hours a week for pocket change and children who work in ways destructive to their health and development. According to UN estimates, there are 250 million working children in developing countries with about 120 million working full time. In addition, child labor is reported to be increasing in Central and Eastern Europe.[6]

The major cause of child labor is poverty. Poverty forces families to send their children out to work. Homelessness or death of parents

TABLE 4.1
Death Rates for the World's Young People: 1994

Region	% Who Die Before Age 15 Boys and Girls
World	10
Africa total	17
Sub-Saharan Africa	18
Northern Africa	10
Asia (except China)	13
China	7
North America	1
Latin America	7
Europe	2
Former Soviet Union	4

Note. From: "The World's Youth," by Population Reference Bureau, in Javier Perez de Cuellar, *Our Creative Diversity: Report of the World Commission on Culture and Development* (Paris: UNESCO, 1995), p. 167.

forces children into employment. According to the World Bank, there are more than 1.3 billion people living on less than $1 a day—the international definition of poverty. Another 2 billion earn slightly more than $1 a day. UNICEF estimated that children account for 50% of people who are poor. In addition, the rich nations are getting richer, and the poor nations are getting poorer. The income difference between the richest and poorest 20% of the world's population increased from 30 to 1 to 78 to 1 between 1960 and 1994.[7]

Some children are held in bondage. According to the International Labor Office, "Although slavery is banned ... child slavery is far from dead."[8] In debt, many parents send their children into bondage to pay off the liability. Banned by national and international laws, this practice persists and is growing because of increased poverty.

In Africa, child labor is on the rise. The International Labor Office estimated that child labor in Africa will reach 100 million by the year 2015. In Africa, 41% of children between the ages of 5 and 14 work. In Asia, 21% of this age group works; in Latin America, 17%.[9] There are several reasons for the growth of child labor in Africa. One is rapid population growth amid economic crises and civil turmoil. War and the epidemic of human immunodeficiency virus (HIV)/acquired immune deficiency syndrome (AIDS) have killed many parents, leaving in their wake thousands of children as heads of households.[10]

In Asia, children are exploited by sex industries. A UN report estimated that in India alone about 500,000 females under the age of 18 are involved in commercial sex, and worldwide the sexual exploitation of boys is increasing.[11] The International Labor Office reported:

> Child prostitution is increasingly widespread, particularly among girls. It has been tolerated if not actually encouraged by those responsible for promoting the lucrative business of international tourism. The situation is becoming even more serious as children are being sold and smuggled secretly across national frontiers for the world sex market. They are often held in prison-like conditions separated from their families in remote foreign countries whose languages, laws and customs they do not know.[12]

Military conflict adds to misery of children. Amnesty International provided this vivid portrait:

> The image of the refugee child is a powerful one. Fleeing, eyes wide with terror, from exploding shells. Fighting for a bowl of grain in a camp. Standing, lost and bewildered, on arrival in a foreign country. At a stage when they should be receiving the care that their vulnerable, dependent and undeveloped state demands, these young children and adolescents have experienced horrors, physical strains and emotional upheavals that most adults would be ill-equipped to deal with.[13]

Amnesty International estimated that 20 million children have been or are currently affected by military combat as refugees, victims, or actual combatants. In recent decades, children have been victims in armed conflicts and civil disturbances in Afghanistan, Angola, Algeria, Azerbaijan, Burundi, Colombia, Guatemala, Lebanon, Liberia, Myanmar, Mozambique, Iraq, Turkey, Rwanda, Sierra Leone, Somalia, Sri Lanka, Sudan, and the former Yugoslavia and Zaire. In some areas, children are killed as part of ethnic or religious "cleansing." Young girls are frequently asked to provide sexual service to combatants.

Besides the death and destruction of war, children face the horrors of forced induction into the military and refugee status. "They recruit in the market place," a young Tamil boy described recruitment into the armed opposition group in Sri Lanka. "One of my friends joined up. He was ten. He banged the drums when someone had died. He said it was very scary in the camp. He held a grenade and had a gun on his shoulder."[14] A 14-year-old Sudanese refugee in Kenya said: "It was something like an accident when I ran away from my village. We were playing at about 5 o'clock when these people, the soldiers came. We just ran. We didn't know where we were going to, we just ran."[15]

War, poverty, and dysfunctional family structures are contributing to the increasing numbers of homeless children. UNESCO estimated that in 1991 there were approximately 100 million street children in the world. The largest concentrations of street children are in Latin America, Africa, and Asia.[16] Even in prosperous nations, such as the United States, homelessness makes it difficult for children to exercise the right to education. In 1999, children constituted 26% of the urban homeless population in the United States. In addition, children *without* families represented 3% of the United States' urban homelessness. Although schooling is available in the United States, homeless children have difficulty attending because of constant movement between homeless shelters, problems with guardianship requirements and transfer of school records, lack of a permanent address, and immunization records. In 1987, when the U.S. Congress passed the Education of Homeless Children and Youth Act, it was estimated that 50% of homeless children were not attending school.[17]

Homeless children face worse circumstances in poor nations. The plight of homeless Brazilian children is well known. Sleeping on the streets, vulnerable to sex crimes and police brutality, they live off garbage dumps and street crime. The 1999 movie, *Central Station*, portrayed a homeless Brazilian child being sold for his body parts. Representing the problem of homeless street children, the following lines were written in 1999 by Mauricio Villela, a Brazilian dentist with a 10-year-old son:

> Sao Paulo is simply unbearable.... Children at the stop lights do not ask anymore, demand and kill, cut, leaving deep scars with their acts, after all, in spite of the acts practiced by them, we can never forget that they are kids my son's age. This becomes very dangerous, when we start to feel rage of children of 10, 11-years of age! In the United States they use a more truthful term (homeless), different of the rude and aggressive used here, little old people, children, heads of household and who knows maybe one of us tomorrow.[18]

CHILDREN'S RIGHTS ASSISTANCE AND PROTECTION RIGHTS

Intended to alleviate the deplorable conditions facing many children, assistance and protection rights were included in the 1966 International Covenant on Civil and Political Rights, the 1966 International Covenant on Economic, Social, and Cultural Rights, and the 1989 Convention on the Rights of the Child. In addition, these documents promised children intellectual rights that help guarantee an education that will empower them to make decisions about their social and economic circumstances.

Children's assistance and protection rights evolved from general discussions about the meaning of human rights and the right to an education. Before 1965, there were continued political disagreements over human rights. In 1965, according to the historian Paul Lauren, the adoption of the International Convention on the Elimination of All Forms of Racial Discrimination broke the "political deadlock that had existed well more than a decade within the General Assembly."[19] Finally, philosophical differences that had undermined implementation of the 1948 Universal Declaration of Human Rights were starting to be resolved. A year after the adoption of the International Convention on the Elimination of All Forms of Racial Discrimination, the General Assembly approved the International Covenant on Civil and Political Rights and the International Covenant on Economic, Social, and Cultural Rights. These documents were important steps in developing a universal concept of education and children's rights.

A central issue facing child-rights advocates was finding a universal justification for treating children as a special class of citizen. Article 24 of the 1966 International Covenant on Civil and Political Rights specifically recognized children as a special class because of their dependent status. Article 24 stated:

> Every child shall have, without any discrimination as to race, color, sex, language, religion, national or social origin, property or birth, the right to measures of protection as are required by his status as a minor, on the part of his family, society, and the State.[20]

Unfortunately, Article 24 lacked a concrete explanation of how a child's "right to measures of protection as are required by his status as a minor" are to be achieved. However, one right specifically identified for children was given in Article 6: "Sentence of death shall not be imposed for crimes committed by persons below eighteen years of age."[21]

Although the 1966 International Covenant on Economic, Social, and Cultural Rights provided extensive rights to children, these rights are undermined by reliance on a state of dependence as a justification. I do not believe that the argument for dependence provides an adequate justification for declaring a universal right for children to be treated as a distinct category of citizen. Concepts of childhood vary from cultural to culture, and, even in European traditions they have varied with historical periods. Also, there are differences between agricultural and industrial societies in the integration of children into the workforce. As I argue later, a universal recognition of children as a class of citizen with special rights can be justified by the right to education under the conditions of a global culture and economy.

While lacking a solid justification for treating children as a special class of citizens requiring their own rights, the 1966 International Covenant on Economic, Social, and Cultural Rights established the basic framework for implementation of children's rights. For the purpose of discussion, I separate children's rights into protection and assistance rights. A *protection right* defends children, because of their dependent status, from exploitation by adults or governments. An *assistance right* guarantees social services by adults or government. The International Covenant on Economic, Social, and Cultural Rights stated: "Special measures of protection and assistance should be taken on behalf of all children and young persons without any discrimination for reasons of parentage or other conditions."[22] The following protection and assistance rights are given to children as a special class of citizens.

Protection Rights

1. Children and young persons should be protected from economic and social exploitation [Article 10, Clause 3].

2. Their [children] employment in work harmful to their morals or health or dangerous to life or likely to hamper their normal development should be punishable by law [Article 10, Clause 3].

3. States should also set age limits below which the paid employment of child labor should be prohibited and punishable by law [Article 10, Clause 3].

4. The widest possible protection and assistance should be accorded the family ... while it is responsible for the care and education of dependent children [Article 10, Clause 1].

5. The State Parties ... recognize the right of everyone to education [Article 13, Clause 1].

6. [State Parties] agree that education shall be directed to the full development of the human personality and the sense of its dignity, and shall strengthen the respect for human rights and fundamental freedoms [Article 13, Clause 1].

7. [States Parties] agree that education shall enable all persons to participate effectively in a free society, promote understanding, tolerance and friendship among all nations and all racial, ethnic or religious groups [Article 13, Clause 1].

8. The State Parties ... [will allow] parents ... to choose for their children schools, other than those established by the public authorities, which conform to such minimum educational standards laid down ... by the State [Article 13, Clause 3].

9. The State Parties ... [will] ensure the religious and moral education of children in conformity with ... [parents'] convictions [Article 13, Clause 3].

Assistance Rights

10. The States Parties ... recognize the right of everyone ... to highest attainable standard of physical health and mental. States ... [will provide for] the healthy development of the child [Article 12, Clauses 1 & 2].

11. The States Parties to the present Covenant recognize that, with a view to achieving the full realization of the right to education:

   a. Primary education shall be compulsory and available free to all,

   b. Secondary education in its different forms, including technical and vocational secondary education, shall be made generally available and accessible to all by every appropriate means, and in particular by the progressive introduction of free education,

   c. Higher education shall be made equally accessible to all, on the basis of capacity, by every appropriate means, and in particular by the progressive introduction of free education,

   d. Fundamental education shall be encouraged or intensified as far as possible for those persons who have not received or completed the whole period of their primary education,

   e. The development of a system of schools at all levels shall be actively pursued, an adequate fellowship system shall be established, and the material conditions of teaching staff shall be continuously improved [Article 13, Clause 2].[23]

In summary, the International Covenant on Economic, Social, and Cultural Rights identified children as a special class of citizen protected against exploitive and physically damaging working conditions and educational systems that ignore their religious backgrounds and that *do not provide* an education in human rights, fundamental freedom, and tolerance. In addition, children were given assistance rights to healthy development and free primary education along with the possible future right to free secondary and higher education. Sadly missing are cultural and linguistic rights.

Despite the absence of cultural and linguistic rights, the Covenant expanded the concept of educational rights to include protection rights. By linking the right to education to teaching about human rights, fundamental freedoms, and tolerance, the child is protected against educational systems of totalitarian and racist states, such as Nazi Germany, that stress obedience to authority and racial superiority. This protects the child from the educational tradition identified by Kandel, which turns schools into boosters of nationalism and racial separatism and superiority.

CONVENTION ON THE RIGHTS OF THE CHILD: LIBERTY RIGHTS

The 1989 Convention on the Rights of the Child reiterated the protection and assistance rights provided by the International Covenant on Economic, Social, and Cultural Rights. In addition, the Convention identified liberty rights that have important implications for the right to an education. Without liberty rights, children are not guaranteed an education that prepares them to make decisions about the effect of the global economy and culture on their lives.

Liberty Rights

1. The child shall have the right to freedom of expression; this right shall include freedom to seek, receive and impart information and ideas of all kinds, regardless of frontiers, either orally, in writing or in print, in the form of art, or through any other media of the child's choice [Article 13, Clause 1].

2. States Parties recognize the rights of the child to freedom of thought, conscience and religion [Article 14, Clause 1].

3. States Parties recognize the rights of the child to freedom of association and to freedom of peaceful assembly [Article 15, Clause 1].

Liberty rights challenge educational systems in developed and developing countries that are nationalistic and organized to indoctrinate students. They also bring into question national examination systems designed to control the curriculum and limit the exposure of students to a wide variety of ideas about social and political change. National or state examination systems are a serious threat to the right of children to access information and ideas. As teachers teach according to the content of national or state examinations, classroom instruction is seriously limited. If the right to education is justified by a universal need to mediate the impact of global economics and culture, then freedom of expression, thought, and access to ideas is essential.

Consider the liberty rights that were denied African children in the school system imposed by the Nationalist Party in South Africa during the years of apartheid. In reference to the education of African children, the Nationalist Party proclaimed: "Native education should be based on the principles of trustee-ship, non-equality and segregation; its aim should be to inculcate the white man's view of life, especially that of the Boer nation, which is the senior trustee".[24]

Without liberty rights and a clear concept of the meaning of education in "the right to education," the Nationalist Party's plan might be considered a fulfillment of the right to education. However, when considered from the standpoint of children's liberty rights and the universal justification for a right to education, the Nationalist Party's educational system violated the right to education. Consequently, children's liberty rights are an important component of a universal concept of education. They provide a guide for ensuring that education is empowering rather than enslaving. Along with children's protection and assistance rights, liberty rights are essential for administering the right to education.

CULTURAL DIFFERENCES AND THE BEST INTERESTS OF THE CHILD

Although the 1989 Convention on the Rights of the Child could be justified as necessary because of children's dependence status and because of providing the conditions for the exercise of the right to education, I believe an added justification is the disruption of family organizations by colonialism and the global economy. The impact of colonialism on family and kinship structures was reflected in discussions about what is the "best interests of the child" as provided for in Article 3 of the 1989 Convention on the Rights of the Child:

1. In all actions concerning children, whether undertaken by public or private social welfare institutions, courts of law, administrative authorities or legislative bodies, *the best interests of the child* shall be a primary consideration [emphasis added].[25]

To interpret the "best interests of the child" in different cultural contexts, UNICEF sponsored "a best interest of the child" project at its International Child Development Center in Florence, Italy. The project was headed by Philip Alston, leading authority on the Convention on the Rights of the Child, senior legal adviser on children's rights to UNICEF, and chairperson of the UN Committee on Economic, Social and Cultural Rights. As a result of Alston's work, UNICEF published a set of papers in 1994 with the descriptive title *The Best Interests of the Child: Reconciling Culture and Human Rights*.[26]

Intensely involved in drafting the Convention on the Rights of the Child, Alston was constantly confronted with the problem of interpreting children's rights in differing cultural contexts. Initially, differing interpretations reflected the ideological split between communist and capitalist countries. With the end of the Cold War, cultural differences became the focus of discussion. According to Alston, important differences existed between what he called "highly industrialized countries" and "traditional societies." In industrialized countries, he wrote, "The child's best interests are 'obviously' served by policies that emphasize autonomy and individuality to the greatest possible extent."[27] In contrast, interpretation of the child's bests interests in traditional societies, where links to family and community are of paramount importance, might require "the sublimation of the individual child's preferences to the interests of the family or even the extended family."[28]

The project's studied reveal a common issue in former colonial countries: Who or what organization is responsible for the best interest of the child as a result of the undermining of traditional responsibility by the imposition of foreign values and social systems?

SUB-SAHARAN AFRICA: CHILDREN'S RIGHTS

Sub-Saharan Africa provides a good example of why universal children's rights doctrines are now necessary because of the effect of colonialism on traditional family practices and child care. Colonialism caused a conflict between the European cultural values of autonomy and individuality and the traditional African values of family and community. When colonialism ended, family organizations were in disarray because of the conflict between traditional and imposed colonial values. The result was family disorganization and neglect of children. This family disorganization, and its effects on children and education, can be resolved only by finding workable family values to replace the chaos left by colonialism.

UNICEF asked Bart Rwezaura, a former professor of law at the University of Dar es Salaam and at the time holding a similar post at the University of Hong Kong, to analyze the problems confronting implementation of children's rights in sub-Saharan Africa as part of the project on cultural differences in the meaning of the best interests of the child. As an expert on both traditional African cultures and current law practices, Rwezaura linked the chaos in contemporary African families to the disruption of traditional customs by colonialism. The present crisis in family disorganization made it difficult to determine the best interests of the child and, more important, what agency would protect the best interests of the child.[29]

Before colonialism, Rwezaura argued, a majority of Africans maintained strong kinship groups based on the social and economic alliances created by marriage. In traditional African society, marriage involved the transfer of bride wealth from the husband to the bride's family. Bride wealth usually took the form of domestic animals or agricultural produce. Essentially, the bride was bought for her reproductive abilities. If the husband's family could not pay sufficient bride wealth then the children belonged to the bride's family.

With the payment of bride wealth, the bride's children belonged to the husband's family, even if the woman had children by another man: The children always belonged to the family that paid the bride wealth.

This practice gave the bride and children economic status. Children were a product of economic investment in the bride. The children provided tangible economic benefits by working in the household, tending animals, and working on agricultural plots. Beginning at the age of 3 years, children were required to herd small animals. Girls as young as 4 years, carried water jugs and helped cook. This work was schooling for adult roles. In addition, boys were often sent to village leaders for developing political skills and learning the people's heritage.

Child pledging provided a means for coping with difficult economic times. Short on crops or animals, a family might agree to a future marriage of a very young girl in exchange for early installments of bride wealth. Although child pledging is now outlawed, it is still practiced and is considered a violation of the rights of women under the doctrines of the Universal Declaration of Human Rights.

In summary, Rwezaura stated, "No matter how we look at the values and beliefs of most African societies, great importance was attached to having children. This is short of saying that the entire social system as well as its survival was organized around and geared towards the objective of acquiring as many children as the community needed."[30] In contrast, he argued, modern Western cultures might consider these values as economically unwise, and they would recommend reducing the number of children. However, Rwezaura contended, the importance of having large numbers of children is ingrained in African traditions.

Colonialism and the global economy disrupted these traditional family practices. Under colonialism, fathers often worked at wage employment away from home. Often colonialists required workers to move from villages to mining centers, transportation and construction sites, and urban areas. For instance, by 1943 almost one half the men in Botswana were employed away from home, and 28% of the total adult population worked in South Africa.

As a result of these economic conditions, there was a sharp increase in the number of female-headed households with dependent children. In addition, the movement of workers undermined family kinship units. Added to this was the role of Christian missionaries in spreading individualist ideas about family and marriage. Rather than children growing up in large kinship units, missionaries held up the European ideal of the nuclear family with one man, one woman, and children. This European ideal contributed to the disorganization of kinship groups.

With a growing cash economy, bride wealth is being transformed from commodities to currency. Accompanying changes in kinship groups, bride wealth now places a burden on the individual groom or family. African courts, a product of colonialism, now deal with many cases involving issues of bride wealth. Some males have sued their fathers for failure to pay bride wealth. Some fathers have sued their sons-in-law for not fulfilling their obligations to meet bride wealth payments. In many places in Africa, divorce now requires the return of bride wealth based on the birth of children. In divorce proceedings, the father-in-law can sometimes demand children as part of the refund for bride wealth payments. Because of the cash exchange, the pledging of young girls in marriage to older men remains a practice.

As a result of the cash economy and the disorganization of kinship relations, the child's status is now unclear. Under traditional practices, children had clear economic value as embodied in bride wealth and in their work for the family. Who was responsible for children's care and who benefited from children were determined by bride wealth.

Now, according to Rwezaura, suits over responsibility for child rearing are common throughout sub-Saharan Africa. Grandparents now sue sons-in-law for the costs of rearing children left in their care by divorced or separated parents. Former husbands now sue for children of former wives and their new husbands when the bride wealth has not been refunded. There are constant legal issues surrounding financial responsibilities of single-parent homes headed by women. Fathers are now suing sons-in-law for the costs of supporting daughters when they return home after a marital dispute.

The confused social position of children as ancestral practices collapse is compounded by their changing economic status. If children are to be of economic value to their families, they must work for cash. Consequently, work can lose its educative function. In the village, the work of the child involves learning the skills required for adulthood. Work in a factory or other business might be exploitative rather than educative. In addition, children are an economic burden. Although Africans might continue to value having large numbers of children, the reality is that they might cost too much to raise. Now families are faced with the costs of school fees, clothing, and medicine.

The second-class status of female children continues as a result of bride wealth. Families tend to invest their resources in educating males, while females are thought of as economically valuable only for their bride wealth. The population of African universities is primarily male. When formal education of women threatens bride wealth, families try to protect their investment by early puberty rites or removal from the school system. In Tanzania, the age of female circumcisions has dropped from 14 to 8 years because parents worry that education leads to early contacts with men and ruins their bride wealth value. Many girls are removed from school before the 6th grade, because parents worry that girls with too much education will rebel and leave for the city.

Today, many girls escape from early marriages by running away to boarding schools such as A.I.C. Girls Primary Boarding School in

Kenya. Interviewed by Ian Fisher for *The New York Times*, 10-year-old Naataosim Mako described running away to the school at the age of 9 after a 30-year-old man paid bride wealth to her father. The bride wealth consisted of 10 cows, 4 goats, more than 200 quarts of home-brewed beer, and more than 6 pounds of sugar and a sack of rice. Another student, Jedida Nkadoyo, was 10 when her mother announced her marriage for a bride wealth of a cow, a crate of bottled beer, and 40 liters of home brew. Priscillar Nangurai, the school's headmistress, described the resistance of parents to educating their daughters. "They feel," she told Fisher, "that when a girl goes to school she gets spoiled because she gets to a point where she is equal to the men. But she's not supposed to be equal.... [They fear that] once she goes to school and gets an education, she will not listen to her elders. She might even elope."[31]

The A.I.C. Girls Primary Boarding School represents European values in conflict with traditional African customs. Recognition of children's rights becomes an imperative in helping societies deal with the impact of global economics and culture. Unfortunately, because of the arrogance of European powers, African societies must adjust traditions to the present conditions. In addition, European powers left a continent in disarray by imposing government organizations and national boundaries on existing tribal cultures. Children face crises in the breakdown of the traditional family and the wars caused by the breakdown of traditional relations between African peoples.

The neglect of child care is reflected in current educational conditions in sub-Saharan Africa. Whereas formal education was unnecessary for existence in postcolonial times, it is now a necessity for participating in a cash economy. In 1999, UNICEF reported the following educational conditions for the region:

> Enrollment: From only 25 percent in 1960, the regional primary enrollment rate climbed to nearly 60 percent by 1980. After declining in the 1980s, enrolment is again close to 60 percent.
>
> Gender: Only a third of women in the region were literate in 1980, now, nearly half are literate.
>
> Effectiveness: In the region, one third of children enrolled in primary school drop out before reaching grade five.
>
> Constraints: Armed conflicts and economic pressures from debt and structural adjustment policies   ... [and] large class sizes, poor teacher education, crumbling buildings and lack of learning materials in a number of countries all reduce the quality of education.[32]

Although UNICEF happily reported an increase in school enrollment since the 1960s, the reality is that 40% of children in sub-Saharan Africa do not attend school and that one third of the 60% attending school drop out before the 5th grade.

In 1990, the Organization for African Unity responded to the problems facing children caught in this vicious swirl of postcolonialism with the issuance of the African Charter on the Rights and Welfare of the Child. The Charter's Preamble expressed "concern that the situation of most African children remains critical due to the unique factors of their socio-economic, cultural, traditional and developmental circumstances, natural disasters, armed conflicts, exploitation and hunger, and on account of the child's physical and mental immaturity he/she needs specific safeguards and care."[33]

Therefore, the African Charter on the Rights and Welfare of the Child justified children's rights by the reality of their treatment and ambivalent status in postcolonial Africa along with their physical dependence. The hope of the Charter was to balance tradition with postcolonialism. The Preamble noted that there must be "consideration [of] the virtues of their [children's] cultural heritage, historical background and the values of the African civilization."[34] However, the consideration of cultural tradition was sharply limited in Article 1 of the Charter: "Any custom, tradition, cultural or religious practice that is inconsistent with the rights, duties and obligations contained in the present Charter shall to the extent of such inconsistency *be discouraged*"[emphasis added].[35]

As the African Charter on the Rights and Welfare of the Child clearly recognized, the social chaos resulting from colonialism and postcolonial global economics and culture justifies the imposition of children's rights even when they are in conflict with traditional cultural practices. The rights annunciated in the African Charter are closely aligned with the rights specified in the 1966 International Covenant on Economic, Social, and Cultural Right and the 1989 Convention on the Rights of the Child.

INDIA AND SIR LANKA: CHILDREN'S RIGHTS AND EDUCATION

A similar justification for universal children's rights applies to India and Sri Lanka. Both nations felt the impact of English rule after 1798 and of earlier incursions by the Portuguese and Dutch. In both countries, there is currently confusion between traditional practices and the judicial practices left by colonialism. The judicial system in Sri Lanka is dominated by a combination of Dutch-Roman and English common law, while India continues to function under traditional English legal practices. In opposition to the dominant legal system is the so-called religious personal law or customary law representing religious traditions, particularly Hindu and Islamic practices.

Indigenous practices in India are more in line with current children's rights than imposed English law. Having been described as showing "brutal indifference to the child's fate," early English common law gave all parental power to the father, "for a mother as such is entitled to no power, but only reverence and respect."[36] In other words, both the interests of children and mother are subservient to the interests of the father in English common law. In contrast, Islamic law gives mothers preferential right to custody of young children and separate property rights. In addition, Islamic law imposes a parental responsibility for support of children, and Hindu, Buddhist, and other indigenous traditions impose a wide family responsibility for child care.

Although traditional practices appear more humane than English law, the issue of child marriages and the selling of child brides are, as in Africa, continuous issues. Islamic tradition allows the father to impose a marriage on a minor child without regard for the age of the child. Hindu tradition places women under the protection of men, and they are considered owned by their fathers or husbands. Because she is owned, a young girl can be given or "gifted" in marriage. In addition, Hindu custom allows "gifting" young girls before puberty. Despite efforts to end this tradition, the gifting of young girls in marriage remains a widespread practice.

Resulting from the mixed brew of English, Hindu, Dutch, and Islamic tradition are large numbers of neglected children. Lost is the broad family responsibility for child care. The present reality, Savitri Goonesekere wrote, is "exploitation of girl children, child marriage and infanticide. Infanticide and child abandonment are reported in the press and by social welfare authorities, even in Sri Lanka, which has comparatively high social indicators for children."[37]

In addition, the right to education suffers. UNICEF reports the following educational conditions in South Asia for 1999:

Enrollment: Primary enrolment has climbed from under 60 percent in 1970 to nearly 70 percent.

Gender: Nearly two thirds of women in the region are illiterate, compared with about one third men.

Effectiveness: About 40 percent of children entering primary school drop out before reaching grade five, the highest regional rate.

Constraints: Nearly half the population in the region lives in severe poverty, earning less than $1 a day. Child labour is a persistent problem, a cause and consequence of low enrolment and high drop-out rates. Pupil–teacher ratios are high in some countries (greater than 60 to 1).

Simple arithmetic shows that a 40% dropout rate combined with 70% enrollment means that 58% of children are receiving no education or less than a 5th-grade education.

For the Sri Lankan legal scholar and professor at the Open University of Sri Lanka, Savitri Goonesekere, recognition and application of the 1989 Convention on the Rights of the Child are necessary because of the social and legal disruption of colonialism. Goonesekere argued, "The colonization of countries in South Asia is part of their historical experience. This period saw the significant modification of personal [religious] law.... It is necessary to recognize that the colonial experience contributed to secularism and uniformity in important areas of child law and policy in these countries."[38]

In searching for culturally relevant definitions of "best interests of the child," child rights advocates are encountering dysfunctional family organizations unable to cope with the changes brought by postcolonialism and the global economy. The results are questions about who assumes responsibility for ensuring the "best interests of the child." Consequently, children need the protection of a universal doctrine of children's rights. Universal rights that include protection and assistance for children are necessary because of disrupted child-rearing patterns and the need to ensure the right to education.

CHILDREN'S RIGHTS AND EDUCATIONAL EXPLOITATION

Paradoxically, given the poor educational conditions facing many of the world's children, there is a growing danger, particularly in developed countries, that educational demands on children are exploitive. This is not a problem of lack of education but just the opposite. In their rush to link education with economic growth, many countries are making increased demands on children to be educated for the workforce. The result is longer schooldays, more homework, and more preparation time for national or state examinations. Although certainly not as debilitating as malnutrition, homelessness, wage labor, and war, too much schooling can rob children of the right to leisure and rest.

Consider the meaning of "the best interests of the child" in Japan. The average elementary student in Japan spends 38 hours a week in school and 8 hours a week doing homework for a grand total of 46 hours. The total for Japanese high school students is 66 hours.[39] Forty-six and 66 hours are certainly above the ideal 40-hour workweek of U.S. labor unions. Parents might proudly boast that their children are spending 66 hours on school work. After all, education is considered a good. However, these students are being denied adequate leisure time in the name of some future employment goal. Japanese schools are geared primarily to educate workers to fit into the economy. Students are not being educated for empowerment or to maximize intellectual pleasures. They are, quite simply, being educated for work.[40]

In addition, there is "examination hell." To prepare for national examinations in Japan, which affect students' future education and employment, 51.6% of children between the ages of 11 and 15 attend cram schools. Twenty-four percent of elementary and junior high school students attend these schools for 2 to 3 hours a week. Six percent spend over 10 hours in cram schools. Paralleling the increasing emphasis on schooling is a decline in sleeping time. Between 1970 and 1990, average sleep time for Japanese elementary students declined from 9.23 hours to 9.03 hours, whereas study time increased from 7.03 to 7.19 hours.[41] Examinations also add to the financial burdens of families. Between 1980 and 1990, the indirect costs (tutors and cram schools) for elementary school students increased from ¥78,899 to 120,463; for junior high students they increased from ¥56,570 to 125,268, and for high school students from ¥38,025 to 70,648.[42]

According to Satoshi Minamikata, professor of law and child rights expert in Japan, the combination of long hours in school and studying and examination hell, is contributing to increased truancy and dislike of school. Since the 1970s, there has been a massive increase in absenteeism with more than four times as many students missing 50 or more days. This increase in absenteeism, Minamikata argued, is attributable to dislike of school. In fact, from 1972 to 1993, there was an actual decrease in the number of elementary school children who were absent because of illness from 57.1 to 24.2%. On the other hand, there was an increase in the number of elementary students absent because of dislike of school from 28.5 to 60.9%. The changes are similar for junior high school where absences for illness decreased from 57.1 to 24.2%, while absences for "dislike of school" increased from 28.5 to 60.9%.[43]

Dislike of schooling appears to be contributing to suicide rates. "However," Minamikata wrote, "a possible dramatic consequence [of dislike of school], a rise in children's suicide, is *not* shown in the statistics.... 1992 ... 27.5 percent were reported to be connected to school or education."[44]

In addition, Japan's long history of abuse of academic freedom and free speech rights in school is a clear violation of the liberty rights provided in the Convention on the Rights of the Child. The Japanese educational system is designed to manipulate students rather than empowering them with skills to evaluate and improve their society. In the 1880s, nationalization of textbooks ensured that censorship, a practice still followed in Japan, would guard against any ideas that might jeopardize the emperor-state. After World War II, traditional justification for censorship appeared in a 1953 magazine article written by a college professor, Kitaoka Juisha. Resurrecting Confucian arguments, he argued for the necessity of state control of morality. "The Japanese people ... are apt to misuse the freedom that they have been granted ... when the control of morals is relaxed, the harlots shamelessly parade the streets, when censorship is abolished, the book-shops bury their counters with erotic magazines. It is doubtful whether such a people should in fact be granted too much freedom."[45] In 1965, the Ministry of Education insisted that in Saburo Ienaga's textbook the word "invasion" be changed to "advance" to describe Japanese military actions in China before World War II. In addition, the government required him to sanitize descriptions of Japanese soldiers killing civilians and raping Chinese women during the 1937 capture of Nanjing. He was also required to remove references to "human body experiments" conducted on thousands of Chinese by the Japanese army. Finally in 1997, Ienaga's struggle was vindicated without invalidating the textbook censorship power of the Ministry of Education.

In summary, the Japanese educational system actually denies childrens' rights by requiring too much time for school, study, and cramming, and by strong censorship of the content of instruction. Disliking education should not be a consequence of exercising the right to education, but that clearly seems to be happening in Japan. The Universal Declaration of Human Rights stated, "Everyone has the right to rest and leisure, including reasonable limitation of working hours."[46] The Convention on the Rights of the Child stated, "State parties recognize the right of the child to rest and leisure, to engage in play and recreational activities appropriate to the child and to participate freely in cultural life and the arts."[47] I believe that Japanese schools and examinations are seriously limiting the right of children to rest, leisure, play, and free participation in the cultural life of the community. I believe that censorship of school materials and the control of learning through national examinations are a violation of the child's liberty rights.

CONCLUSION: JUSTIFICATION FOR THE UNIVERSAL RIGHT TO AN EDUCATION AND CHILDREN'S RIGHTS

Besides binding the world together in a network of commercial and cultural trade, colonialism and the resulting global economy and culture, for better or worse, affect all lives. Colonialism created the conditions requiring human rights doctrines to protect language and cultural minorities. The existence and universal impact of a global culture and economic system require a right to education if human rights are to be protected. This requires that people of all cultures have the knowledge and skills to determine the benefits and liabilities of global culture and economics. In turn, the exercise of the right to education requires a universal concept of children's rights. Based on this argument, and drawing from my discussion of the various UN Declarations, Covenants, and Conventions related to education and children's rights, I propose the following "Justification for the Universal Right to An Education and Children's Rights".

Justification for the Universal Right to An Education and Children's Rights

1. A universal right to an education is justified by the necessity for all people to know how the global culture and economy created by colonialism and postcolonialism affect their lives and what benefits or harm might result from it.

2. A universal right to an education is justified by being necessary for achieving other human rights that guarantee equal economic and social opportunities in the global economy.

3. Universal assistance rights for children, such as government provision of high-quality health care, proper nutrition for normal development, housing, and free schooling, are justified as necessary for children to exercise their right to an education.

4. Universal protection rights for children, such as protection against economic and social exploitation, and employment in work harmful to their morals or health or dangerous to life or likely to hamper their normal development, are justified by being necessary for children to exercise their right to an education.

5. Universal liberty rights for children, such as freedom of expression; freedom to seek, receive, and impart information and ideas; and freedom of thought, are justified as necessary for understanding the impact of the global or dominant economy and culture.

6. Universal right to an education that *does not* serve nationalistic or particular political ends by indoctrination, propaganda, or the use of national examinations to control teacher and student learning is justified by the rights of children to freedom of expression; freedom to seek, receive and impart information and ideas; and freedom of thought.

7. Universal right to an education that *does not* make any distinction, exclusion, limitation, or preference based on race, color, sex, language, social class, religion, or political beliefs is justified as necessary for children to exercise their right to an education.

⇜ 5 ⇝

A Universal Concept of Education:
Human Rights Education and Moral Duties

Implementation of the right to education requires a universal concept of education that is appropriate to differing cultures and languages and helps people make decisions about the advantages and disadvantages of the world's economy and culture. What should all people be entitled to when exercising their right to an education? If groups or persons claim a right to education, what are they claiming? What is the meaning of *education* in the "right to education"? Part of the answer is human rights education. The right to education requires protection of human rights.

"Education in and for human rights is a fundamental human right," proclaimed the Guidelines for National Plans of Action for Human Rights Education issued in 1997 by the UN High Commissioner for Human Rights.[1] However, it is meaningless to simply declare the right to an education in human rights without identifying the agency, person, or government responsible for ensuring its actualization. Who is responsible for securing the right to education? Who ensures that schools do not violate the liberty, cultural, and language rights of children: an international agency such as the UN? Can supervision be agreed on by international treaties that bind governments to protect rights?

The answer, I believe, is that we must rely on all people or on as many as can be taught a moral duty to protect human rights. The fulfillment of universal rights depends on all people's having an obligation to guarantee that all other people's rights are protected, including the right to education. Human history, with its endless tragedies of war and exploitation, demonstrates that concentrations of power cannot be trusted with the responsibility of championing human rights. Human rights will be assured by the actions of all people working collectively or individually.

In their "Introduction to Human Rights Education," Nancy Flowers of Amnesty International and Kristi Rudelius-Palmer of Partners in Human Rights Education stressed that responsibility in human rights education means active protection of the rights of all. They stated: "The responsibilities of all citizens in a democratic society are inseparable from the responsibility *to promote human rights*. To flourish, both democracy and human rights require people's active participation. Human rights education includes *learning the skills of advocacy—to speak and act everyday in the name of human rights*" [emphasis added].[2]

Despite my hope that all people will be active guardians of human rights, I am not a utopian. I believe that the imperfect and fallible human will never be able to create a perfect world. The frailty and quixotic qualities of human emotions and psychological states diminish the chances of humans ever achieving a world free from human rights violations. On the other hand, we can make improvements while unsuccessfully trying to reach an ideal. We should try to imagine the possibility a world where everyone actively works to ensure that all people are able to enjoy their rights. As Pam Costain asserted in "What Are Human Rights?"

> Human rights are both inspirational and practical. Human rights principles hold up the vision of a free, just, and peaceful world and set minimum standards for how individuals and institutions everywhere should treat people. Human rights also empower people with a framework for action when those minimum standards are not met, for people still have human rights even if the laws or those in power do not recognize or protect them.[3]

My choice of all people rather than global or national organizations is based on distrust of concentrated power. Often, concentration of power in international organizations or governments tends to be self-serving. The history of rights debates is filled with governments defining and recognizing rights according to their own self interests. During the Cold War, as I discussed before, human rights efforts were often frustrated by arguments between capitalist and communist powers over the meaning of rights. Both sides had their own interpretations based on political and economic interests. As I previously argued, the UN Education for All made compromises, in the name of cultural rights, to make its programs acceptable to cultures that clearly violate the human rights of women and children.

I am not dismissing governments and international organizations as allies in the struggle to make human rights a reality. They certainly can help people protect rights. However, the effort must be focused on people and not institutions. Governments and other organizations will follow the lead of a universally held moral ideal. Admittedly, my choice is debatable, but I place my bet on the potency of an individually held moral belief rather than gambling on the outcome of organizational behavior. Also, I limit my hope to progressing to universal human rights rather than actual accomplishment of the goal. Reaching for a dream is important even if it cannot be completely achieved.

My concern with relying on institutions is illustrated by the recent use of human rights education as a forum to enlist support for the UN. Similar to overzealous supporters of a nation state, some international leaders, blinded by their belief in the righteousness of UN actions, asserted that human rights education should include teaching students the value of the organization's peacekeeping efforts. As I will argue, all citizens should be taught to be as critical of the United Nations as they should be of any other political organization.

Consequently, I begin with a critical analysis of the UN official proposals and guidelines for human rights education. Following this discussion, I present my arguments for a human rights education that includes the teaching of a moral duty for all people to actively protect the human rights of others.

THE UNITED NATION'S DECADE FOR HUMAN RIGHTS EDUCATION

After declaring human rights instruction part of the "right to education," the 1993 Vienna World Conference on Human Rights, as well as later initiatives, intertwined human rights with other ideas such as democracy, the rule of law, and UN peacekeeping efforts. Officially issued on July 12, 1993, Article 79 of the Vienna Declaration & Programme of Action "calls on all States to include human rights, humanitarian law, *democracy and rule of law as subjects in the curricula of all learning institutions in formal and non-formal setting*" [emphasis added].[4] In Article 80, the document stated: "Human rights education should include *peace, democracy, development and social justice* as set forth in international and regional human rights instruments" [emphasis added].[5] My question, as I discuss later, is whether democracy and the rule of law should be included in human rights education. This question is important because later wording on human rights education included support of the UN international peace efforts. Should human rights education include support of the United Nations?

In a broader context, delegates to the Vienna meeting debated the question of who or what organization would take responsibility for ensuring the enforcement of human rights, including human rights education and the right to education. Those attending the meeting worried about the applicability of human rights to all national circumstances and the lack of enforcement. According to the report of the *Human Rights Tribune*, delegates from China, Iran, Malaysia, Singapore, Indonesia, Yemen, and Syria wanted to slow efforts to protect political and civil rights until their countries could solve social and economic problems. Representatives from these countries maintained that authoritarian governments were necessary for economic development. In addition, Islamic nations were concerned about the failure of the UN to fully protect Muslim residents of Bosnia and Herzegovina from ethnic cleansing and genocide by the Serbs.[6] Complaining about enforcement, legal activists urged the UN to create a High Commissioner for Human Rights and an International Criminal Court to protect human rights. After much debate, delegates recommended that the UN General Assembly create the position of High Commissioner for Human Rights and that the International Law Commission develop a plan for an international criminal court.[7]

There were mixed reviews of these efforts to enforce human rights doctrines. The International Centre for Human Rights and Democratic Development in Canada reported: "The major battle that was fought and ultimately won in Vienna concerned 'universality'–whether or not fundamental human rights transcend cultural peculiarities."[8] In contrast, others complained that nondemocratic institutions were resisting the spread of human rights. "The efforts of the predominantly Asian governments [China, Iran, Malaysia, Singapore, Indonesia, Yemen and Syria]," wrote Douglas Payne of Freedom House, "managed to impede efforts by democratic nations and non-governmental organizations to strengthen UN human rights enforcement mechanisms."[9] While Reed Brody, director of the U.S.-based Human Rights Law Group, expressed relief that the Vienna meeting reaffirmed the universality of human rights and recognized the rights of indigenous peoples, he worried: "We don't see new measures, we don't see a clear commitment to the United Nations to give a certain percentage of money to human rights.... All of the wonderful words in this document will be illusory if the money is not there to back them up and to pay for the mechanisms."[10]

Although many people complained about the outcome of the Vienna meeting, one important result was the General Assembly's approval of the recommendation to establish the post of High Commissioner for Human Rights in December 1993. One specified duty of the High Commissioner was "to coordinate relevant United Nations education and public information programmes in the field of human rights."[11] This responsibility was reiterated in March 1994 by the Commission on Human Rights in a resolution requiring the High Commissioner "to include among his specific objectives a *plan of action* for the United Nations decade for human rights education."[12]

In March 1995, the General Assembly issued its official resolution proclaiming the UN Decade for Human Rights Education. This resolution emphasized that human rights education should include broader topics than just information about the rights protected by international covenants and declarations. Human rights education, the resolution stated, "should constitute a comprehensive life-long process by which people at all levels in development and in all strata of society learn respect for the dignity of others and the means and methods of ensuring that respect in all societies."[13] In this context, human rights instruction included attitudinal (dignity of others) and activist (ensuring the respect in all societies) objectives.

It is clear from the Plan of Action for the Decade for Human Rights Education submitted to the UN General Assembly by the first appointed High Commissioner for Human Rights, Jose Ayala-Lasso of Ecuador, that the UN intended to broaden the concept of human rights education to include the general policy objectives of the organization. Unfortunately, from my perspective, it is possible that the addition of other objectives could delude and create unnecessary controversy. On the other hand, many others might agree that human rights education should, as expressed in the Plan of Action, promote human rights and "understanding, tolerance, peace and friendly relations among nations, and all racial or religious groups, as well as *encourage the development of United Nations activities in pursuance of those objectives*" [emphasis added].[14]

My problem with the mandate that human rights education support UN activities on issues such as "peace and friendly relations among nations" is that this sounds similar to nationalistic forms of education used to indoctrinate students to support various government institutions and activities. Rather than owing allegiance to a national organization, human rights education, as suggested in the Plan of Action, prepares the student to hold an allegiance to an international government, namely the UN. Are UN efforts to promote peace always in the best interest of all people? Are UN peacekeeping efforts free of the political interests of powerful member nations?

In 1996, Cuba raised a similar objection to linking human rights education to peacekeeping efforts. The Ministry of Foreign Affairs of Cuba called attention to paragraph 49 of the Plan of Action, which stated: "Centre for human rights will continue and enhance its activities aimed at assisting peace-keepers."[15] The Ministry demanded that clear distinction be maintained "between peace-keeping activities and human rights activities."[16] The only connection between the two, the Cuban government suggested, was that peacekeepers should be educated in human rights and should respect human rights when carrying out their activities.

Although I applaud many of the activities of the UN and in particular its role in creating and promoting universal human rights, I think human rights education requires teaching people to question and be skeptical of the actions of any government or international power, including the UN. It is possible that in the future the UN could actually violate human rights in the name of international justice.

I have the same problems with the interjection of ideological issues that I consider separate from the concept of human rights. Referring to the 1993 Vienna World Conference on Human Rights, the action plan stated: "Human rights, humanitarian law, *democracy and the rule of law* should be included as subjects in all formal and informal learning institutions."[17] I have already raised objections to the consideration of democracy as an ideal form of government. While I consider democracy an important step in the evolution of political institutions, I believe, as stated previously, that there is room for improvement. I have also suggested that there are cultural issues, particularly about those cultures that seek guidance from the wisdom of elders.

I have the same feelings about the concept of the rule of law. I applaud the role of the concept in protecting people from the arbitrary actions of rulers and in ensuring equality before the law. However, the rule of law is meaningless without specifying the nature of the laws. The rule of law is a principle that can easily be recognized and supported by the most ruthless dictators. The rule of law can also be used to protect vast amounts of wealth held by corporations and individuals even when that wealth results in extreme deprivation for the rest of the population. In addition, the rule of law might be in conflict with cultural practices that rely on tradition and custom.

An emphasis on the rule of law also supports passive forms of citizenship. Consider the results of relating citizenship and law in an 8th-grade textbook, *We, the World and Human Rights,* published jointly by the Netherlands Helsinki Committee and the Jann Tonisson Institute with financial support of the Dutch Foreign Ministry. The textbook was written as an introduction to human rights as specified in the Universal Declaration of Human Rights. After declaring Estonia an example of a democratic country, the textbook quoted Article 19 of the Estonian Constitution: "In exercising their rights and liberties and fulfilling their duties, everyone must respect and consider the rights of liberties of other persons and *observe the law*" [emphasis added].[18] First, regarding passive citizenship, it should be noted that the Estonian Constitution calls for only respecting and considering human rights as opposed to actively seeking to protect the human rights of all.

Second, immediately following the constitutional requirement to "observe the law" is the statement, "But the laws will remain only documents.... People who ... follow the laws and contribute to the development of welfare of all people, are considered to be good citizens."[19] Mere obedience to the law is a very passive form of citizenship. In addition, what happens if a law violates human rights? Should students not be told to violate the law if it is a violation of human rights? Should a more active form of citizenship be defined that obligates citizens to change laws when they violate human rights?

Amnesty International's *First Steps: A Manual for Starting Human Rights Education* suggested a passive form of citizenship in its lesson "Rights and Responsibilities." The lesson's goal is "Learning point— Every right has a corresponding responsibility."[20] One interpretation of responsibility in this goal is that everyone should ensure that all people are able to exercise all their rights. In my mind, this is what it means to say that all rights have responsibilities. Responsibilities vary according to the right. If the government or some group infringes on the right to free speech, then my responsibility is to actively combat this infringement of free speech rights. If a worker does not have adequate leisure time or health care, then it is my responsibility to actively help the worker obtain these benefits. In contrast, the Amnesty International manual's discussion of responsibilities emphasized not interfering with the rights of others and limiting the exercise of rights. For example, *First Steps* stated:

Information about Rights and Responsibilities

Every right has a corresponding responsibility. For example, your right to freedom of speech is limited by *your responsibility not to say untrue things which will degrade another person and abuse their right to dignity and good reputation.*

The balance of our rights and our responsibilities to respect the rights of other people *means that we usually have to exercise our rights within certain restraints* [emphasis added].[21]

The oddly passive quality of Amnesty International's manual of human rights education is highlighted by its complete neglect of the Vienna Conference's mandate that the right to education includes an education in human rights. Rather than actively calling for national school systems to include human rights education, the manual stressed the importance of trying to squeeze the topic into curricula controlled by national testing and educational administrators. Consider the manual's following curricular guidelines:

Primary Curricula

In primary schools, because there is less exam pressure on children and staff, and because teachers usually teach several subjects to one class, teachers have often found it quite easy to get the Principals' *permission* to teach human rights in a way which involves many subjects.

Secondary Curricula

Introducing teaching for human rights at this level can be *more difficult*. A lot depends on the *attitude of the Principal and the educational authorities*, who are often worried about the already- overcrowded timetable and the students' need to prepare for major examinations [emphasis added].[22]

Words such as "permission" and "attitude of the principal and educational authorities" jump off the page at anyone familiar with the Vienna Conference's mandate. Teachers should not be told to seek "permission."Teachers should be told to "demand" from authorities the time and resources necessary to provide all students with their right to an education in human rights. If one is truly militant about human rights, then one should urge teachers to strike until education authorities complied with the right to human rights education.

The peace efforts of the UN, democracy, and the rule of law are certainly appropriate topics of discussion in any educational forum. However, should they be part of human rights education? Based on previous arguments, I believe that discussion of these topics should be part of the "right to education" as matters of speculation about ways of achieving the good life. For instance, I consider it important for students to examine the accomplishments and problems facing democratic governments and to consider possible improvements. On the other hand, I do not believe democracy should be taught as having equivalent value to the idea of human rights. Certainly, the Convention on the Rights of the Child protects students from such blatant attempts to limit freedom of thought by trying to persuade students that democracy, rule of law, and UN policies offer the best hope for the protection of human rights.

I am critical of the potential damage of the interjection of these ideas and support of the UN as unquestioned elements in human rights education, but I applaud the mandate that all governments prepare national programs for human rights education. Unfortunately, the target of the mandate is already established governments, many of which are violators of human rights. The Plan of Action called on "all Governments to contribute, in cooperation with NGOs, educators and the media ... to consider the establishment of a national focal point for human rights education and the creation of a national resource and training centre for human rights education."[23] The Commission on Human Rights approved this proposal with two resolutions in 1995 and 1996 asking member nations to plan human rights education programs.[24]

Despite the objections of the Cuban government to linking human rights education to UN peacekeeping efforts, the High Commissioner for Human Rights continued to make this connection. In 1997, the High Commissioner distributed "Guidelines for National Plans of Action for Human Rights Education." Section 5A of the document defined human rights education as the imparting of skills, knowledge, and attitudes directed to:

a. The strengthening of respect for human rights and fundamental freedom,

b. The full development of the human personality and the sense of its dignity,

c. The promotion of understanding, tolerance, gender equality and friendship among all nations, indigenous peoples and racial, national, ethnic, religious and linguistic groups,

d. The enabling of all persons to participate effectively in a free society,

e. The furtherance of the activities of the United Nations for the maintenance of peace [emphasis added].[25]

Similar to previous statements, the Guidelines included under "General Principles" the "importance of human rights education for *democracy, sustainable development, the rule of law,* the environment and peace" [emphasis added].[26]

I believe that these general principles highlight the problem of total reliance on governments, the United Nations, and private agencies in the protection of human rights and the creation of human rights education programs. There is a tendency for people to confuse their own beliefs and feelings of righteousness with human rights doctrines. Human rights doctrines provide the opportunity to open the floodgates of creative thinking about alternatives to existing political, social, and economic organizations. The very principles of cultural rights guarantee diversity of institutions and ideas. Although the link between human rights and UN peacekeeping efforts is reminiscent of governments using schools to teach patriotism, the introduction of democracy, sustainable development, and the rule of law into human rights education simply reflects the ideology of some UN leaders. As I have stated previously, these ideas are worthy of debate but they are far from defining a perfect world.

Some instructional materials come close to repeating the worst errors of nationalism by building emotional loyalty through symbols and holidays. The greatest violation of human rights has occurred under governments, such as Nazi Germany, that stressed emotional attachments to symbols of the state. It would be an error to repeat this fostering of blind support in the name of human rights. For instance, a report "Human Rights and Citizenship Education—A Czech Classroom Experience" recommended recognizing "UN Day" and "the Anniversary of the Convention on the Rights of the Child and Earth Day" and using Council of Europe and Amnesty International posters.[27] These might provide opportunities for discussion, but these anniversary celebrations days could easily slip into emotional public displays similar to the 4th of July in the United States. Unthinking patriotism should be avoided in the quest of human rights.

Of even greater concern is the resistance of government-operated school systems to human rights programs that challenge educational efforts at building patriotic and nationalist sentiments. Sometimes teachers believe human rights are a threat to their own authority and the authority of other adults. For instance, human rights educators found teachers in post-Soviet Russia wary of human rights instruction because they "did not believe students could understand human rights; in some cases they even thought that learning about human rights could be harmful because it could result in increased conflicts between children and adults in their community."[28] Similar to many other authoritarian-government teachers around the world, Russian teachers were uncomfortable with free and open discussions. "Classroom traditions," the Human Rights Education Association reported, "reflected 'direct' or 'didactic' teaching, whereby Russian teachers saw their role as imparting the correct knowledge to students. Classrooms tended to be teacher-centered, and educational programs rarely employed activity-based methods, such as discussions and role plays."[29]

Reflecting the clash between human rights education and indoctrinating-nationalistic education, Russian teachers balked at educational methods that threatened feelings of patriotism. In one role- playing lesson on the topic of freedom of movement, students were divided into two groups representing a democratic and a nondemocratic country. The Human Rights Education Association reported, "The students' task was to move from the non-democratic country to the other, collecting all appropriate documentation, and so forth. Observations revealed that the students were quite actively and emotionally engaged in the role play; *however, some teachers found the lesson 'unpatriotic'.* As a consequence, the role play script was revised to include additional explanation about freedom of movement" [emphasis added].[30]

The problem for human rights education in existing government-operated school systems is compounded by traditional notions of civic education. Felisa Tibbitts of the Human Rights Education Association compiled a list of teaching materials that could be infused in traditional civic education courses. In the introductory statement, Tibbitts justified the list by referring to the UN Decade for Human Rights Education and the High Commissioner's previously discussed three components of human rights education: knowledge; values, beliefs, and attitudes; and action. Immediately following the listing of these three components, Tibbitts stated, "Teaching democratic citizenship involves *instilling a commitment to a system of government, valuing the rule of law* and showing tolerance towards other people's opinions."[31] Certainly, traditional civics education has involved committing students to a system of government and laws. In the context of a nationalist school system, this would mean a commitment to the existing system of government and laws. However, nothing in human rights documents suggests people should be committed to any particular system of government. I argue that people should resist government systems and laws that infringe on human rights. However, the reality of government-operated schools is that they are not in the business of educating future citizens to revolt against the government or to reject the government's laws.

Consequently, human rights education needs to be protected from the self-interest of organizations such as the UN and nationalistic governments and also from those in power who want to interject their own ideologies into human rights principles. Human rights provide the opportunity for all people to participate in discovering the good life. Human rights doctrines must be protected from sloganeering terms, such as democracy, rule of law, and sustainable development. One mechanism for achieving this protection, I believe, is to include in human rights instruction the moral duty to protect the human rights of all. This avoids the problem endemic in human rights education of preaching a passive form of citizenship which defines responsibility as avoiding interference into the rights of others rather than a citizenship that actively works to protect the rights of all.

PROTECTION OF HUMAN RIGHTS AS A CLAIM RIGHT

Central to encouraging a moral duty to protect human rights is the concept of claim right. This is contained in the High Commissioner's guidelines for human rights education that divides instruction into three components:

   a. Knowledge: provision of information about human rights and mechanisms for their protection,

   b. Values, beliefs and attitudes: promotion of a human rights culture through the development of values, beliefs and attitudes which uphold human rights,

   c. Action: encouragement to take action to defend human rights and prevent human rights abuses.[32]

I believe that the real protection of human rights depends on the actualization and elaboration of the third instructional component—

ACTION. This requires teaching that all people have a MORAL DUTY to defend human rights. The implementation of human rights requires a commitment by all people to the protection of the human rights of all. Consequently, it can be argued, actualization of the right to education depends on all citizens' assuming the responsibility of ensuring that all people receive an education. As I argued in the last chapter, this means an education that does not violate cultural and language rights or children's rights to free access to information and freedom of thought.

In this dependent relation between human rights and moral duties, I am treating human rights as claim rights. Claim rights place a responsibility on all people and institutions, including government, to ensure that people have the ability to exercise a right. In contrast, other definitions of rights, such as liberty rights and assistance rights, lack the requirement of political activity by all citizens.

Liberty rights are usually thought of as freedom from interference, particularly from the intrusion of government into private lives. In many ways, early Stalinists were correct in arguing that liberty rights are necessary only if there exists a tyrannical government or other dominating social organization. Liberty rights do not need to be called on if one agrees with government actions. However, liberty rights do provide an important protection against unwanted intrusion and they do serve to place important constraints on education, namely that education cannot take away the right of students to information and intellectual freedom.

Compared with claim rights, liberty rights do not place a burden on individuals, organizations, and government to ensure the fulfillment of rights. For instance, the right to an education as a liberty right guarantees that individuals and government do not interfere with people pursing their right to education. As a liberty right, the right to education does not guarantee that a person or child can actually receive an education. No burdens are placed on individuals, organizations, or government to ensure that people can exercise their right to an education.

Assistance rights, on the other hand, do place a burden on government and society to ensure that all children receive an education along with adequate shelter, nutrition, and health care. Assistance rights are similar to claim rights in that they obligate society to provide certain types of social services to help people achieve their rights. The 1948 Universal Declaration of Human Rights contained important assistance rights as exemplified by Article 25:

1. Everyone has the right to a standard of living adequate for the health and well-being of himself and of his family, including food, clothing, housing and medical care and necessary social services,

and the right to security in the event of unemployment, sickness, disability, widowhood, old age or lack of livelihood in circumstances beyond his control.

Motherhood and childhood are entitled to special care and assistance. All children, whether born in or out of wedlock, shall enjoy the same social protection.[33]

The combination of liberty and assistance rights imposes on governments or other organizations the duty of ensuring that children receive an education, that educational resources are provided, and that freedom of information and ideas is protected in schools. The missing element in this combination of liberty and assistance rights is identifying the person or organization with responsibility for ensuring the fulfillment of these rights and all other human rights.

Claim rights place a responsibility on all people to act to protect the rights of others. Claim rights create an imperative that citizens are active as opposed to being passively obedient to laws and concerned only with not interfering with the rights of others. Claim rights place a burden on all people to actively work to ensure human rights.

The right to education, as a claim right, places a duty on society and government to ensure that everyone can exercise that right. If I am taught human rights as claim rights, then I am taught that I have a duty to ensure that all people have the ability to carry out their right to an education. It is my duty and the duty of all people to guarantee that all people can acquire an education. If the right to an education includes an education in human rights, then, as a claim right, everyone has the duty to unite in a common struggle or to act individually to ensure that everyone has the opportunity to exercise this right!

If a child was unable to receive an education, then, as a claim right, every person who knew of the child's condition would feel obligated to correct the situation. The cause of the child's educational deprivation could be the result of the government's failure to provide schooling or the neglect of the parents. In either situation, all citizens would feel a responsibility to actively work to ameliorate the child's condition. What about a violation of the child's liberty rights to free access to information as a result of the actions of parents, teachers, or school administrators? Considered as a claim right, this violation would require citizens that know about the situation to directly act to protect the children's liberty rights. Let us assume that the parents are interfering with the child's liberty rights. Then teachers, school administrators, and other citizens have the obligation to do something to stop the parents from violating the child's rights. If it is a teacher infringing on children's liberty rights, then the child's parents, school administrators, and all other citizens should be committed to actively end the process.

THE MORAL IMPERATIVE OF HUMAN RIGHTS: GUILT AND SHAME

Guilt and public shame are the energizing emotions that provide universal protection of human rights. Citizens should feel guilty and face public shame if they do not defend others against violation of their human rights. Instilling a moral duty to protect human rights should result in a feeling of guilt when a person fails to carry out this duty. Jewish and Christian traditions have demonstrated the power of guilt to maintain minimal levels of social control. In the 19th century, Japanese leaders argued that Christian nations had a distinct advantage in controlling their populations because of religious practices that promoted feelings of guilt by punishing behaviors with threats of eternal damnation. In contrast, the Confucian traditions of some Asian countries rely on public shame for social control through the approval or disapproval of the group. Despite the concerns of 19th-century Asian leaders, public shame continues to be an important means of group control.[34]

I want people to feel guilt and public shame if they fail to protect the rights of others. I want these feelings to fuel the psyche and to force people to act to preserve people's rights. Just as Christian crusaders were motivated by the mythology of Christ's death and salvation, I want all people to be human rights crusaders who believe in the possibility of world justice and peace. However, unlike Christian crusaders, who, it can be argued, violated their own religion by conducting wars and killing others, human rights crusaders will be constrained by their own belief in human rights. While working to protect human rights, people will not violate human rights. In this case, the means do not justify the end.

What does this imply for the right to education? Motivated by feelings of public shame and guilt, people should feel obligated to ensure that everyone has the right to education. In addition, people should be aroused to actively guarantee that schools do not violate human rights. The moral duty to protect human rights puts everyone on guard against the denial of education to other people. Consider this proposition in the framework of the previously stated "Universal Right to An Education and Children's Rights." Directed by a moral imperative to act, all people are obligated to ensure that all others receive an elementary and secondary education according to this universal definition of education.

ALL HUMAN BEINGS ...
MANUAL FOR HUMAN RIGHTS EDUCATION

What does instruction in knowledge, values, beliefs, attitudes, and moral duty look like in practice? A good starting point in answering this question is UNESCO's instructional manual *Human Beings ... Manual for Human Rights Education: The Teacher's Library.* Written in response to the Vienna Conference's call for human rights education, the 50th anniversary of the Universal Declaration of Human Rights and the United Nations Decade for Human Rights Education, the *Manual* was composed by a team of educators and experts from around the world working under the direction of Kaisa Savolainen, director of UNESCO's Section for Humanistic, Cultural and International Education. Designed for primary- and secondary-school teachers and informal educational institutions, UNESCO representatives tested the *Manual* in schools throughout the world.[35]

Therefore, the *Manual* is an important document to analyze because it represents what UNESCO leaders consider to be the best practices in human rights instruction. Also, because of its significance for human rights education, the *Manual* provides a good starting point for considering the integration of human rights education into the basic right to education and its place alongside the universal guidelines for literacy and numeracy instruction.

Written primarily for teachers, the first part of the manual focuses on essential concepts that will make, according to the *Manual*'s foreword, "human rights education ... rigorous, have a scientific basis, expand knowledge and promote thought."[36] Part 1 is designed to introduce teachers to basic human rights ideas in preparation for instructing students. Consequently, this section highlights the ideas UNESCO's writers believe are essential for human rights education. The second part makes suggestions on how various school disciplines can incorporate human rights themes. The third part provides instructional examples.

DEMOCRACY AND EDUCATION

Despite the foreword's claim of providing a "scientific basis" for human rights education, the first part of the *Manual*, without providing any scientific proof, asserted an interdependent relation between human rights education and democratic schooling. Unfortunately, the authors seemed unaware of the many debates over this issue, particularly the issue of democratic control versus democratic culture. Although the text made the distinction between democratic political structure and culture, it did not recognize the problems inherent in combining the two in educational institutions.

The *Manual* asserted: "Human rights, the rule of law and DEMOC-RACY are closely intertwined." The word "DEMOCRACY" is capitalized to indicate a definition provided in the margin of the page.

> Democracy: A political system based on the participation of the people. It foresees, among others, the separation of powers among the judiciary, the legislative and the executive authorities, as well as free and regular elections.[37]

Apparently realizing that this political definition of democracy highlighted in the margin does not guarantee human rights, the authors added a cultural definition of democracy in the actual text:

> Democracy is a way of living together and an expression of respect for other people; it must be rooted in a genuine democratic culture, a culture of debate and dialogue.... A critical attitude should therefore be developed in children and young people towards the institutions that govern a State or regulate life in a given society.[38]

In translating these democratic concepts into school practices, the *Manual* created a problematic situation by combining the democratic concept of control with that of democratic culture. Quoting the Integrated Framework of Action on Education for Peace, Human Rights and Democracy approved by the General Conference of UNESCO in 1995, the *Manual* called for "implementation of democratic school management, involving teachers, pupils, parents and the local community as a whole."[39] At the same time, the *Manual* proclaimed the importance of a democratic classroom culture based on "freedom of expression, thought, assembly and association."[40]

What happens if a democratic management votes—including administrators, parents, students, and other community members—to exclude certain ideas from discussion in the school? In the United States, democratically elected school boards and state legislatures have voted to exclude all sorts of ideas from free discussion in the classroom, including political and economic ideas related communism, anarchism, and socialism and even ideas related to human reproduction such as birth control and abortion. In fact, as I discussed earlier in the book, a democratically elected Congress refused to ratify the Universal Declaration of Human Rights.

Simply stated, democratic political control can be in conflict with the maintenance of a democratic culture that stresses critical debate and dialogue and freedom of expression and thought in the classroom. This is the problem raised by the philosopher Amy Gutmann in her book *Democratic Education*. Similar to the *Manual*, she defined democracy as a state in which all adults share in power. However, she recognizes the possibility that this democratic control can restrict freedom of ideas and result in possible domination of the school curriculum by the ideas of the majority. She argued that the government, families, majority rule, and individuals can all interfere with freedom of ideas and nondiscrimination. It is possible that a majority of citizens might decide to limit freedom of expression in the classroom and to establish laws and institutions that restrict the rights of minority cultures. In other words, political democracy does not guarantee human rights.[41]

Gutmann believed, and I agree with her, that the two hallmarks of a democratic education are freedom of ideas and nondiscrimination about race, gender, religion, ethnic origin, political affiliation, and disabilities. Basic to democracy, she argued, is the ability of people to deliberate among alternative concepts to the good life. In this context, she articulated a concept of "nonrepressive" education. A nonrepressive education, she contended, allows students to consider different concepts of the good life. Nonrepression requires freedom of thought in the classroom.

However, she argued, nondiscrimination does place some limits on the freedom of speech of teachers. She argued that educators have the authority to teach children racial, ethnic, and religious tolerance because these virtues are necessary for a democratic society. Expanding on this concept of nondiscrimination, I would include the obligation of teachers to teach and support human rights doctrines. Of course, this does not preclude critical discussions of human rights.

Therefore, Gutmann argued, the principles of nonrepression and nondiscrimination should place limits on the democratic management of education. In other words, control by the majority is limited by these principles. Democratic control is not allowed to interfere with students' consideration of different versions of the good life and the teaching of human rights.

The problem, therefore, is creating a political structure for education that allows democratic control but restricts interference with the principles of nonrepression and nondiscrimination. Gutmann's answer is to vest authority in what she refers to as "democratic professionalism" among teachers. She wrote: "The professional responsibility is to uphold the principle of nonrepression by cultivating the capacity for democratic deliberation."[42] In the framework of democratic professionalism, teachers become the protectors of nonrepression and nondiscrimination in the classroom against the potential interference of democratic majorities. In this context, I would change the concept of democratic professionalism to include a moral duty to protect human rights.

Applying Gutmann's reasoning to the concept of democratic management would restrict the ideas presented in the *Manual for Human Rights Education*. School administrators, the community, students, and teachers should all be governed by feelings of guilt and public shame if they allow democratically arrived at decisions to interfere with human rights, particularly the right to freedom of thought.

Of course, this leads to the age-old problem of utopian visions. How do you get the system running if each part is dependent on the other? In this case, teachers and school administrators must be taught a moral duty to protect human rights. Where do they receive this instruction before operating schools dedicated to teaching human rights? Who will jump-start the system?

Because I am not a utopian or believer in the perfectability of humans or society, I can only hope that democratic management would be limited by the moral duty of teachers and school administrators to protect human rights. It is something humans should strive to accomplish. It should be part of the education of teachers and school administrators. While perfection might not be possible, but the goal is something worth trying to achieve.

"NATIONALISTIC" AND UNCRITICAL HUMAN RIGHTS EDUCATION

Oddly missing from Part 1 of the *Manual* is any discussion of the problems associated with justifying the existence of universal human rights. Designed to introduce teachers to basic human rights concepts, the section fails to achieve the goal of democratic education, which includes, in the words of the *Manual,* "a critical attitude" and "dialogue and debate." In other words, human rights are presented as universal values which require no justification. It seems logical that if a democratic classroom culture is to be developed then the very nature of universal rights should be open to debate.

In fact, UNESCO's *Manual* is similar to nationalistic forms of education that attempt to win support through indoctrination. The very history of human rights and the UN is presented in an uncritical format. Resembling the worst forms of nationalistic history, the *Manual* never suggests to readers that there were major controversies surrounding the Universal Declaration of Human Rights and that countries, such as the United States, refused to ratify the document.

The *Manual* gives the following celebratory history of human rights:

As the nations were convinced that the effective protection of human rights was essential to achieving these objectives [of the UN], on 10 December 1948 the United Nations General Assembly proclaimed the Universal Declaration of Human Rights.

Even today, the Universal Declaration of Human Rights is regarded as the cardinal document that enshrines and gives impetus to the promotion of human rights. The authority and moral value that it has acquired over the past fifty years make it a fundamental reference point. Nearly all documents concerning human rights quote the declaration and some states refer to it directly in their national constitutions.[43]

This quotation is similar to nationalistic histories designed to win patriotic allegiances by presenting their constitutional histories as a consensus of values. Words such as "enshrines" conjure up sacred utterances that are beyond criticism. In the United States, nationalistic school textbooks neglect discussions of the possibility of the U.S. Constitution being a product of concerns about protecting property rights. Very seldom in nationalistic school systems is the national constitution a target of critical discussion in the classroom.

In the case of the *Manual*, both the United Nations and the Universal Declaration of Human Rights are exempt from critical deliberation. The *Manual* justifies universal human rights by claiming they are inalienable values. The problem of cultural differences is skipped over with glib sentences such as "These values [human rights] are universal. Cultures and societies differ so much that their expression takes varying forms but diversity in no way affects the foundation of inalienable values constituted by human rights."[44] The *Manual* then precedes to describe dignity, freedom, equality, and justice as fundamental human values without providing any justification.

Other human rights texts tend to sanctify human rights documents. The 8th-grade textbook *We, The World and Human Rights* jumps from a one-paragraph history of slavery in Egypt and the United States to the uncritical and misleading statement:

> Only after World War II people came to an understanding that all people should have equal rights to live and to be happy. In order to achieve that an organisation uniting all people of the world was established in 1945— the United Nations Organisation (UNO). In 1948 the Universal Declaration of Human Rights was adopted. It consists of 30 articles.[45]

Admittedly, this text is for 8th-graders. However, it should have been stated that there were and are important controversies about the universality and content of human rights documents. In addition, the quotation suggests that all "people came to an understanding." Such simple-minded histories restrict rather than encourage critical thought.

Even when the *Manual* highlights issues associated with human values, there is no suggestion that they are open for critical discussion. For instance, consider the discussion of equality described as "an underlying principle of the universality of human rights." Using bold and capital letters, the *Manual* stated:

> EQUALITY is a value, an ideal for people who live a hard day-to-day life of economic inequalities—unemployment, sweat-shop labour—social in-

equalities caused by the privileges enjoyed by some people and the exploitation of others, and inequality of educational opportunity. Equality must always be fought for. Freedom and equality are both indispensable: it is out of the question, from the point of view of human rights, to combat inequalities by abolishing freedom. When this happens, the result is dictatorship, the absolute and arbitrary power of some human being over others. Imprisonment, torture, ill-treatment—in short, any form of arbitrary power that destroys the freedom of other people—are fundamentally opposed to equal rights between human beings.

As a universal value, equality concerns the freedoms and rights of each individual: other people are different from me but are my equals, and I respect their freedom in the same way as I assert my own.[46]

In this case the word "equality" is used almost like religious dogma. Like the word "God," equality is presented as an unquestioned good with universal value. However, the *Manual's* text suggests a wide-ranging and debatable use of the word *equality*. In the previous passage, the word EQUALITY is used in four differing contexts, each with its own discrete meaning: namely, economic equality, equality of educational opportunity, political equality, and social equality.

Similar ideological statements appear in Part 3, which is devoted to classroom activities. A classroom activity devoted to "Learning about democracy" suggests, "In secondary schools, describing the nature and main characteristics of *parliamentary* and governmental institutions. Showing in what sense they are *mainstays of democracy*. Setting up an experimental 'students parliament' is an excellent opportunity to take stock of the resources and the difficulties involved in the democratic process."[47] Rather than presenting parliamentary government as a "mainstay of democracy," the lesson might raise this as a question. Besides the question of the desirability of democracy, there is the issue of whether or not a parliamentary government is in fact democratic because it depends on elected representatives to express the wishes of citizens. Some might argue that representative government is not a democracy and that a true democracy requires the direct voting of all citizens on laws. In addition, the lesson seems particularly Eurocentric because it does not take account of cultural differences. Some cultures might prefer a community meeting and consensus as a means of governance.

The most startling example of unquestioned ideas is the *Manual's* almost Stalinist use of the concept of "solidarity." The writers claim that "human rights do[es] not encourage individualism. On the contrary," it is asserted in Part 3, "they [human rights] ... are rooted in solidarity with other people's history and future in a commitment to 'a spirit of brotherhood.'"[48] In a section on classroom activities, the reader is told, "Teachers should ... encourage solidarity-based activities and the organization of events (exhibitions of the children's work on a given human rights, for example). Such projects are in keeping with the philosophy of human rights, which calls for *cooperation between individuals and States*."⁴⁹

Sometimes I think there is a confusion of traditional values of Western progressive education with human rights education. The following "Assessment of Developing Values" appears without any critical analysis in Amnesty International's *First Steps: A Manual for Starting Human Rights Education*:

> How do you rate yourself on the items listed here?
> (A = very good, B = good, C = ok, D = very poor)
> * respect for others
> * interest in others
> * listening to others
> * sticking to the job
> * sensitive to others' needs
> * fair judgement of others
> * cooperating with others
> * thinking before acting
> * being honest
> * admitting errors⁵⁰

Most Western readers might feel sympathetic toward this list of values, but they should realize the complicated cultural differences in meaning. For instance, "sticking to the job" and "interest in others" seem to have little relation, as far as I can discern, to human rights education. One appears to be a value taken straight from the Protestant ethic, while the other sounds like good Victorian manners. All the other items could easily undergo critical discussion about the meaning related to different cultures. Why did the writers for Amnesty International put these items in their human rights education manual?

It could be that the writers of the manual were engulfed by the existing sea of educational babble, which they simply accepted without critical interpretation. For instance, the assessment list is footnoted as being taken directly from a U.S. social studies textbook (John Michaelis, *Social Studies for Children: A Guide to Basic Instruction*, 10ᵗʰ Edition [Englewood Cliffs: Prentice Hall, 1988], p. 377). One certainly should be critical of the relation between human rights education and a textbook written and published during the Reagan years of the 1980s.

I am not opposed to the inspirational sound of words such as equality, democracy, sisterhood/brotherhood, and cooperation. The words indicate the best of human intentions. However, they are complicated concepts that may or may not contribute to the advancement of human rights. Is individualism in conflict with human rights? Perhaps, human rights could be advanced with less rather than more cooperation between individuals and the state. These should be topics of debate and not presented as dogmatic truths.

CULTURE AND HUMAN RIGHTS EDUCATION

Human rights education must be sensitive to cultural differences if it is to recognize cultural rights. The *Manual* demonstrates an amazing lack of cultural awareness. For instance, the *Manual* contends that classroom debates should be conducted in what many might call a Eurocentric manner with a rational and positivistic style and without the expression of emotion. The authors link this debate method to the requirements of a democratic society. In Part 2, devoted to classroom methods, the teacher is informed about debates: "Human rights are not subjective or emotional impressions, but principles underlying positive law and precise texts with legal implications."[51] The *Manual* asserts under the heading "Debate is a constituent element of a democratic society" that "The teacher should encourage pupils to be detached and not to make personal remarks.... This means helping pupils to learn how to build up their personality while at the same time respecting the requirements of truth, ethics, and the law."[52]

The writers of the *Manual* seem unaware that public speech takes different forms in other cultures. Everyone does not agree that public persuasion involves detachment and a lack of personal remarks. In addition, the *Manual* suggests that human personality should be formed around a positivistic and detached approach to the pursuit of truth and to public rhetoric. To understand the cultural problems presented by the *Manual*'s approach to debate and the search for truth, consider the differences in ways of knowing expressed in Table 5.1.

As expressed in Table 5.1, Hawaiian cultural traditions do not separate feelings and emotions from knowing. In fact, emotional detachment from both speech and understanding might appear to traditional Hawaiians as false and untrue. In traditional Hawaiian culture, public speech relies on the expression of emotion and the interweaving of spiritual stories and metaphors. Western- style debate using unemotional references to supposed facts and statistical truths would have a difficult job persuading an audience accustomed to hearing richly ornamented and ambiguous rhetoric. Could a person with Hawaiian cultural background believe someone who expressed facts in a detached tone?

TABLE 5.1
Comparison of Western and Hawaiian Ways of Knowing

Concept	Native Hawaiian Ways	Western Rational View
Intellect	Na'au: Thinking comes from the intestines; the "gut" links the heart and the mind. Thus, feelings and emotions are not separate from knowing, wisdom, and intelligence.	Separation of intellectual activity (cognitive domain) and emotion (affective domain). Thinking comes from the head/brain.
Relationship	When love is given, love should be returned. Because one is spiritually and physically connected to others, good relationships and reciprocity are highly valued. The connections between people must remain unbroken, harmonious, and correct.	Individuals are disconnected from one another. Because knowledge is seen more as a concrete set of ideas and skills that can be quantified, individual grasp of knowledge is highlighted. This lends a commodity quality to knowledge that leads to individually focused learning and being.
Knowledge	All learning must have aesthetic or practical use. Knowledge must link the spirit and the physical and must maintain relationships.	Knowledge for knowledge's sake has problematized Western education as the bridge between theory and practice has not been resolved.
Analysis	Kaona. This establishes a tolerance for ambiguity often viewed in the use of symbol and metaphor.	Concrete analysis and objectivity clearly explain subject matter.

Note. From: *Culture and Educational Policy in Hawai'i: The Silencing of Native Voices,* 1998 (p. 33) by Maenette K. P. Benham and Ronald H. Heck, Mahwah, NJ: Lawrence Erlbaum Associates.

Hawaiians relate personality development to an understanding of emotions, myth, spiritualism, harmony, and symbols in contrast to the *Manual*'s suggestion that personality be developed around positivistic and unemotional debate.

The *Manual*'s lack of cultural understanding is highlighted by its recommendations on teaching history and social studies. This section blends indoctrinating approaches to history instruction with a Eurocentric focus. The section opens: "It is essential for history teaching to be presented in the light of evolving human rights. Movements to promote human rights, and the proclamation of standards and principles in declarations, conventions and protocols can be traced through history." The focus of human rights history is not inappropriate because the *Manual* is about human rights education. On the other hand, there is no suggestion in the opening or in the rest of the section that the history of human rights is open to critical review or discussion. The cultural bias is evident in the suggested topics that give the impression that human rights must be understood from the vantage point of Western history.

In addition, the historical method is to evaluate history according to modern human rights standards rather than to critically explore the evolution of these standards. The *Manual* recommends five historical epochs for human rights education.

1. The early eighteenth and nineteenth century in Europe and America can be presented in the light of the rights stated in the Covenant of Civil and Political Rights.... It should be noted that the progress of these standards and concepts occupies a fundamental place in the political history and the burgeoning philosophy preceding the major revolutions that left their mark on the world between 1776 and 1917. [These dates are obvious references to the American and Soviet revolutions, and the allusion to "the burgeoning philosophy" refers to the European Enlightenment.]

2. Similarly, the history of the industrial revolution and of other social movements can be introduced by a review of the issues linked to economic, social and cultural rights. [I assume from the context that the industrial revolution being referred to is the one beginning in the West in the 18th and 19th centuries.]

3. The period of major discoveries and waves of imperialist expansion can be used to study the rights of indigenous peoples. For example, it may be observed that back in the fifteenth century a Spanish missionary denounced the enslavement of the indigenous peoples of Latin America and asserted that they were the equals of Europeans. [This is teaching the history of colonialism from a European perspective.]

4. The Second World War can be introduced, along with the Universal Declaration of Human Rights, to illustrate the relationship between human rights and peace. [Why not a critical history of the actual disputes over whether or not there are universal rights during the writing of the Universal Declaration?]

5. The study of the fight for national independence and the ejection of colonialism can be used to discuss the right of peoples to self-determination. [Again, history is being used to illustrate a set of rights rather than teaching how the struggle over colonialism delayed the issuance of the Covenants until the 1960s.]

The first three recommendations focus on Western history except in the case of the effect of Western expansion on the rest of the world. The fourth and fifth recommendations present an uncritical history of human rights documents.

Surprisingly, Amnesty International's *First Steps: A Manual for Starting Human Rights Education* exhibited the same Eurocentric bias. Its section "Ideas for Teaching Human Rights in Core Subjects" recommended:

> When teaching history, human rights can be introduced around traditional subject matter. Here are some examples.
>
> •Documents: Magna Carta (1215, England)
>   US Declaration of Independence (1776, USA)
>   The Declaration of the Rights of Man (1789, France)[53]

The narrowness and Eurocentric focus of these recommendations make me wonder whether the authors themselves were very well versed in the history of human rights. In *The Evolution of Human International Human Rights: Visions Seen*, Paul Gordon Lauren examined a number of historical documents to understand the evolution of human rights ideas across cultures, including the Koran; various Buddhist scriptures such as Tipitaka and Anguttra-Nikaya; Confucian texts including the *Analects* and *Great Learning*; the documents of the Mohist school of Chinese moral philosophy; the 10th-century Islamic philosopher Al-Farabi's *The Outlook of the People of the City of Virtue;* and the legal codes of King Hammurabi of ancient Babylon.[54] In addition, textual and oral traditions from Africa and Native Americans could be included. From North America, I would include the various Ghost Dance traditions that deal with the rights of indigenous people against invading Europeans.

The writers of the Universal Declaration of Human Rights were aware, as I discussed in chapter 2, of conflicting cultural traditions of human rights. Also, the impetus for the document emerged from a world community and, in particular, the post–World War II revolt against colonialism. Most of the world's cultures focused their intellectual traditions in different ways on the issue of human rights. Western documents and rights traditions were an important influence, but other cultures also approached human rights from their particular history and intellectual framework.

It is conceivable that a student in Africa and Asia might walk away from these Eurocentric lessons with confused feelings of gratitude and a convoluted belief that Europe provided the philosophical underpinnings for a human rights movement that contributed to the overthrow of European imperialism! On the other hand, a European or North American student might leave these lessons convinced of the superiority of their intellectual traditions and might arrogantly believe that their traditions are a model for the future of human history. It is also conceivable that students might leave these lessons with an uncritical allegiance to human rights documents in the same manner that a student leaves a nationalistic history course with unquestioned patriotic feelings and loyalty to his or her country.

CRITICAL THOUGHT AND HUMAN RELATIONS EDUCATION

Human Beings ... Manual for Human Rights Education and another teaching guide distributed in 1998 by the High Commissioner for Human Rights, *ABC, Teaching Human Right: Practical Activities for Primary and Secondary Schools,*[55] provided examples of activities designed for developing human relations. Admittedly, human relations are an important aspect of reducing conflict and building respect for other people. However, I often feel uncomfortable with these types of exercises. I use the word "uncomfortable" because I do not dismiss their potential value, but I am often offended by the saccharine quality of human relations exercises designed to build tolerance, trust, and community. In some cases, highly complex issues are reduced to feeling good about others. My preference is to link human relations exercises with critical thinking. Many exercises in the manual and booklet do make this connection.

Consider the educational example of religious tolerance from Dakar that is cited in *Human Beings ... Manual for Human Rights Education.* The activity is for children ages 8 to 14 and has the goal of encouraging "respect for the beliefs—or lack of beliefs—of others."[56] In the activity, pictures and photographs are shown depicting persons with visible signs of their religious affiliations. The following methods are recommended:

Method

- The teacher shows the photographs and pictures.
- Ask the class to identify the figures in terms of their religious affiliation.
- By means of questions, the teacher encourages the children to:
  - Cite cases of religious intolerance,
  - Say whether they experience such situations in their neighborhood or village,
  - Say what they think about this kind of behavior,
  - Show that tolerance is a factor of peace.

- Conclude by saying that everyone has a duty to respect their neighbor's religion.[57]

I agree that religious intolerance has been the source of many wars and remains a major global problem, but I think it is necessary to confront conflictual issues. Avoidance only leads to a "feel good" lesson that provides little understanding of human rights issues and the causes of religious conflict. Most religions do not recognize the right of children to freedom of thought. In fact, many believe that parents and educational institutions should restrict freedom of thought to allow for religious indoctrination. Should children be allowed freedom of thought so that they can choose their religious affiliation? Most religious leaders would probably reject this right as irreligious. Some religions are intolerant of others because they believe they are the only true religion. This is true of different groups in Judaism, Christianity, and Islamic religions. How does one resolve the conflict between religious intolerance embedded in religious dogma and at the same time respect that religion? What about religious conflict over abortion? What about the potential conflict, from a religious point of view, between the right to life, women's rights, and abortion? What about the conflict between women's rights and religious practices that delegate women to second-class roles?

My point, of course, is that religious tolerance is not simply a matter of teaching that all people have a duty to respect their neighbors' religion. The issues are much deeper than simply feelings of respect.

An example of an uncritical form of human relations instruction is a lesson titled, "A Call to Practice Solidarity." The lesson is for students aged 15, and it originates from the Instituto Tecnico Industriale Statale in Rome, Italy. The goal is "To raise awareness of the need for international co-operation." The following, and I would argue simple-minded, methods are recommended. I think the obvious limitations of this lesson for promoting international cooperation do not require explanation:

Method

- Meet a lonely, unhappy person, out of school, then in school.
- Discuss remedies for this situation and ways of being supportive.
- Suggest making an appeal for solidarity in the school magazine.
- Collective drafting of an article (see example in box) [the example deals with the loneliness of an African war refugee].[58]

Besides superficial treatment of issues, human relations approaches can often overlook cultural differences. A cultural anthropologist could no doubt cite some societies that would be disturbed by the following exercise recommended in *ABC*:

Blind Trust

Divide the class into pairs. Have one student blindfold the other and have the sighted member of the pair lead the "blind" one about for a few minutes. Make sure the leading child is not abusing the power to lead, since the idea is to nurture trust, not to destroy it.... Once the activity is over allow the students to talk about what happened. Discuss how they felt—not just as "blind" partners, but their feelings of responsibility as "leaders" too.[59]

In this exercise, the teacher must be aware of whether or not local cultural practices might make blindfolding taboo or cause children do anxiety.

On the other hand, the recommended discussion following the exercise is a model of critical thought. Following the exercise, the booklet recommended "a discussion of the importance of trust in the whole community. This can lead in turn to a discussion of world society and how it works, and how it can fail to work too."[60] These are all deep questions, worthy of group discussion. They avoid turning the activity into mere instruction in teaching trust. After all, trust should be given only when it will be beneficial. By raising critical issues after the exercise, the instruction moves from indoctrination to critical thinking.

In contrast, the following activity may not lead to critical thinking about human relations. This exercise is placed under the general question, "How do I live with others?"

Buddy

Teachers should arrange for their students to have a senior buddy from an upper class. An activity should be arranged to encourage children to seek out the help of their buddy if they have a problem. Ways should be devised to encourage the senior buddy to take an interest in his or her small colleague by showing games and helping with activities.[61]

This exercise would be more valuable if followed by a discussion of questions, such as: Can we benefit from the wisdom of older students and adults? Should we always trust older students and adults? How should we go about selecting friends that will help and not harm us?

Human relations can initiate important discussions about specific issues. Consider the exercise recommend by the Institut Moulant Bokolo (UNESCO-Associated School) in the Democratic Republic of the Congo for children between the ages of 10 and 15. Under the title "Equality Between Men and Women in Marriage," the activity was described as combating forced marriages and creating awareness of the right to choose one's husband or wife. The following instructional methods were recommended:

Method

- The children divide up into groups. One group represents the parents; a second represents a girl who wants to get engaged to a young man of her choice; a third represents the family elders.
- Presentation of the scene to be acted: a girl feels old enough to become engaged and wants to marry the man of her choice. Her parents want to make her marry a rich man.
- Exchanges between the groups which put forward their arguments for or against the marriage insisted on by the parents.
- Conclusion of the game: the girl will marry the man she chooses. The parents finally accept that the girl has the right to a private life once she is adult.[62]

The role playing in this exercise would certainly enhance the reality of the situation. Groups would have to think like the bride, groom, and parents. On the other hand, the discussion at the end of the exercise could be broadened. Besides the human rights principles associated with freedom, gender equality, children's rights, and the right to choose one's own mate, there are the broader questions related to cultural differences and the concept of marriage, such as: How do marriage practices differ around the world? What about polygamy and polyandry? What would be the ideal relationship between humans for the purpose of reproduction?

Of course, a broad discussion of this type might offend religious and cultural sensibilities. An important part of most religions and central to many cultural practices is the regulation of human reproduction and, consequently, the relationships between genders. The previous exercise on forced marriages is clearly designed to change local cultural practices. In this case, there is a clash with human rights doctrines. According to the argument made earlier in the book, however, the protection of local cultures now depends on the expanding protection of human rights. Consequently, when there is a clash between culture and human rights, human rights must carry the day. This is also true for religious practices.

LET OUR CHILDREN DREAM ABOUT A PERFECT WORLD OF RIGHTS

The criticism in the preceding section is designed primarily to alert readers to the potential danger of human rights education's repeating the traditions of indoctrinating-nationalistic education and ignoring cultural differences. On a more positive note, *ABC, Teaching Human Rights* offered examples of a more critical approach to instruction. The booklet made a distinction between teaching "about" human rights, which focuses on learning the content of human rights documents, and teaching "for" human rights, which involves learning to be actively involved in protecting human rights. The difference between instruction "about" and "for" is underscored by the contrast between "teaching and preaching."[63] To avoid "preaching" about human rights, this booklet offered practical activities to "teach" human rights to prepare students "for" the active pursuit of human rights goals.

One activity recommended asking students the following question:

> Imagine that it is your job to draft the basic principles for society as a whole. The society includes you, though you don't know what kind of person you are going to be in this society. You may be male or female, young or old, rich or poor, disabled in some way, or living as a member of any contemporary nation, race, ethnic group, religion or culture that is not your own. You simply don't know.[64]

The beauty of this question is that it requires students to grapple with a question of central importance to a critical understanding of the universality of human rights. This approach is a vast improvement over a simple presentation of human rights documents and a recounting of human rights history. In fact, this question could lead to a study of the historical debates about whether there are universal human rights. In addition, the question of universality leads naturally to the meaning of human rights in different cultural contexts.

The booklet suggested that the result of this exercise be compared with the actual Universal Declaration of Human Rights and the International Covenants on Economic, Social and Cultural Rights. This comparison depends on the ages of the students. The booklet offered a plain language version of the Declaration that could be used with older elementary students. This comparison could help students critically evaluate the different parts of the Declaration.

The same process was recommended for Children's Rights. When I first read this suggestion, I imagined young children declaring, "All children have the right to candy." At first glance, this seems rather frivolous. On the other hand, thinking about rights should involve utopian dreams. Young children might envision a world of unlimited candy as their ideal, and why not? Everyone should have the right to pleasure. Older children and youths may express their utopian dreams as part of this exercise.

Teachers should not dismiss or censure statements such as "All children have the right to candy." Children should be encouraged to dream about their rights and the world they want. In comparing this wish with actual UN documents on children's rights, it could be discussed in the context of the right to leisure and nutrition. The dreams of children and youths might actually improve and augment concepts of human rights. It should be constantly stressed to students that UN human rights documents are the product of fallible humans and there is always room for improvement.

This type of critical exercise helps students evaluate rather then simply accept current human rights documents. *ABC, Teaching Human Rights* linked this approach to developing a sense of claim rights. In the words of the booklet, "The basic principles of a human rights culture will survive only if people continue to see a point in it doing so." Understanding the necessity of human rights, the booklet argued, results in students saying, "I have a *right* to this. It is not just what I want, or need. It is my right. There is a *responsibility* to be met."[65] In this case, "responsibility" refers to the responsibility to claim one's rights and the rights of others. Unless all people are taught this responsibility, *ABC, Teaching Human Rights* contended: "We will not *claim* our rights when they are withheld or taken away, or feel the need to meet *rights-claims* made upon us. We have to see for ourselves why rights are so important, for this in turn fosters responsibility."[66]

Let children and adults dream about a perfect world of rights. Let them compare their fantasies with historical debates about human rights and contemporary documents. Motivate them to want a world where they can achieve happiness with others. Make them feel a responsibility to themselves and others to ensure that visions of the good life come true. Fantasies of the good life can be added to the psychological energy provided by guilt and public shame. What better way to motivate people to assume the moral duty of ensuring the rights of all than a combination of desire, guilt, and public shame?

CRITICAL DIALOGUE ABOUT HUMAN RIGHTS EDUCATION

Imagination and fantasy generate scenarios that can be subjected to critical thought and dialogue. In recent years, the Brazilian educator Paulo Freire has increased our understanding of the uses of dialogue for understanding differing scenarios when presented as thematic representations of life. Freire argued that a dialogue about thematic representations will raise the consciousness of people about the causes of economic and political inequalities. Living in a "culture of silence," as Freire coined the term, people have little cognizance of cause and effect in human relationships. In a culture of silence, people simply accept their misery and make few conscious choices to improve their conditions. Breaking the silence requires confronting people with an imaginative objectification of their plight in the form of photographs, text, or some other thematic representation. Dialogue about these thematic representations forces people to become conscious of their lives as objects that can be understood and changed. At the first stage of the dialogue, the simple structure of the thematic representation is discussed, such as village or city life or the discussants' relationship to the events in the representation. As the dialogue progresses, both the leader and participants gain greater clarity about the inter-relationships depicted in the thematic representation. An important factor in the dialogue is that the teacher never assumes more knowledge about the thematic representation than the student have. Both students and teachers embark on an exploratory dialogue.[67]

Imagination should be combined with critical thought in discussing thematic representations. Consider the following thematic representation used by the Centre de Rechereche et de Formation en Sciences de L'Education et d'Intervention Psychologique in Port-au-Prince, Haiti. In view of the years of political turmoil and economic deprivations in Haiti, the thematic representation written by Esery Mondesir, an education student, appropriately depicts the difficulties faced by a 10-year-old girl named Melissa as she struggles through an average day. The story begins with Melissa, living as a household servant because her parents could not afford to support her, being awakened. 'She stirred on her pile of urine-soaked rags; it was four in the morning and for her a new day of violence was beginning."[68] The story continues with a description of Melissa's tasks and her whippings by her employers:

> Melissa loses count of the number of slaps she receives in a day. As for the humiliating names she is called, they are best passed over in silence. She is never caressed, never kissed on the cheek and never gets any thanks. Finally the sun sets in a blaze of glory in the west, but for Melissa it has yet to rise.[69]

Ideally, from Freire's standpoint, this story would be read for discussion by Melissa or children in similar situations. It would be a thematic representation of their lives that would be used as an object for discussion. Both the presenter and Melissa would engage in a dialogue to understand why these conditions exist and how they can be improved. Again, the presenter would assume that they do not understand the causes or possible future actions. These understandings would emerge from the discussion.

In a variation of Freire's methodology, Haitian educators centered the dialogue on human rights issues. Appropriately, their target audience was children ages 9 to 10. In addition to the story, students were provided with photographs of street children and children in domestic service and the text of the Convention on the Rights of the Child. Unfortunately, the proposed method violated an important Freirian principle that a dialogue should take place without any preconceived plan about its final direction and conclusion. The methodology of the lesson required instructors to "Emphasize the concern felt by the international community for children in general and for underprivileged children in particular (e.g., describe the work of the UNICEF)."[70] This is blatant use of propagandistic education to win allegiance to UNICEF, and it violates the principle that everything should be an object for critical discussion.

Disregarding the obvious attempt to steer the dialogue in a particular direction, the lesson did create a useful context for a critical discussion of children's rights by using the following method. It also requires children to use their own imaginations in depicting similar situations:

- Read the text to the class.

- Divided into small groups, the class examines Melissa's situation in the light of the Convention on the Rights of the Child.

- Ask the children: Do you know of any cases like Melissa's in your country? Are children ill-treated only in ... [the story's] country?

- Ask children to write an account of a real-life case similar to Melissa's involving children whose rights are ignored.

- The groups pool their conclusions and a class discussion is held.

- The class makes proposals about respect for children's rights.

A more Freirian dialogue would begin with an open discussion about Melissa's situation and possibilities for improvement. This might or might not lead to children's rights issues. On the other hand, this lesson does give pupils an opportunity to critically discuss children's rights from the perspective of a concrete example. It also requires them to use their imaginations in providing other examples and proposals for children's rights.

Combining thematic representations with role playing can be very effective in prompting critical dialogue and imagination. This combination was recommended in a lesson from the Inter-American Institute of Human Rights in Costa Rica. The following situation was presented as a thematic representation:

Your name is Youssef, Pierre, Nadia or Linda. You are a journalist. You report in your newspaper an incident implicating quite well-known people and you comment on it. This annoys these people, whom you do not know. The next day the people come to your home and take you off somewhere and give you a violent beating. No one knows where you are. You cannot get away from the place.[71]

The added ingredient in this lesson was student dramatization. Students are asked to write a scenario based on this story and act it out. The role playing enhances the reality of the situation and adds emotional energy to answering the following questions: "What to do in Youssef or Linda's situation? Would you have written what you thought if you were the journalist? Would you have decided to keep quiet to avoid having problems? Do you know of any cases of kidnaping, torture or illegal detention?"[72] These questions could cause students to combine critical thinking with fantasy to imagine a means for curbing political torture. This might lead to a general discussion of human rights and human rights documents.

In "Learning Activities about the Universal Declaration of Human Rights," Amnesty International suggested another method of combining imagination and critical thought by having students create thematic representations of human rights. This requires students to give careful consideration to the real and complicated meaning of a particular right as indicate in the following lesson.

Human Rights and Art

Overview: By having to think about how to represent a human right the participant has to integrate the concepts expressed in the human rights article s/he has chosen to portray.

Materials: This depends on the art medium you are working with. A copy of the UDHR [Universal Declaration of Human Rights] or the simplified version.[73]

Amnesty International's *First Steps: A Manual for Starting Human Rights Education* provided a lesson using imagination and critical thinking by presenting students with the following scenario:

Imagine that you have discovered a new country, where no one has lived before, and where there are no laws and no rules. You and the other members of your group will be the settlers in this new land. You do not know what social position you will have in the new country.

Each student was asked to formulate three rights that he or she thinks are important for them to have in this new country. Working in different groups, students selected the 10 most important rights from their individual list of rights. Then each group presented its list of rights to the class for discussion. The rights agreed to by the entire class were then compared with a simplified version of the Universal Declaration of Human Rights. The comparison was followed by a series of critical questions: "Did your ideas about which rights were most important change during this activity? How would life be if we excluded some of these rights? Are there any rights which you now want to add to the final list? Did anyone list a right themselves which was not included in any of the lists?" One advantage of this exercise is that it can be used in any cultural context. The cultural background of the students determines their selection of rights and discussion of those rights.

A Dutch textbook for Grades 6 and 7, *It's About Me and Human Rights*, combined photographs and stories as thematic representations to teach children's rights. The lessons were specifically related to conditions in the Netherlands and Estonia. However, the stories and photographs could be changed to fit any cultural context and to address local social issues. For example, one lesson consisted of two case studies and one photograph. The first case involved an alcoholic mother who abandons her 1-year-old toddler. When the mother fails to appear at a court hearing about the matter, the court takes away her parental rights to the child. In the second case, a 3-year-old girl is abandoned by her mother. Eventually, the mother sends a letter from Japan to friends saying that she did not plan to return home (Estonia). Eventually, social workers find a letter from the girl's grandmother in Moscow where she eventually goes to live. The photograph depicts two children working as street musicians. The bigger girl is playing an accordion, while the smaller girl stands next to an open box containing donations from passersby.[74]

These two cases and the photographs provided powerful thematic representations for young school children to discuss. Unfortunately, the lesson tried to steer the direction of the discussion by asking leading questions such as "Why does a family need a state and laws?" However, a critical dialogue could be achieved by simply entertaining students' reactions to these thematic representations. One discussion question did achieve this critical level:

> Merike's father often beats her brother Mart. Merike would like to help her brother but she is very much afraid of their father. And she does not know who to turn to, because mother is on father's side, and Merike does not trust her class teacher either. Can you give some good advice to Mart and Merike?[75]

Thematic representations also provide a means for a critical dialogue about children's rights in education. An important issue is the right of children to freedom of thought and expression. The Dutch text provided the following story for discussion by 5th and 6th graders:

Mati wrote an article for the school newspaper, where he says he does not like the rules for students' behavior established for that school. The headmaster said this article could not be published. Should there be a law or instruction, which would give the headmaster the right to decide, whether to publish Mati's article or not? Why?[76]

This story provided a good opportunity to discuss a child's right to freedom of thought and expression. For the discussion to be truly dialogical, the teacher must let the students decide the direction of the discussion and any final conclusions.

Thematic representations followed by open discussions provide the best opportunity for combining imagination with critical thought. The fostering of critical dialogue is essential, because human rights, and political and economic systems are constantly evolving as we seek a better world.

CONCLUSION: UNIVERSAL GUIDELINES FOR HUMAN RIGHTS EDUCATION

So far, my discussion of human rights education has combined a number of cautions with promising instructional methods. A central problem is the tendency to preach human rights and attempt to win the allegiance of students to UN endeavors. And, because of the assumptions of some human rights educators, issues such as democracy and the rule of law are erroneously equated with human rights. There is also a tendency to treat words such as democracy, equality, tolerance, and solidarity with the reverence usually given to religious dogma. This process of enshrinement leads to confusion over the difference between democratic management and culture in schools. In addition, some of the previous examples demonstrate a gross insensitivity to cultural differences.

On the other hand, I have highlighted effective methods involving the consideration of human rights as claim rights, the use of imagination and fantasy as psychological energy for choosing and contemplating a better world, the use of critical dialogue, and the critical examination of the history of human rights documents. To avoid the tendency to use indoctrinating and nationalistic types of education, all human rights statements and documents should be presented to students for critical discussion and possible improvement or dismissal.

My most challenging suggestion is creating a sense of guilt and moral shame for failure to actively protect the human rights of others. In advocating this moral duty, I run the risk of following the same path of indoctrination as religions and governments. However, I think an important lesson of patriotic and religious education can be found in its failures. No amount of preaching converts all listeners into zealots or patriots. No amount of indoctrination or emotional manipulation makes all people assume the moral duty of protecting human rights. Recognizing the impossibility of converting all to the cause, I propose accepting this limitation and the possibility of even less general acceptance by maintaining open and critical dialogical methods.

Therefore, the concept of a moral duty governed by public shame and guilt should be an object of discussion for students to accept or dismiss. Thematic representations and role playing about efforts to protect human rights would be effective means of generating discussion about this moral ideal. This moral duty should be *chosen* and not imposed.

The following guidelines for human rights education contain cautions against dogmatic instruction and suggestions for critical approaches to teaching human rights as part of the universal right to an education. Similar to this book's other guidelines, these are only *minimal* suggestions intended to have universal applicability. Obviously, local conditions and teachers will foster other and more expansive approaches.

Universal Guidelines for Human Rights Education

Cautions

1. Human rights education *should avoid* "nationalistic" forms of education designed to win the allegiance of students to organizations that claim protection of human rights, such as UNICEF and the UN. The value of all institutions should be an object of critical exploration and discussion.

2. Human rights education *should avoid* binding human rights with ideas, such democracy, the rule of law, equality, tolerance, and solidarity. These should be considered as separate and complex ideas that should be subjected to critical analysis and discussion.

3. Human rights education *should avoid* treating human rights documents as sacred texts to be "enshrined" and worshiped. These documents should be presented to students as imperfect beginnings that are open to criticism and improvement.

4. Human rights education *should avoid* cultural insensitivity as highlighted in this chapter by Eurocentric historical treatments of human rights and assumptions about the cultural appropriateness student activities.

Methods

1. A critical analysis of the history of human rights documents.

2. A critical discussion of human rights documents.

3. The use of thematic representations and role playing to generate critical dialogue about human rights situations.

4. The use of critical thinking, imagination, and fantasy to generate students' visions of ideal human rights.

5. A critical discussion of student-created human rights documents as compared with existing documents.

6. The use of thematic representations and role playing to generate discussion about the moral duty to protect the rights of all people.

7. The use of thematic representations and role playing to generate discussion about the role of public shame and guilt in fostering a moral duty to protect the rights of all people.

These guidelines for human rights education along with the universal guidelines for literacy and numeracy instruction discussed in the next chapter provide the basic components of a universal definition of education as guaranteed by the universal right to an education. These minimal guidelines are formulated to fulfill the universal justification for the right to an education, namely, the necessity for all people to know how the global culture and economy created by colonialism and postcolonialism affect their lives; what benefits or harm might result from it; and how human rights can help provide equal economic and social opportunities in the global economy and culture.

ᐊᑭ6 ᑭᐊ

A Universal Concept of Education:
Guidelines for Literacy and Numeracy Instruction

My universal guidelines for literacy and numeracy education, along
with human rights education, are intended to be *minimum* curriculum
guidelines for schooling children under the age of 18. Based on human
rights, cultural and linguistic rights, the Convention on Biodiversity,
and children's rights, I can justify only certain aspects of schooling as a
universal right while leaving decisions about other details of education
to local communities or governments. For instance, one element of traditional schooling missing from my universal curriculum is job training or vocational education, which should be determined by local
needs and economic conditions. On the other hand, the broader issue
of understanding the nature of work in a global economy I consider a
universal need and part of a curriculum that fulfills an important requirement of the universal right to education.

A universal concept of education as embodied in the right to education must incorporate children's rights to freedom of thought and access to the world's knowledge. These liberty rights are essential for the
exercise of the right to education. Because the right to education is justified by the need for people to weigh the advantages and disadvantages
of the world's economy and culture, then access to the knowledge of
that economy and culture and freedom to think about it are necessary
for fulfilling this right. Liberty rights protect students from educational
systems that are indoctrinating, propagandizing, nationalistic, and
discriminatory. Consequentially, a universal concept of education
must include children's rights.

Educational principles that are applicable to all societies must recognize cultural and linguistic rights as long as those rights do not interfere with the assistance and protection rights of students or support

educational practices that are indoctrinating, propagandizing, nationalistic, and discriminatory. The implementation of the universal right to education depends on the actualization of children's assistance and protection rights.

Literacy and numeracy are treated as a function of the overarching goal of understanding one's place in relation to one's culture, the world, and human rights. Again, I want to stress that I am outlining only a minimum universal curriculum with additional subjects and topics to be determined by local groups and nations.

UNIVERSAL GUIDELINES FOR LITERACY INSTRUCTION

Literacy and numeracy are necessary tools for understanding the world. They also provide the means for considering alternatives to existing conditions. If the universal concept of education entails understanding and freely choosing from the benefits and disadvantages of the global economy and culture, then universal guidelines for literacy and numeracy instruction should serve as aids in accomplishing this end. In this context, there are two important aspects to literacy and numeracy instruction. First, students must be provided with the words and mathematical tools that help them understand themselves and their culture in relation to the rest of the world. Second, words and mathematical tools should serve as instruments for adapting to the world economy and culture. This second aspect of literacy and numeracy instruction entails the ability to think about alternatives to contemporary economic and social conditions. Successful adaptation requires an ability to think about differing models of economic organization and growth.

Universal guidelines for literacy instruction are intended to provide a starting point for basic instruction. Literacy instruction should begin by naming the world with words that help readers understand their social and cultural situation. Learning to read, as Paulo Freire argued, is a process of naming the world. Words become the means for reflecting on the causes and consequences of human action.[1] All children and adults should be taught to read with words that name and help them to understand their surroundings. This means that reading instruction must begin in the mother tongue. Initial reading instruction uses students' own words for describing the world they know. It should include fiction and nonfiction writings about familiar objects and social situations.

Consequently, the choices of words to be learned and literature to be read are extremely important. The English understood this during their rule of India. In the 19th century, they made the decision to use an English-based education for training a local administrative cadre. The Indian students who went on to help English colonialists maintain control learned to read by using textbooks and literature from England. They learned to name their world from the perspective of a foreign culture. Potentially lost in this education were the words that would help them to understand the past and present of their local culture. They learned to think like their masters. This form of education was typical of English colonialism. When the English returned Hong Kong to Chinese rule in the 1990s, local textbooks were still filled with references to foxes and other aspects of the English countryside.[2]

Control of language is an important mechanism for controlling minds. Colonial masters understood that exporting their languages, literature, and schools could serve as a means of dominating local populations. By learning words associated with a foreign and distant culture, colonial populations were taught to think of their masters as culturally superior. The U.S. government recognized this when instituting an English-only policy in Puerto Rican and Hawaiian schools after conquering and annexing these countries in the 1890s. Before the English-only policy, the Puerto Rican and Hawaiian governments conducted schools in Spanish and Hawaiian respectively. Local resistance defeated the English-only policy in Puerto Rico, but in Hawaii the policy effectively caused the decline of Hawaiian culture and language and the reduction of the Hawaiian people to third-class status below resident Anglo and Asian populations. By 1990, there were only 8,872 speakers of Hawaiian out of a Native Hawaiian population of 200,000.

The restoration of Hawaiian language and culture has accompanied demands for Hawaiian sovereignty and return of lands. As the anthropologist Sally Engle Merry stated, "The political movement demanding sovereignty grew out of a much larger and older renaissance of Hawaiian culture, language, arts, dance and music."[3] In 1987, as a result of political activities by Native Hawaiians, Ka Lahui Hawai'i was established as a sovereign Native Hawaiian nation-within-a-nation with its own constitution and officers. In the same year, a Native Hawaiian language-immersion program was initiated with the majority of the students having English as their mother tongue. The study of English was delayed until the 5th grade. In 1993, the Hawaiian language-immersion program was extended to the 12th grade, and by 1995 there were 11 Hawaiian immersion schools serving 1,000 students.[4]

Of course, access to a native tongue does not guarantee political action. There is also the content of instruction. The restoration of Hawaiian culture could simply be limited to dancing the hula and playing the ukelele. However, culture also includes traditional institutions, such as the Hawaiian constitutional monarchy that existed before 13 White businessmen in 1893 declared a provisional government and petitioned the U.S. government for annexation. Knowing this history can energize groups to demand restoration of their power, such as a history (that was not taught in Hawaiian schools when I attended them in the 1950s) that includes the 1898 annexation of the provisional government despite protests from the legitimate government ruled by Queen Lili'uokalani. At the time, the queen demanded that the United States "undo the action of its representatives and reinstate me in the authority which I claim as the Constitutional Sovereign of the Hawaiian Islands."[5] In 1993, the U.S. government recognized the illegality of the act, and President Bill Clinton signed a formal apology for the overthrow of the Hawaiian Kingdom.

Language also provokes strong emotions. Tears streaked down my face in 1999 when I heard the Hawaiian slack-guitarist Dennis Kamakahi sing the chant and mourning song originally composed for the return of King David Kalakaua's body from San Francisco in 1891. Hawaiians, along with many tourists, are filled with love of the islands as they listen to *Aloha Oe'* composed by Queen Lili'uokalani. However, most tourists do not realize the song was written by Hawaii's last monarch. In fact, few realize that she was a great songwriter. One of her most beautiful songs, *'lkd La Ladana*, was written after visiting Queen Victoria in London (*Ladana* means London). The words pluck the strings of the Hawaiian heart.

At the 1997 gathering of indigenous educators in Santa Fe, New Mexico, instruction in the mother tongue was a common theme in the 14 models of native education presented for discussion. Knowledge of the mother tongue, it was stressed, was key for understanding a person's relation to both the past and the present. "The gathering's participants," Benham and Cooper argued, "suggested that one's native language leads to understanding positionality and context because it carries the double entendre meanings of the past and is filled with metaphor, which helps to define our present."[6] One conversation that was reported from the gathering emphasized the role of language as a key element in liberation: "We should make the native language a priority. It is language that makes you what you are. Our models should be centered around children and include liberation."[7]

Therefore, restoration of language and history provides access to the existence of previous political power, and to the possibility of regaining power, and energizes the emotions. In addition, it creates visions of alternatives to existing conditions. For instance, learning the Hawaiian language opens doors to an optional lifestyle and to the possibility of considering traditional Hawaiian concepts of family and community as possibly superior to those imposed by Anglo values. It prompts people to think about changing their conditions.

Restoration of language and history provides access to alternative value systems, such as those offering options to the Western technological visions now gripping the world. If people are going to understand the benefits and drawbacks of the present global economy, they must deal with the environmental issues associated with technological development. Consider the importance of the oral traditions of the Hopi people. Despite many attempts at cultural destruction by the U.S. government, Hopi traditions have survived in written and oral forms. Taught in their mother tongue, Hopi children have access to the environmental wisdom and purpose of the Hopi people.

Traditional Hopi beliefs center on the assignment given by the Great Spirit Maasau'u, Guardian of the Earth, to maintain the natural balance of the world. Hopis were alarmed after World War II when the atomic bomb fulfilled prophecies about a gourd full of ashes signaling the earth's destruction. In 1948, the tribe selected four messengers to warn the world of its impending doom from environmental destruction. Speaking before the UN in 1992, the last of these messengers, Thomas Banyacya, warned, while holding a ceremonial rattle representing Mother Earth:

> The line running around it is a time line and indicates that we are in the final days of the prophecy. What have you as individuals, as nations and as the world body been doing to take care of this Earth? In the Earth today, humans poison their own food, water and air with pollution. Many of us including children are left to starve. Many wars are still being fought. Greed and concern for material things is a common disease.[8]

Before the UN General Assembly, Banyacya held a photograph of a large rock drawing from Hopiland and explained:

> This rock drawing, shows part of the Hopi prophecy. There are two paths. The first with high technology but separate from natural and spiritual law leads to these jagged lines representing chaos. The lower path is one that remains in harmony with natural law. Here we see a line that represents a choice like a bridge joining the paths. If we return to spiritual harmony and live from our hearts we can experience a paradise in this world. If we continue only on this upper path, we will come to destruction.[9]

The loss of Hopi language and culture would deprive the world of this alternative vision to the good life. Hopi spiritual beliefs place the balance between the human and the environment ahead of the technological race. The loss of this powerful vision would restrict freedom of thought by limiting the ideas available for students to think about.

Literacy instruction can serve the same purpose in countries that dominate the world economy, such as the United States, the European Union, and Japan. While reaping the economic rewards, the populations of these countries feel the negative effects of environmental destruction, the commodification of every aspect of life, and dehumanized work. Have the global culture and economy made the populations of these countries happier? Is there a lost history and system of values that would compel people to search for alternative directions for technological and economic development?

David Noble suggested that Western technological development grew out of a messianic vision that paradise could be restored on earth. In the monasteries of the Middle Ages, monks searched for the knowledge that was supposedly lost with the Garden of Eden. The monks' search sparked a technological revolution that evolved through the Renaissance and Enlightenment. At each stage, inventors and scientists claimed they would bring paradise back to earth. Technological development, they argued, would create the good life and increase human happiness. Promoters of electricity and computers, for instance, promised people greater leisure and more satisfying lives. What happened? Often technology was directed by another set of values, namely the desire for increased profits. Rather than paradise, technology spawned a world of consumerism and environmental destruction.[10]

Similar to the Hawaiians and Hopi, literacy can reveal alternative value systems and visions of the good life to the major economic benefactors of today's global society. These citizens can also be energized by words that reveal lost dreams. On the other hand, these populations can also learn words that function only to fit them into the existing productive machinery and to distract their imaginations by visions of consumption rather than happiness.

Words can be used to name and promote human rights. UNESCO offered the example of "A Treasure Box of Children's Rights." The goal of this educational method is to teach children under the age of 6 that they have rights. "By collecting objects representing the rights of the child," UNESCO's *Manual for Human Rights Education* stated, "and putting them in the treasure box, the children understand the importance of the rights of the child. The treasure box project should be continued until the end of primary school."[11] In the class and personal treasure boxes, students deposit UNICEF pictograms illustrating children's rights, dolls, and newspaper articles. The pictograms and newspaper articles stimulate the learning of words related to human rights. Learning to read these words provides access to an understanding of human rights.

In summary, learning to name the world can be used for political and economic enslavement or for liberation and control over external forces. Students can be taught words designed to wed them to existing systems of domination or words that help identify the forces shaping their lives. Words can be used to recapture a history of lost political power and to provide the emotional energy to search for alternatives to the good life. Words can rekindle legends of alternative value systems that can be woven into plans for a better world. Words are the sustenance of both domination and freedom. Literacy is the key that opens the door to social and economic improvement and protection of human rights.

Therefore, the right to education—learning to judge the benefits and disadvantages of a global economy and culture—justifies universal guidelines for literacy instruction. Based on the previous discussion, these universal guidelines for literacy instruction should include the following:

Universal Guidelines for Literacy Instruction

1. Initial language instruction should be in the mother tongue.
2. Initial language instruction should use words that name the world surrounding the student.
3. Initial language instruction should use words associated with human rights.
4. Initial reading material should include the history and culture of the student for the purpose of presenting alternative lifestyles, political and economic arrangements, and value systems. This material should not be written to indoctrinate the student, but to present possible alternatives to the good life.
5. Initial reading material should present real life problems that force students to think about their present situation.

These guidelines acknowledge cultural and language differences by stressing initial instruction in the mother tongue, the use of words that name the student's world, and the use of literature that draws on local culture and history. On the other hand, the guidelines restrict literacy instruction to materials that promote thinking about alternatives to the good life as opposed to indoctrinating literature.

It is assumed that literacy instruction will be like a spiral moving from the student's immediate world to eventually encompassing the world. As the student's vocabulary increases, his or her range of literature increases. Students whose mother tongue is not the dominant language of the region or nation, will receive instruction in this dominant language. Again, literacy instruction in the dominant language should follow the previous guidelines with the purpose of providing students with the tools to improve their conditions and possibly unlocking the door to the good life.

UNIVERSAL GUIDE TO NUMERACY INSTRUCTION

Are there universal guidelines for numeracy instruction? Learning to count opens doors of understanding in our highly numerical world.

However, in many cultures numbers have mystical meanings and can represent a striving for a higher ideal. In the global economy, the primary use of numbers is for control and regulation of commerce and human activity. Alternative concepts of numbers are another means by which people can reflect on present conditions. For instance, the Tsimshian of North America have seven distinct sets of numbers, which reflected their way of naming the world. They have different number sets for flat objects, long objects, round objects, animals, humans, canoes, and no specific objects. The North American Blackfoot have different numbers for the living and dead.[12]

Some cultures attribute mystical value to numbers. In the 1998 movie *Pi*, an obsessed mathematician teamed up with Hasidic Jews, members of a mystical branch of Judaism, to find the right combination of numbers representing Hebrew letters that spell out a lost name for God. In the *Republic*, Socrates proposed instruction in numbers and arithmetic to better understand ideal forms. While recognizing the practical use of numbers, Socrates believed thinking about numbers was a step in learning the ideal good.[13] The ancient Roman scholar Cicero compared the differences between Romans and Greeks: "By them [the Greeks] geometry was held in the very highest honor, and none were more illustrious than mathematicians. But we [the Romans] have limited the practice of this art to its usefulness in measurement and calculation."[14]

The search for infinite numbers was often a product of religious rather than economic or practical concern. In India, number towers or temples rise as testimonials to the linkages between religion and mathematics. In the story of Buddha's temptation, Buddha was rejected by Gopa, the daughter of Prince Dandapani, until he could publically demonstrate his abilities in writing, wrestling, archery, running, swimming, and number skills. To prove his number skills, Buddha was challenged by the mathematician Arjuna to list all the numerical ranks above 100 *kotis* (a *koti* was 10^7 or 10 million). Buddha answered by giving a numerical ladder that led to the number 10^{421}. Then Buddha was challenged, in the words of Karl Menninger, "to name all the divisions or atoms of a yoyana (a mile). Buddha ... [responded that] one mile ... contains ... $384,000 \times 7^{10}$ atoms, a number I [Menninger] gladly let the reader work out for himself."[15] Similar to Socrates, Indians were not interested in the practical aspects of infinite numbers; they were interested in achieving a thought process that would allow people to grasp purely abstract concepts.

In contrast, numbers can exercise power over people through such things as taxes and census. As the previous quote from Cicero indicates, the Romans were primarily interested in the practical use of numbers to extend their empire through conquest and taxation. Numbers were used to count coins and people as wealth was brought from the empire back to Rome. The knotted cords, called quipus, of the Inca were used to maintain the absolute power of the monarch. The knots were tied in various fashions to indicate numbers that represented imperial transactions. Each Inca settlement had four quipu keepers who submitted the knotted cords to the central government. The quipu was the ancient Peruvians' only system of numbers, and knowledge of quipus was limited to the keepers. Consequently, as Menninger stated, 'There is no doubt that this perhaps intentionally obscure manner of recording numbers, which only initiates could read, was a strong support for the monarchical absolutism of the Inca ruler."[16]

As the so-called father of ethnomathematics, Umbiratan D'Ambrosio, argued, class distinctions in developing countries are, in part, supported by an artificial distinction between pure and applied mathematics. This distinction results in maintaining social and economic privilege. In many developing countries, academic systems are modeled on those of former colonial powers which results in reserving so-called pure mathematics for a privileged intellectual class. In D'Ambrosio's words, "Ideology, implicit in dress, housing, titles ... takes a more subtle and damaging turn ... when built into the formation of the cadres and intellectual classes of former colonies.... We should not forget that colonialism grew together in a symbiotic relationship with modern science, in particular with mathematics and technology."[17]

In the global economy and culture, numbers are used to objectify human behavior and to account for the exchange of goods and services. Desiring control and predictability about human behavior, organizations use statistical research to measure consumers habits and workers' actions. The World Bank and the Organization for Economic Cooperation and Development are leading advocates of applying human accounting procedures to school systems. They hope to equate investment in education with measured outcomes that are usually in the form of standardized testing. Human capital accountants want to be able to predict that if X amount of money is invested in education then schools will produce Y skills that will grow the economy by Z amount. In this formula, students are reduced to human resources to be educated for the good of global businesses.[18] What seems to be lost in current rhetoric about human accounting is the concern expressed after World War II that centrally administered and standardized examinations were a mechanism of totalitarian control because they controlled the content of the curriculum. Certainly, academic freedom and freedom of thought disappear as tests control the content of the curriculum and statistical methods are used to measure student compliance with authoritarian dictates about what should be learned.

Learning about the contemporary usages of numbers helps students make decisions about the impact of the global economy and culture. Consider how automated teller machines (ATMs) in Malaysia significantly changed family structures so that women can be more fully used in the labor force. In Malaysia, Moslem women were recruited from the countryside as a well-disciplined and inexpensive workforce for factories outside Kuala Lumpur, which represented international corporations such as Motorola, Canon, Sanyo, Panasonic, and Minolta. After studying the global semiconductor industry, Jeffrey Henderson concluded that companies deliberately recruited these young women for "the sense of discipline ... [they] acquired through subjection to patriarchal domination in the household." Requiring that female recruits be unmarried, the companies offered perks such as "completely furnished hostels, free transportation, and subsidized meals." These female workers were, according to Henderson, "likely to remain the unskilled recipients of relatively low wages."[19]

Motorola executives decided to use ATMs to change Malaysian cultural patterns. These efforts represented the tension between traditional female subjection to authority and a minimum level of independence required for factory work. The manager of Malaysia's Motorola plant, Roger Bertelson, said, "We had to change the culture because the Malay home does not encourage women to speak out."[20] To undercut the patriarchal culture, the company deposited wages directly into bank accounts that are accessed through ATMs. Bertelson explained, "We had to change the pattern. She had to go home and tell her father: 'I'm not going to bring my money home in a pay envelope any more. It's going into the bank.'"[21]

In this situation, the hard numbers used to calculate wages and access money through ATMs pushed female workers into a whirlwind of cultural forces. Unprepared, the workers were caught between the forces of tradition, economic exploitation, and the requirements of the modern factory. Commenting on these conflicting forces, Bertelson stated, "The government would like to maintain Islamic principles and protect people from Western values, but whether the government likes it or not, the people are becoming westernized."[22] Interviews with Malaysian workers conducted by William Greider revealed the complexity of the social changes they were experiencing. One worker, Rosita, explained, "I had no intention of working for the company, but the company came to my kampong (rural village) and approached my father and he suggested that I work." Razian told Greider, "I changed jobs three times because the salary was not as big as it was promised.... I want to better myself, but I've got no money for classes." Another female laborer, Sansiah, explained, "Initially, I was helping my father in the paddies. When my friends started leaving I felt lonely and bored, so I went, too."[23]

The experiences of these young women could be classified as liberating, at least liberating from a patriarchal family. However, they were unprepared to protect themselves from exploitation and cultural manipulation. They lacked the intellectual tools that would make it possible for them to control and make decisions about the cultural changes they were experiencing as they moved from the village to the factory and city.

One important requirement of Malaysian factory work is that female workers be able to read and write and do basic arithmetic. As I have suggested, literacy should prepare people for the dynamics of cultural change. The teaching of numeracy should be directed toward the same goal. This goal is important for village women who make a transition from a world of small-scale cash transactions where economic decisions are in the hands of men to a world of paychecks, banks, ATMs, and credit.

Today, numeracy is tied to hand calculators and computers. As a result, there is a social division between those with and those without knowledge of and access to mathematical technology. Historically, the Romans, Chinese, and Japanese pioneered number technology with various forms of the abacus. Even as late as the 1940s, the *soroban*, the Japanese form of the abacus, was proved superior to electrical means of calculation. In 1947, a contest was held between a U.S. Army finance clerk operating a $700 electric machine and a Japanese Communications Ministry clerk flipping the wooden beads on a 25-cent *soroban*. The *soroban* easily won in competition for speed and accuracy in adding columns of four to six digits.[24]

Today, the hand calculator can easily beat the abacus. However, similar to Inca quipu keepers whose power depended on their exclusive knowledge of rope tying, the operators of hand calculators and computers have a distinct advantage in the global economy. The ability to use, along with the ability to purchase a hand calculator or use other number-oriented technology such as ATMs, provides important social and economic power in the global economy. In fact, the ability to use number-oriented technology is another means of separating the haves from the have-nots.

Ability to function in the global economy requires that numeracy instruction be linked to concrete social situations as opposed to abstract rote learning. As John Dewey suggested, students should learn that numbers exist because of social need. In his school, he taught children to count by having them set the table for the midmorning snack. The children discovered that they had to match the number of students with the number of spoons. Of course, this required them to learn how to count. Each step in the learning of numbers and arithmetic was linked to real-life situations. The Dewey method and the later project method were characterized by student-operated stores where children learned to add, subtract, multiply, and divide as they calculated purchases and handled change. Often, student savings banks were used for teaching arithmetic and for basic economic instruction.[25]

Numeracy instruction can also be a means of resurrecting a lost past or sustaining a dying culture as the educational anthropologist Jerry Lipka discovered while working with the Yup'ik Eskimos in Alaska. Through ethnographic research, which included discussions with tribal elders, Lipka developed a mathematics education program based on Yup'ik numeration and geometric patterns that could be used to teach the dominant mathematical system of the global economy and to preserve cultural traditions. This unique program demonstrates the possibilities of using numeracy education to help people understand the impact of outside forces on local cultures.

As Lipka explained:

> This approach to teaching mathematics is additive; it can supplement traditional math instruction or it can be a basis for teaching certain parts of the math curriculum. This approach can move Yup'ik knowledge from the margins of schooling toward the center; math is always a core academic curriculum.[26]

Yup'ik mathematics and science evolved to solve problems associated with living and traveling in the difficult world of the tundra. As a result, the human body became the center of mathematics. The number 20 was called *yuinaq* or whole person. The numbering system was on a base 20, which referred to the fingers and toes. The number 10 was *qula* which means "above", referring to the 10 fingers above the toes. Higher numbers were additions to the whole person: 30 was *yuinaq qula*, which meant a whole person plus "above." There were no written numerals for the Yup'ik number system.[27]

To use Yup'ik counting as a mathematical bridge to the dominant global-numbering system, Lipka and his researchers created a visual representation. After consulting Mayan and Egyptian number systems and examining Yup'ik cultural symbols used in masks and drums, the researchers presented their symbolic representations to tribal elders. After debating the acceptability of the number symbols, the elders practiced counting by using the symbols.

One of the interesting discoveries was that the Yup'ik numbering system had already been influenced by the global economy. Early Russian traders influenced the construction of numbers beyond 400. *Tiisitsaaq* was identified as a word borrowed, or in Yup'ik "loaned," for the number 1,000. Variations of this word are used to identify numbers over 400. Lipka concluded, "Yup'ik counting today is 'pure' between 1 and 400 and beyond 400 is strongly influenced by the Russian language."[28] In addition, English influenced the counting system because many people preferred shorter English words to longer Yup'ik words.

Out of this research, Lipka created a Yup'ik math tool kit using the new number symbols. Yup'ik clothing patterns also provided a means for teaching geometry and could be used to teach literacy. Traditional geometric patterns on parkas were walking stories that told about legendary people, identified regions, and indicated families.

This method of numeracy instruction conveys important cultural values. For instance, instruction in measurement creates harmony between the individual and the outside world. Yup'ik measurement was based on the proportion of a person's body size. In making a smoking rack for fish, heights were gauged by the size of the body of the user. The same proportional measurements were used to construct kayaks. Among the Yup'ik, Lipka concluded, "Measurement is a process of achieving balance based on visualizing, local materials, and specific tasks."[29] The builder uses measurements to create tools that are in harmony with her or his body and nature.

Jerry Lipka's work with the Yup'ik provides a good example of how mathematics instruction can demonstrate the influence of the global economy on one's culture—in this case the borrowing of Russian and English words—and how it can be used to preserve and restore local cultures. In addition, Lipka's work demonstrates cultural differences about the use of mathematics and the ways that local numbering systems can be used to understand the dominant global system.

Do all people have a right to their own mathematical systems in the same manner that they have the right to their own mother tongues? I believe the answer must be Yes! Similar to language, mathematical systems reflect cultural values. Students should learn about the effect of numbers on cultural change. Alternative mathematical values can be sources for thinking about alternatives to current social and economic conditions. Similar to language, mathematics can provide differing visions of the good. Mathematics also opens the door to an understanding of the benefits and disadvantages of science.

Unfortunately, colonialism displaced many local mathematical and scientific systems. As George Joseph wrote, "For many Third World societies, still in the grip of an intellectual dependence promoted by European dominance during the past two or three centuries, the indigenous scientific base that may have been innovative and self-sufficient during precolonial times is neglected or often treated with a contempt that it does not deserve."[30] Besides demonstrating the fallacy of European nations as the major sources for the development of mathematical ideas, George listed major cultural differences in solving mathematical problems. The Eurocentric approach has emphasized formal proofs based on deductive axiomatic logic while dismissing empirical and intuitive methods. Eurocentrism is also compounded by Westerners' ignoring African, Arab, Indian, and Chinese contributions to the evolution of mathematics in Europe.[31]

Charting one's life in the global economy requires a vast assortment of numeracy skills that should be linked to concrete situations and problems. Culturally based instruction should also be used as a bridge for understanding the dominant global mathematics. The growing economic gap between users and nonusers of hand calculators, computers, and other electronic devices requires the introduction of these mathematical tools in fulfilling the right to education. Students should also learn the political uses of numbers and calculations as represented by the Romans and Incas. Protection against government and business exploitation through manipulation of numbers should be an important part of mathematics instruction.

Similar to the universal guidelines for literacy instruction, my numeracy guidelines are intended as minimum requirements for fulfilling the right to education. The universal guidelines for numeracy instruction provide a means for understanding the effect of the global economy and culture through the world of numbers. Similar to literacy guidelines, numeracy guidelines should help learners think about alternatives to present social and economic conditions:

Universal Guidelines for Numeracy Instruction

- Initial numeracy instruction should be in accordance with the culture of the student, or, stated in terms similar to literacy guidelines, initial numeracy instruction should be in the mother numbering system.
- Culturally based number systems should be used as a bridge for learning the numbering system of the global economy.
- Instruction in the dominant-global number system should be linked to concrete social situations involving the exchange of goods and money, government taxes, and the measurement of goods and basic building structures.
- Instruction should include the operation of electronic calculators and computers.
- Instructions should include literacy in the language of modern electronic and computers.
- Instruction should include how numbers are used as means of political, economic, and behavioral control.

A UNIVERSAL CONCEPT OF EDUCATION

Embodied in my discussion of universal guidelines for literacy and numeracy education are answers to the broader questions: What should all people be entitled to when exercising their right to an education? If a group or person claims a right to education, what are is he or she claiming? What is the meaning of "education" in the "right to education"? The answers to these questions about literacy and numeracy instruction are summarized in the following list; literacy and numeracy education should include, but not be limited to:

The Meaning of 'Education' in the 'Right to Education' Literacy and Numeracy Instruction

1. Literacy in the students' mother tongues.
2. Literacy in the official language in the country where they are resident if the official language is not a student's mother tongue.
3. The use of the mother tongue in classroom instruction if desired by the parents and/or students.
4. Knowledge of the numbering system of their cultures.
5. Knowledge of the numbering system of the global economy.
6. Knowledge of the dominant-global number system.
7. Knowledge of the use of electronic calculators and computers.
8. Literacy in the language of modern electronics and computers.
9. Knowledge of the dominant-global number system.
10. Knowledge of the use of electronic calculators and other electronic numbering devices.
11. Knowledge of how numbers are used as means of political, economic, and behavioral control.
12. Knowledge of the students' own cultures and their relations to them.
13. Knowledge about the impact of global culture and economics on their lives.
14. Knowledge of the environmental web of life.
15. Skills for assessing the value of the world's knowledge and what benefits or harm might result from it.
16. Knowledge of human rights.
17. Classroom practices that respect the students' rights to freedom of expression; freedom to seek, receive, and impart information and ideas; and freedom of thought.
18. Classroom practices that are based on the students' cultures as long as they do not violate human rights or the rights of students

to freedom of expression, freedom to seek, receive, and impart information and ideas, and freedom of thought.

19. The moral duty to protect human rights.

CONCLUSION: LITERACY AND NUMERACY AS METHODS FOR REFLECTING ON THE GOOD LIFE

We hardly have a perfect world with perfect governments and economic systems, and, given the fallibility of humans, we will probably never achieve utopia. On the other hand, there is room for improvement on all fronts. Schooling can certainly play a role in preparing people to think about alternatives to the good life.

A real danger is that education will be used by economic and political interests, whose power depends on maintaining the status quo, to indoctrinate students into a complacent belief that current thinking offers the best solutions for achieving the good life. Have we achieved the best form of government? One could certainly defend the U.S. government and others as having improved on the barbaric political conditions that existed in ancient Roman and Chinese societies. By and large, political conditions have improved for some humans with the recognition and defense of human rights. The Universal Declaration of Human Rights is an important political step in improving the lives of many human beings. However, we can still improve on existing conditions.

Despite the claims of some that the free market or socialism is an ideal economic system, it is difficult to imagine that anyone could seriously argue that the world economic system is the best that can be achieved or that current economic theories offer any final solutions. For years, global economic discussions have been divided between free market and socialist ideas. We need to move beyond these paradigms. We need to think of new ways to more equitably distribute goods and to maintain the environmental web of life.

Consequently, the right to education must foster social imagination and thinking about new ways of organizing the good life for all people. Literacy and numeracy should be tools that help people navigate through the complexities of modern life while freeing their creative powers to imagine better ways of structuring social, political, and economic organizations. As part of the process, people should be able to use their imaginations to reflect on the past and the present. People should be able to think about models of past and present cultural ideals, twist them in their minds so that they can see them from every perspective, and then reflect on the contribution of these ideals to the good life. In this process, the very meaning of the good life becomes an object of reflection. This process of imaginative reflection should be engaged in by all people, from indigenous cultures to the world's economic elites.

A guiding principle in the process of imaginative reflection, I believe, should be the moral duty of all people to protect the human rights of others. How best, people should ask themselves, can various forms of political and economic organizations protect the rights of others? I consider that a basic part of the justification of a universal right to education and of a universal concept of education is an education that includes the teaching of a moral duty to protect the rights of others. This is an activist position that moves beyond a concept of a passive citizen who simply obeys the law and does not violate the rights of others. This moral duty requires all people to actively think about and act to protect human rights. This moral duty is the topic of the next chapter.

ᵈᙏ 7 ᙏᵉ

Mediating the Effects
of World Culture and Economy

The right to education is justified by the universal necessity for everyone to determine the benefits and use of the world's knowledge. So far, I have focused on human rights, literacy, and numeracy as basic to the fulfillment of the right to education. However, these basic skills and knowledge provide only a minimal competence in coping with the world's economy and culture. In addition, the right to education requires learning to mediate between one's own culture and international pressures. This ability, I argue, requires centering oneself in one's own culture and language. It is from the advantage of "cultural centeredness" that people can become competent in dealing with the whirlwind of global forces. In addition, cultural centeredness unlocks a diversity of ideas and dreams that can play a vital role in finding new ways to improve political and economic systems.

Words, such as "culture" and "world culture," often invoke the 19th-century European image of discrete and homogenous societies.[1] This image is a product of 19th-century nationalism, which attempted to build patriotic feelings around claims of shared beliefs, customs, languages, and history. For the nationalist, culture in a given political sphere is homogenous or should be homogenous. This concept of culture existed in the imagination of 19th- and early 20th-century Europeans, but not in reality. In fact, culture, as I have previously discussed, is related to a variety of factors including social class and gender. The manners, customs, and history of upper class English males differs from that of lower class English females. Even though they can communicate, their language is divided by accents and colloquialisms. Also, culture is dynamic, particularly in the modern world. Therefore, as I am using the term in this chapter, *cultural centeredness* refers to social class and gender along with shared customs, values, language, and beliefs that are constantly changing.

Again, I want to remind readers, I am outlining only the requirements for fulfilling the universal right to education. I am not detailing every aspect of elementary and secondary education guaranteed by the right to education. Only the universal aspects of schooling are being discussed including literacy, numeracy, human rights education, and in this chapter, mediating the effects of the world's culture and economy. Other aspects of education, such as vocational training, literary traditions, science, advanced mathematics, civic education, and other subjects, will be determined by local school systems. However, I am arguing that the universal right to education guarantees all people an education according to the guidelines so far established in this book.

THE MEANING OF CULTURAL CENTEREDNESS

"I dream in Chamicuro, but I cannot tell my dreams to anyone," Natalia Sangama, a Peruvian, explained to a reporter visiting her village of thatch huts clustered on the bank of a sky-blue lake in the Amazonian jungle. Sangama was the last speaker of Chamicuro, and, consequently, she had to converse with the rest of her family in Spanish. "Some things cannot be said in Spanish," she lamented, "It's lonely being the last one."[2]

When a language is lost, so is much of a culture, Michael Krauss, a University of Alaska linguist informed the reporter. Commenting on the concern of linguists with the potential death of 50% of the world's 6,000 languages in the next century, the reporter wrote, "Each language contains words that uniquely capture ideas, and when the words are lost, so are the ideas."[3]

Also lost are distinct ways of looking at the world, which could energize and contribute to creative thinking. These differing views of the world are often present in the emotional and buried meaning given to words. For Pueblo Indians the word *scientist* connotes "a disturbance" because of the damage archeologists did to their culture.[4] In contrast, for most other English speakers, the word *scientist* defines an occupation and carries with it a feeling of prestige and wisdom. A common American phrase is "it doesn't take a rocket scientist," which refers to something that does not take a high level of intelligence to do or understand. In this case, "rocket scientist" is alluded to as the highest form of intelligence. However, to think of science and scientists as "a disturbance" forces most English speakers to evaluate the meaning they have associated with the word. This could lead to a critical evaluation of the worth and role of science in the present world. After all, science and technology have brought "disturbances" along with benefits.

Sangama's loneliness as the last speaker of her language highlights the cultural and linguistic confusion resulting from colonialism and current events. Her problem was not unique as she negotiated different languages and cultures, but it is more difficult than that of an English citizen whose family's ties reach back into centuries of English history. Sangama was losing her traditional language and culture, while the English person watches the triumph of her or his language. Still, the English citizen experiences constant cultural change because of the impact of immigration into England, global media, and participation in world markets.

The right to education guarantees both Sangama and the English person access to the world's knowledge. The danger for both is that nationalist systems of education will deny access to the world's knowledge. Certainly, the English person might benefit from the ideas that will be lost with the death of Chamicuro language. The ideas embedded in that language might provide new ways of imagining a better world. In addition, the English person also needs to be centered in her or his own culture in order to make decisions about global forces. This process of centering is easier for the English person than for those experiencing linguistic and cultural extinction.

My concept of cultural centeredness is derived from the work of Molefi Asante who focused on the African-American experience. Asante ascribed many of the social problems in the African- American community to the cultural dysfunctionalism resulting from enslavement and forced migration to a foreign land. Epitomizing the most brutal expression of colonialism, the African diaspora to the Americas forced the integration of differing African cultures and languages. In the United States, cultural and language problems were exacerbated by laws forbidding the education of enslaved Africans. As a result, enslaved Africans had to negotiate a world in which the owners spoke English and other slaves might or might not speak a common mother tongue. In this situation, enslaved Africans fabricated a language, Ebonics, to communicate with the owners and between themselves. After several generations, many mother tongues of enslaved Africans were embedded in Ebonics. Adding to the linguistic confusion was the clashing of African cultures in the context of slavery. African-American culture emerged from the creative energies required to adapt to this linguistic and cultural mixture.[5]

The forced and rapid cultural adaptation of enslaved Africans and their descendants resulted, according to Asante, in some members of the Black community being socially dysfunctional as expressed in high crime rates, unstable families, and drug usage. Other members of the Black community adopted the culture of the dominated White elite and, in recent years, joined that elite in large corporations and in the government. Some adopted the economic values of the Protestant ethic and became successful entrepreneurs and professionals, particularly in business and schools serving the Black community.[6] However, even socially and economically successful African Americans still feel uncertain about their cultural place in U.S. society.[7]

The solution for any culture experiencing the demands of rapid change or invasion by another culture, Asante argued, is to gain "cultural centeredness." The uniqueness and power of Asante's argument can be illustrated by a comparison with Cornel West's claim that problems in the Black community are the result of a nihilistic philosophy of self-destruction caused by black rage at white racism and the blocking of economic opportunity. "Nihilism," West wrote, "is to be understood here not as a philosophical doctrine that there are no rational grounds for legitimate standards or authority; it is, for more, the lived experience of coping with a life of horrifying meaninglessness, hopelessness, and (most important) lovelessness."[8] The existence of nihilism, West argued, is proved by the self-destruction by many members of the Black community through crime, drug usage, and violence. The solution, according to West, is a combination of economic changes that open up windows of opportunity for the Black community along with meeting "the nihilistic threat head-on."[9] West wanted to openly confront the "self-destructive and inhumane actions of black people" by a "politics of conversion" that builds hope in the future and provides an affirmation of self-worth. Self-love, according to West, provides a counterpunch to the power of nihilism.[10]

West's identification of anger and rage as a source of nihilistic destruction would be true of any group undergoing forced subjugation through colonialism or racism or experiencing social class or gender discrimination. Despite his own privileged position as a Princeton and Harvard professor, West reported feeling rage as a victim of racism as he stood on a corner in Manhattan unable to flag down a taxi while all around him cabs were stopping for White people. Even for professional African Americans, rage fueled by memories and realities of racism and oppression simmers below the surface waiting to erupt. Turned inward, the rage can become self-destructive.

However, West's solution of self-love is inadequate against a historical memory of cultural uprooting, enslavement, economic exploitation, segregation, and racism. Certainly, self-love and a positive self-image are potential antidotes for many self-destructive behaviors. It is hard to disagree with West's statement, "People, especially degraded and oppressed people, are also hungry for identity, meaning, and self-worth." Despite these obvious truths, one can hardly imagine West's politics of conversion remedying the social dysfunctionalism appearing in global societies that have experienced rapid cultural change as a result colonialism, war, migration, and world economics.

Cultural education programs invoking West's politics of conversion focus on building self-esteem and identity through teaching African-American history, literature, and culture. Translated into other societies and conditions, this means teaching, for instance, aboriginal or immigrant groups in any country their history, literature, and culture as a means of building self-respect. In fact, this is the professed goal of many multicultural education programs.

The only thing wrong with West's proposal is that it *does not go far enough* in remedying the cultural havoc caused by colonialism and world economics. One thing missing from West's analysis, and that of others who propose simple multicultural education programs to build self-esteem, is that rage and nihilism are also a result of the internalization of the values of the oppressor. Stated simply in the context of the United States, Black people might internalize White images of African-American inferiority. If African Americans or any colonized group, as Frantz Fanon vividly described in the *Wretched of the Earth*, let the oppressor colonize their minds, then they come to believe that they are inferior and deserve to be ruled.[11] This results in a self-hatred, it can be argued, that is expressed in forms of self-destruction or violent acts against the oppressor.

Is cultural centeredness just a matter of expelling the negative self-images and ideas adopted from the oppressor? Do educators simply work to eliminate from the world's media negative images of all cultural groups? Can the use of classroom materials presenting positive images of the students' culture end nihilism? How do educators help students gain a cultural centeredness that allows them to understand their relation to the global culture and economy?

Molefi Asanti believed students can break through their uncertainties about themselves and their culture by understanding the cultural transformation that has taken place among their own people. For African Americans, Asante believed, this means understanding the cultural values that originated in Africa and still remain part of their community. In addition, cultural centeredness means understanding how African cultures were changed through the experience of enslavement and intersection with other cultures in the Americas.

Therefore, one issue is understanding the continuation of traditional values when they are not recognized by the dominant culture. "Although," Asante wrote, "our traditional values [meaning African values] such as harmony, justice, equality, patience, diligence and good-naturedness are not foreign to us today, they are rarely represented in the media, which instead produces a flood of images and ideas about how nihilistic we have become."[12]

This approach adds another twist to the idea of expelling the negative self-images implanted by the dominant group. For instance, in the case of African Americans or any colonized group, the dominant media and schools have historically presented images of White people, or the dominant group, and their cultures as the ideal to be emulated by all people. Accompanying these ideal images are ones that present a negative image of the subjugated group. Absent from these images are the traditional values of the subjugated group.

The term *cultural centeredness*, as I am adapting it from Asante, goes one step beyond expelling the images implanted by the oppressor. It involves centering people's understanding and perspective in their traditional cultural values. To be "uncentered" in this context refers to the psychological confusion resulting from acting according to cultural values that find no representation in the schools, media, government, economic system, or surrounding society. In addition, people are "uncentered" when they do not understand their actions and beliefs in relation to their heritage. To be centered, therefore, people understand and accept their actions as a product of their cultural traditions despite the neglect of these traditions in school and other social and political institutions.

The idea of "perspective" is crucial component of cultural centeredness. As Asante explained, "Afrocentricity is a perspective which allows Africans to be subjects of historical experiences rather than objects of the fringe of Europe."[13] In the case of African Americans, they experience, according to Asante, schools and institutions that impose a "Eurocentric perspective on every subject and theme as if the Eurocentric position is the only human and universal view."[14]

The difference between the Afrocentric and Eurocentric perspectives is primarily one of interpreting data. For instance, interpreting the phenomena of the American Civil War would be different from an Afrocentric as opposed to an Eurocentric perspective. In this case, there would be no *right* interpretation, only a different set of concerns and questions. A Eurocentric perspective might raise questions about the causes and effect of the war with regard to dominant political and social institutions, while the Afrocentric perspective might focus on the causes and effect with regard to their own society and culture.

Asante used the example of the difference between Eurocentric and Afrocentric perspectives in interpreting cultural changes under slavery. His example is drawn from the work of the White anthropologists Sidney Mintz and Richard Price who argued, about the development of an African-American culture, "We believe that the slaves were confronted with the need to create new institutions to serve their everyday purposes."[15] The issue, according to Asante, is that Mintz and Price think of enslaved Africans as "slaves" and not as "Africans." As slaves thrown together without a common language and without traditional institutions, Mintz and Price argued that they had to create a new culture to survive in the world of slavery. Therefore, from their perspective, understanding African-American culture requires knowing why and how slaves created this new culture. From the Afrocentric perspective, enslaved Africans had a culture or cultures. Understanding African-American culture requires understanding how African culture changed under the conditions of slavery. The Afrocentric perspective links present-day African-American culture to the world of enslaved Africans and, before enslavement, to Africa.

There is nothing inherently radical about the concept of cultural centeredness. It appears radical and disturbing only to those who cling to one cultural perspective. In the United States, the Afrocentric idea was greeted by an avalanche of almost hysterical prose by White conservatives. The most widely discussed criticisms were Arthur Schlesinger Jr.'s *The Disuniting of America* and Mary Lefkowitz's *How Afrocentrism Became an Excuse to Teach Myth as History.*[16] The major fears of these conservatives are that cultural centeredness results in atomizing society and creating greater ethnic conflict, and that it displaces traditional White Anglo-Saxon values. Arthur Schlesinger Jr's argument focused on the necessity of cultural unity to maintain social stability. His vision of cultural unity focused on educating people in the values underlying dominant political and social institutions. Also, Schlesinger and Lefkowitz argued that an Afrocentric education disadvantages students wanting to compete in the dominant economic system.

Of course, these arguments represent a rejection of the human rights doctrines that protect minority languages and cultures. They also ignore the right of people to a cultural choice. In India, Africa, North America, and other regions, some members of minority cultures have chosen complete immersion in the culture of the dominating group. They have rejected their culture for the purpose of belonging to the ruling order. For instance, in the United States many Native Americans and African Americans have been assimilated into the dominant European culture. Cultural centeredness, from my perspective, does not reject that choice. On the other hand, there are many African Americans and Native Americans who have not made that choice. Indeed, they are seeking some understanding of their cultural position in the existing society.

Cultural centeredness is not a militant plea for separation or revolution. As Asante noted, "Afrocentricity seeks no special advantage and asks no special quarter. It does not promote racial supremacy of blacks nor is it based on biology. *It is not anti-anyone.*"[17] It does not mean the rejection of the dominant society. The reality for all minority cultures is that they have been influenced by the dominant group just as the dominant group has been influenced by them. India and England will never be the same as a result of English colonialism. Cultural centeredness requires recognition of the continual interplay and complexity of relationships between cultures, including cultures defined by social class and gender.

Speaking from the perspective of an African American, Asante stated, "Does this mean that we are not Americans? Of course not. We share in the contributions and achievements of this society, but we are different and difference does not have to mean hostile. Does this mean that we have no influences from others? Of course not. Yet we are separate in our historical paths because of the differences in our coming to America and the reception we have received in hegemonic situations."[18]

The same concept of cultural centeredness can be applied to Americans of English descent. The only difference is the assumption, and I want to emphasize the word *assumption*, that English cultural traditions dominate U.S. society. People of English descent are centered in their culture when they understand how their historical path and cultural changes were distinct from those of African Americans and Native Americans. Those of English descent must understand how English cultural traditions were modified by immigration and contact with African and native cultures.

The historical path of African Americans takes a different route from that of English Americans. Before enslavement, the ancestors of African Americans lived in cultures that were only beginning to undergo rapid change as a result of colonialism. They experienced a world where their actions were governed by recognized cultural norms. There was access to cultural traditions, and there was some understanding of how actions reflected traditions. In most cases, the ancestors of African Americans were part of the dominant cultures of the societies in which they lived. This changed situation with enslavement and the diaspora.

The experience of enslavement and forced migration, Asante argued, separated the Africans of the diaspora from those remaining in Africa. Enslavement resulted in a new ethnic African group called African Americans. As a result of enslavement, Asante suggested, all African Americans share a distinct cultural experience. In distinguishing African Americans from Africans, Asante wrote:

All African peoples have not experienced the same set of oppressive conditions as the Africans of the Americas. I possess all the pathos of the slave ships, the cotton fields, the spit in the face, the segregation, and the multitude of miniviolences in deed and word found in the Americas, and yet I do not find the same pathos in the voice of my brother from Mali or my sister from Kenya. In the Cuban, the Jamaican, the Brazilian, the Columbian, the Barbadian, the Haitian, the Trinidadian—yes, I recognize what Leon Phillips calls the "cadences and tonal variations that energize, envelop, and stir audiences to communal synthesis."[19]

CENTERING A CULTURE: LANGUAGE

Gaining cultural centeredness, I maintain, is an essential step in learning to judge the impact of global systems. Cultural centeredness makes it possible to judge the advantages and disadvantages of the world's economy and culture. Of course, because of the fluid and changing nature of culture, absolute cultural centeredness is not possible. The process is like a ship that tries to maintain a course despite the shifting winds and sea. The helmsperson must constantly adjust the rudder. In the same manner, people trying to be centered in their culture must continually adjust their cultural position to accommodate changing circumstances.

Language is an important aspect of cultural centeredness. I have already discussed the right to education in one's mother tongue and the official or dominant language. As I suggested at the beginning of the chapter, however, the meaning of words can vary between cultures and through time. Therefore, in the context of cultural centeredness, I would expand the meaning of language rights to include sociolects, which refer to dialects associated with social factors such as social class and culture. I am including in the study of sociolects slang, argot, jargon, and pidgin. Slang refers to nonstandard and informal words, argot to words used by secret groups, and jargon to specialized words of particular professions or trades. Pidgin refers to languages that are created when groups are forced, such as African Americans, to rapidly develop a means of communication without an opportunity to learn one another's languages.

The study of the sociolects of English is particularly important as English becomes the world language. For instance, consider the development of jargon associated with computers. Japanese educated before the 1980s must learn new words to be able to read computer manuals. Nicolas Kristof reported, "For middle-aged and elderly Japanese, life these days is a perplexing struggle through what seems like an endless language." Today, Japanese is written with a combination of Chinese characters, Roman letters, a Japanese alphabet called *hiragana*, and *katakana*. *Katakana* is a written phonetic version of foreign words. Computer manuals contain the following *katakana words* derived from English: *konpyutaa* (computer), *kiiboudo* (keyboard), *mausu* (mouse), *daburu-kurikku* (double-click), and *aikon* (icon).[20] In a Costa Rican store, I watched the owner learning to operate a computer when a group of Germans entered. Looking over my shoulder, one German, in the context of a German sentence, exclaimed, "Windows 95."

In many cases, understanding the sociolects of English is important for cultural centeredness. The combination of the English and American empires, world media, and global trade has resulted in the development of what Braj Kachru called, "Non-native Englishes."[21] Kachru was concerned with English becoming a "restricted code of communication that has rapidly become a symbol of power, authority, and elitism in the non-Western world."[22] In addition, he worried about how "English has become a vehicle of values not always in harmony with local traditions and beliefs."[23]

Consider the sociolects of English in the context of Afrocentricity. In this case, cultural centeredness requires understanding the evolution of Ebonics, which could, according to the previous definitions, be considered either as a pidgin or a dialect of one of the world's Englishes. In 1997, the Linguistic Society of America issued a resolution criticizing the treatment of Vernacular Black English as "'slang,' 'mutant,' 'lazy,' 'defective,' 'ungrammatical,' ... [and] 'broken English.'" The resolution called these labels "incorrect and demeaning."[24] According to the resolution,

> The variety known as "Ebonics," "African American Vernacular English" (AAVE), and "Vernacular Black English" and by other names is systematic and rule-governed like all natural speech varieties. In fact, all human linguistic systems—spoken, signed, and written—are fundamentally regular. The systematic and expressive nature of the grammar and pronunciation patterns of the African American vernacular has been established by numerous scientific studies over the past thirty years.[25]

Whether Ebonics is a dialect or language is debatable. According the resolution of the Linguistic Society, "The distinction between 'languages' and 'dialects' is usually made more on social and political grounds than on purely linguistic ones."[26] For instance, different varieties of Chinese are often referred to as "dialects" even though their speakers cannot understand each other. On the other hand, Swedish and Norwegian are treated as "languages" even though their speakers can generally understand one another.

Where as Asante considered the study of Ebonics important for cultural centeredness, the Linguistic Society of America considered it important for learning so-called standard English. The Society's resolution stated, "There is evidence from Sweden, the U.S., and other countries that speakers of other varieties can be aided in their learning of the standard variety by pedagogical approaches which recognize the legitimacy of the other varieties of a language ... [such as using] *the vernacular of African American students in teaching them Standard English is linguistically and pedagogically sound*" [emphasis added].[27]

One of the defining stylistic characteristics of Ebonics is the "call-and-response" between speakers and audiences. Embedded in the call-and-response style is a set of cultural, or as Asante suggested, political values. Call-and-response, combined with the improvisational form of the speaker, gives the audience an active role in determining the animation of the speaker and the content of the speech. Callouts, such as "That's right!" "You can say that again!" and "Make it plain!" act as cues for the speaker. This mode of presentation is quite different from that in traditional European audiences where people sit silently (in their minds politely) and listen to a prepared speech. The lack of participation reflects, as Asante pointed out, a political relationship. The speaker exercises authoritarian control of the situation by delivering a fixed text that is not usually modified by continual audience participation. On the other hand, the combination of improvisation by the speaker and call-and-response by the audience creates an atmosphere of greater equality of power between the speaker and audience. The speech becomes a group effort.

Improvisation and call-and-response have their origin in African cultures. Improvisation has also separated African from European music. A major contribution of African-American culture has been jazz, which is a blend of the African improvisational style and music with European traditions. Asante detailed many other examples of rhythm and styling among African Americans, such as signifying and rapping. He argued that there is a basic lyrical code to Ebonics. Asante stated, "But it is not only the preacher who combines brilliant imagination with music to make a lyrical style; this combination also predominates among public platform orators whose roots are firmly in the secular rhetoric of the urban streets."[28] In recent times, this lyrical style was characteristic of Malcolm X and Martin Luther King Jr.

I could spend many pages recounting the grammatical and cultural origins of Ebonics. The point I want to stress is its relationship to cultural centeredness. As Asante argued, "The closer a person moves to the white community psychologically, the further he or she moves from the lyrical approach to language."[29]

The right to education guarantees African-American children in the United States the right to learn Ebonics and the right to learn what is called "standard English." The right to learn Ebonics is necessary for cultural centeredness. African Americans wanting to achieve cultural centeredness should study Ebonics as a sociolect of African and English languages. In this way, African Americans can understand how African traditions blended with and modified the language and culture that evolved in North America. By reflecting on their linguistic traditions, African Americans can understand the relation between the cultural traditions associated with their language heritage and the cultural traditions associated with standard English.

As I stressed in previous sections on language rights, I believe the official or dominant language of a country is important to learn to be able to participate in the political and economic system. The study of Ebonics as a sociolect of African and English languages is primarily intended to center African Americans in their cultural traditions and to preserve an important language. Embedded in Ebonics are cultural styles and ideas that could possibly unlock creative ways of viewing current global issues. However, it is still important in the United States to learn so-called standard English to be able to participate in the dominant financial and political system. Asante, as an academic who writes in standard English, represented the possibility of being Afrocentered and working in the dominant system.

Cultural centeredness for other groups is also complicated by the historical evolution of "Englishes," "Spanishes," and other transplanted European languages in former colonies. For instance, the politics of language is a major issue in Guatemala where the largely Mayan population saw their languages banned in the public schools and were forced by Spanish-speaking authorities to change their names and traditional clothing. In 1999, after 36 years of civil war, a measure was put on the ballot that would have extended official recognition to Guatemala's 24 Indian groups. The measure reflected the demands of guerilla groups that had opposed the government during the war. An important part of the measure was the provision of government services in indigenous languages. However, only 18.5% of qualified voters participated in the election. The majority of this 18.5% voted against the measure. Leopoldo Mendez, priest of the traditional Mayan religion, blamed the poor turnout by Native American voters on a lack of time to inform them in their native languages of the vote on the measure.[30] Ironically, because there were no laws requiring the government to provide information in native languages, there was not a large enough voter turnout to force the government to provide that service. Native American turnout was also limited by the lack of a voting tradition.

In the case of Guatemala, there are several language issues to be untangled to achieve cultural centeredness. Exercising the right to education in their mother tongue and in the official Spanish language, Native Americans must understand how their languages have evolved under the influence of Spanish-speaking rulers. Of particular importance is the understanding of how sociolects or creolized Spanish might have developed as a result of the interaction between the various languages. Similar to Asante's focus on the development of Ebonics as a means of achieving cultural centeredness, Native American and Spanish-speaking groups in Guatemala must examine their languages and sociolects to understand the source of their various rhetorical styles and the changing meaning of words.

In most if not all languages, there are sociolects affiliated with social class. Often, the sociolect of the elite economic, political, or religious group is treated as the "correct" or "appropriate" sociolect. England has various sociolects identified with particular social classes. These sociolects are denoted by differences in grammar, word meanings, slang, and pronunciations. Usually, the sociolect of the elite is the language of the schools, with the sociolects of nonelite social classes being treated as inferior.

In the case of sociolects affiliated with social class, it is important for students to understand that so-called proper language usage is the sociolect of the elite. It is important for students speaking nonstandard versions of the national language to understand that their speech is not "inferior" but is a sociolect. Wolfram, Adger, and Christian contended, "Mainstream groups—roughly corresponding to the middle and upper class—are considered to exhibit socially acceptable behavior, both linguistically and culturally. As with language, their norms for behavior define a standard because they control access to attractive educational and work opportunities."[31]

For instance, in working-class communities in the United States, there is a frequent use of double negatives, such as "We didn't go nowhere," "They couldn't find no food," and "It don't never run good."[32] Appalachian sociolect provides another example. The following quote is from a ghost story told by an elderly White woman living in West Virginia. "I was always kindy afraid to stay by myself, just me, you know, it was gettin' about time for me to get in, so Ingo, he'd went over to this man's house…. I hear hem a-talkin', a-settin'."[33] In most U. S. public schools, according to Wolfram, Adger, and Christian, these sociolects are treated as signs of "students' incompetence or lack of interest in education" rather than as cultural differences.[34]

The meanings of words and the rhetorical style of sociolects should be investigated and understood. Cultural centeredness, as related to social class, requires students to understand the evolution and meaning of their particular sociolect. Again, I want to emphasize that this study is for the purpose of cultural centeredness and is not meant to deny students a knowledge of the official language or standard language usage.

CULTURAL CENTEREDNESS AND CULTURAL VALUES

In addition to language, understanding transitions in behavior patterns and beliefs is essential for cultural centeredness. Similar to language, behavior patterns and beliefs can also vary by social class and gender. African-American behavior patterns and beliefs originated in Africa; they were changed by enslavement and forced migration; and they were influenced by contact with other cultures in the Americas and by Christianity. The degree of preservation of African culture in the Americas is a function of the cultural repressiveness of each particular slaveholding country. For instance, relatively early compared with the United States, enslaved Africans in Haiti gained their independence and freedom after a slave revolt led by Toussaint-Louverture in 1804. In Haiti, enslaved Africans were for the most part a culturally compact group transported from homes in the kingdom of Dahomey. Among these former Dahomeans, there emerged Voodooism which combined their belief in spirits, the importance of trances and dreams, and traditional symbols from Roman Catholic rituals.

By the late 20th century in the United States, African behavior patterns and beliefs were enmeshed with the cultures of European immigrants. However, as Asante argued, for African Americans to gain cultural centeredness, they must understand which of their behaviors and beliefs originated in Africa. In addition to creating cultural centeredness, this process allows for the consideration of alternative ideas about the present organization of society.

For instance, the African commitment to "sudicism" or harmony shapes concepts of economic individualism. In the Protestant ethic and in capitalist ideology, the value of economic individualism is measured by growth in personal wealth. In the framework of sudicism, economic individualism is valued in terms of its contribution to the good of the group. In this context, economic activity is measured by group benefits rather than individual gain. Understanding sudicism helps African Americans understand the contradictory attitudes guiding their actions in American society. On the one hand, African Americans inherited a tradition emphasizing a commitment to the economic well-being of others. On the other hand, African- American culture was shaped by an economic system that focuses on the importance of individual gain.[35]

Sudicism also pertains to harmony in the individual. The African perspective, according to Asante, is that disharmony within the person results in disharmony in society. In this cultural tradition, the search for harmony pervades "all literary, rhetorical, or behavioral actions; the sudic ideal, which emphasizes the primacy of the person, can only function if the person seeks individual and collective harmony."[36] To become human, in this cultural perspective, requires a person to perform actions that lead to harmony within her or himself and the group. In Asante's words, "This is why the black church exudes a collective sense of harmony."[37] In contrast, in the European tradition, dating from Roman times to the rise of capitalism, individuals are constantly in battle between the forces of good and evil or are competing for economic gain. Any harmony supposedly experienced by society is a by-product of this struggle.

Harmony is also related to the African idea of "possession." People become possessed when they achieve perfect harmony with self, nature, and the universe. Possession is, according to Asante, related to the spirituality of the person. Possession is reflected not only in the intense spirituality of the African-American church but also in phrases such as "Boy, they worked themselves up" and "Girl, he worked himself into a frenzy."[38]

Another context for possession is music. The music of slavery reflects a continual striving for harmony. The embodiment of the African tradition is in jazz where the musician improvises while possessed with harmony. Asante quoted the musician and scholar Wynton Marsalis about the meaning of jazz to the Black community. "It is the most modern and profound expression of the way Black people look at the world.... Jazz is something Negroes invented and it said the most profound things not only about us and the way we look at things, but about what the modern democratic life is really about. It is the nobility of the race put into sound"[39]

Another cultural contrast, according to Asante, is the "spiritual dimension" in African tradition and the positivist tradition in European thought. In the African tradition, the material world is an illusion, and reality is in the spiritual. The spirit of the dead do not depart to heaven or hell but remain among the living to influence day-to-day life. In contrast, the positivist sees reality as the material world and dismisses the spiritual as mere superstition.

In addition, in the African tradition, "personalism" or the activating energy in each individual makes possible the spiritual and material worlds. In other words, humans carry the energy of the world in them. "That is why," according to Asante, "the drummer recites an incantation to the trees before he cuts them down to make his drums; that is why the people of the Niger always stalk a lion with words of praise and incantations before they shoot it."[40]

Personalism, spiritualism, harmony, and possession are examples of cultural perspectives that were influenced and changed by the horrors of enslavement, the struggle against racism, the imposition of Christianity, and the contacts with Europeans. These experiences fabricated African-American culture and constituted African Americans as a separate ethnic group different from other Africans and other Americans. For African Americans to be culturally centered requires understanding the evolution of their culture.

The African-American example provides insight into cultural centeredness as a process of understanding how world events shaped, and currently affect, thinking and actions. This cultural centeredness provides the starting point for mediating the influences of the current world culture and economy. In some ways, the African-American expe-

rience is an extreme example of the difficulty of gaining cultural centeredness because of the cultural disruption caused by enslavement,
forced migration, and domination by a foreign culture.

CULTURAL CENTEREDNESS IN A MANAGED CULTURE

Quite different from the African American experience is the conscious
attempt by leaders of the European Union and Singapore to create a
unified culture from many different cultures and languages. In these
cases, the fabric of a new culture is being consciously woven together.
What does it mean to have cultural centeredness under these conditions? I have dealt with the evolution of education and culture in these
communities in another book.[41] However, I did not consider there the
problem of cultural centeredness.

In both these communities, economic goals underlie the attempt to
manufacture cultural unity from diverse populations. In Singapore,
multiple language groups—Tamil, Malay, Chinese, and English—were
brought together under the banner of English imperialism. Following independence in 1965, Singapore's leaders tried to resolve cultural differences by establishing separate primary schools for each language group
while retaining English as the language of higher education. During the
1990s, the Singapore schools engaged in a program of nationalist education with the goal of creating "unity within diversity." Comparing this
effort to U.S. schools, Deputy Minister Lee Hsien Loong made the in-
sightful comment, "And it [the U.S. school system] is so successful that
many Americans are completely convinced that American values are
universal values of mankind."[42] Similar to traditional nationalist approaches to education, the goal of Singapore schools is to create an emotional bond among all citizens. Different from past nationalist efforts,
the goal is to support the political structure of the economy. Minister of
Education Teo Chee Hean proclaimed that a nationalist education will
teach "why we must continue to work together and outperform others
[other nations] to succeed in the future."[43]

The European Union evolved from a series of trade agreements beginning with the founding of the Organisation for Economic Cooperation and Development (OECD) in 1948 and culminating in the 1992
Treaty on European Union (Maastricht Treaty). The major reason for
forming the European Union was to create an economic block that
could compete with the United States and Japan in world markets. In
1996, Romano Prodi, president of the Council of Ministers of the European Union, explained, "The competitive challenge coming from the
rest of the world, today particularly from Asia, should be tackled
openly by placing in common the capacities, the inventiveness and the
production quality of the Union's members."[44] Similar to Singapore,

European Union leaders approved a plan for building nationalist unity within the Union between historically antagonistic cultures. In the union, this effort engendered many questions: Are there common European values? Is there a common European culture? What, for instance, do Italians, Germans, and French have in common? To answer these questions, the Union has supported academic conferences, media events, school programs and curricula, and cultural programs designed to fabricate an emotional bond to the European Union. Similar to Singapore, the schools have been enlisted in this nationalist project for economic purposes. Again the call is for "unity within diversity."

What does cultural centeredness mean in the context of strong nationalist educational efforts directed at improving competitiveness in the global economy? How is the call for "unity within diversity" related to cultural centeredness? Theoretically, the phrase "unity within diversity" suggests that citizens retain their identity with their particular culture while joining with other cultures to strive for economic success. It is quite possible that under the banner of "unity within diversity" schools could emphasize cultural centeredness. For instance, French schools could help students center themselves in their culture in relation to language, social class, and gender.

It is also possible for Singapore's schools to achieve the same cultural centeredness under the rubric of "unity within diversity." In Singapore's case, Asante's methodology for understanding Afrocentricism could be used to center Chinese, Tamil, and Malay cultures. Both the Chinese and the Tamil were brought to Singapore as workers by British colonialists. Similar to African Americans, although they did not experience the terrors of enslavement, they were displaced persons and victims of colonialism. Cultural centeredness as conceived by Asante would ensure that the word "diversity" in "unity within diversity" is truly meaningful.

ECONOMIC UNITY AND UNDERSTANDING
THE GLOBAL ECONOMY

The really troublesome part of the catchy phrase "unity within diversity" is the unity part. For both Singapore and the European Union, unity means some form of economic bonding for the purpose of competing in global markets. I argue that many nations, including Japan and the United States, are replacing traditional notions of political nationalism with economic nationalism. People are being taught not to die for the state, but to work hard to protect national currencies and financial systems.

The invasion of economic nationalism into schools has made it difficult for students to separate their economic interests from those of national industries. I argue that what is good for General Motors and Daimler-Chrysler is not necessarily good for workers. Unfortunately, from my perspective, economic nationalism is now linked to a human resource and human capital model of schooling.

In this model of schooling, students are treated as a resource to be developed for the good of the economic system. Education becomes career education in the sense that all schooling is intended to prepare students for occupations. Students are sorted in the educational system by ability, aptitude, and achievement tests according to the needs of the labor market. Ideally, in the human resource model, all graduating students will enter jobs that match their education, interests, and aptitudes. As I have written in several other books, the human resource model of schooling now dominates most of the world's school systems.[45] As a result, it represents a major obstacle to helping students understand how to protect their own economic interests.

Human capital accounting has become the dominant method for evaluating the effectiveness of the human resource model. Used by national governments and international organizations such as the World Bank and the Organization for Economic Development and Cooperation, human capital accounting measures the economic return on schooling by external and internal efficiency.[46] Money spent on schooling is treated as an economic investment that should produce economic gains in the form of better workers. External efficiency is measured by the ability of school graduates to get jobs that are appropriate for their education. In this conceptual framework, an educational system is very inefficient if PhDs in literature become cab drivers or students educated to be airline mechanics spend their lives painting landscapes. Internal efficiency refers to the cost of educating each student. For instance, a school system is internally inefficient if students do not graduate on time or if they must repeat grades or subjects.

Unfortunately, the results of the human resource and capital models are authoritarian educational systems dominated by national testing or, in case of the United States, by statewide testing. As Kandel noted during the original discussions about the Universal Declaration of Human Rights, human rights are threatened, particularly those of freedom of speech, expression, inquiry, and access to information, by school systems that are nationalistic, unequal, authoritarian, examination controlled, and having prescribed methods of instruction and curricula. In test-driven educational systems, subject matter is controlled by the content of the examinations. Teachers must teach to the test. National or state tests control the content of instruction.

Therefore, national testing and human resource and human capital accounting models, violate childrens' rights and the principles underlying the right to education, while blurring the lines between individual or group economic interests and the economic interests of the nation and international corporations. Consequently, strict limits should be placed on national or state examinations. These limitations should be according to the types of subjects to be examined.

Can there be national examinations without violating basic human rights doctrines? I think it is possible to use national examinations in ways that do not infringe on human rights. For instance, I think national or state testing is appropriate for certain professions and for certain skills. It is in the interest of the general welfare of the world's population that professionals, such as airline pilots, doctors, nurses, and civil engineers, are tested and certified by the state. Also, it is not a violation of human rights for governments to assess job skills, such as word processing, accounting, and industrial trades.

On the other hand, it is a violation of human rights for governments to administer national tests for subjects such as history, culture, economics, government, philosophy, and literature. The content of these subjects should not be controlled by national or state examinations. For these subjects to enlighten students rather than indoctrinate them, they must be free of the tyranny of the test and must be taught in an atmosphere that promotes freedom of thought, expression, and access to information.

For cultural centeredness to serve a role in helping students understand their relation to the global economics and culture, governments should abandon efforts to use schools to create economic nationalism. The use of schools to create emotional bonding with a nation's economic enterprises should be replaced with discussions of its benefits and disadvantages. Rather than building unthinking economic patriotism similar to the patriotic feelings promoted by Nazi and other nationalist school systems, students should be allowed to arrive at their own conclusions. This approach does not deny the possibility that after careful reflection a student might embrace and support her or his nation's economic endeavors.

ECONOMIC MORALITY: THE SEARCH FOR THE GOOD LIFE

As one aspect of culture, economics includes human relationships associated with the production, distribution, and consumption of goods. Studying economics as human relationships that are governed by cultural and moral rules helps people to better evaluate the benefits and disadvantages of differing monetary and financial systems. This approach to economics results in two important outcomes. One is an awareness of inherited economic attitudes and behaviors in relation to current economic thinking. The second involves new ways of thinking. Currently, many people's economic thinking ranges between two systems—the free market or state regulation and ownership. The primary emphasis in both approaches is on production and distribution of goods. Neither of these paradigms, I argue, has proved completely satisfactory in serving human needs and creating equitable living conditions.

In the global economy, there is a great deal of cultural confusion about the economic exchange of goods and services. In the United States, neoclassical or Austrian economics advocates that all goods and services be regulated by the free market. Unlike the 19th century, as I discuss later, contemporary advocates of the free market are concerned only about contractual relationships protected by law and not about the personal morality of transactions.[47] In contrast, many public leaders and politicians are calling for corporations to show responsibility toward their community and workers and for the economically fortunate to engage in acts of community service. Even public school systems have added requirements of community service for graduation from high school. During the administrations of Presidents Bush and Clinton, the public heard calls for "a thousand points of light" and "corporate responsibility."[48] How do we help students make sense of this and other conflicts over cultural values associated with economic exchange?

To illustrate how students might gain an understanding of the effect of economic doctrines on human relationships, I examine Marcel Mauss's anthropological essay, *The Gift: The Form and Reason for Exchange in Archaic Societies*[49] and Jerry Martien's *Shell Game: A True Account of Beads and Money in North America*.[50] I have selected these works because both are reflections on human values and economics. Written in the 1920s, Mauss's essay provides insights and alternative ways of thinking about economic systems. His findings and arguments are open to criticism but have provided an important source of discussion about economic relationships.[51] As Mauss concluded, "These facts [referring to his discussion of economics in various societies] not only throw light upon our morality and help to direct our ideals. *In their light, we can analyze better* the most general economic facts, and even this analysis helps us dimly to perceive *better organizational procedures applicable in our societies*."[52] Martien's *Shell Game* is a personal account of a search for understanding of contemporary economics in the United States by tracing the conflict and mingling of Native American and colonialist methods of exchange and distribution. Similar to Mauss, Martien's study leads to important insights and new ways of thinking about economic organization.

Keeping in mind that the goal is to educate people so that they can evaluate the advantages and disadvantages of world culture and economics, let us consider the current situation where there is a concentration of money among a few and an absence of money among others. I do not intend to launch a liberal, socialist, or communist critique of capitalism by pointing out disparities in the ability to participate in the exchange of goods. My intention is to focus on the evolution of human relations as related to the economic exchange of goods and services. Fundamentally, it is a question of cultural values related to monetary transactions.

For a student in the United States, this process requires understanding the changing nature of cultural values governing economic exchanges. This is where Martien's book provides important insights. Among colonialists and 19th-century Americans, disparities in the ability to obtain goods was acceptable; however, these differences were governed by Christian doctrines regarding charity, just prices, and just wages. As the Puritan leader John Winthrop told New England colonists, "God Almightie in his most holy and wise providence hath soe disposed the Condition of mankinde, as in all times some must be rich some poore, some highe and eminent inpower and dignities; other meane and in subjection."[53] However, this doctrine was balanced by a Christian obligation for the rich to give alms to the poor. In the context of the 19th-century Protestant ethic, the rich were trustees of wealth and had an obligation to be charitable. Exchanges were also governed by a moral obligation to adhere to a just price and wage. As John Winthrop preached to his fellow New Englanders, "A man may not sell above the current price, i.e., such a price as is usual in the time and place."[54] These moral principles governing economic exchanges took on added meaning when considered in the context of clashes between European and Native American cultural values over the exchange of good and services. This is where Mauss's essay *The Gift* becomes important.

Mauss's essay opened with an old Scandinavian poem that illustrates the moral obligation embodied in the exchange of goods. The exchange of presents in the poem includes the obligation to reciprocate. It is in the reciprocity of these exchanges of goods that friendships are maintained. Among Polynesians and Northwest Indians, Mauss found two other obligations binding participants in an exchange of goods— the obligation to give and the obligation to receive. The obligation to receive places an important burden on all members of the community. Mauss wrote, "For a clan, a household, a group of people, a guest, have no option but to ask for hospitality, to receive presents, to enter into trading, to contract alliances, through wives or blood kinship ... [there is] a whole system of law and morality based upon the duty one has not to fail to share in the meal at which one is present or that one has seen in preparation."[55] It is important to understand that gifts consist of both usable and decorative goods and services, such as fish, oil, timber, labor, necklaces, and clothing. Gifts are the means of economic exchange.

These three forms of obligations (I would call them moral obligations)—to reciprocate, to give, and to receive—create a complex system that knits communities together and provides for a more equitable distribution of goods. They are similar to what I have called "claim rights" in the sense that everyone has a claim to one another's goods. Mauss wrote, "To refuse to give, to fail to invite, just as to refuse to accept, is tantamount to declaring war; it is to reject the bond of alliance and commonality."[56]

Imagine a student in the United States reflecting on these three obligations. Today, reciprocity involves a monetary exchange that might have little to do with maintaining the bonds of the community. For instance, if I walk into a store and receive candy from the clerk, then I am obligated to give the clerk money. This could be considered a basic exchange of gifts. However, the exchange of goods and personal obligations ends when I receive the candy and the clerk receives the money.

The obligation to give has been stripped from modern economic science. If I see a street beggar, I am not obligated, unless motivated by religion or personal morality, to give her or him money. More important, in Christian traditions, the beggar is not obligated to reciprocate my gift. Consequently, the relationship becomes one-sided as opposed to being mutually binding.

In addition, there would be no beggars if everyone acted according to these three obligations. Economic exchange might actually hold communities together and at the same time rectify disparities in wealth. Rather than accepting a society divided between the rich and poor, as contained in Christian doctrines, society could be swept up in a frenzy of giving and receiving. This happened during the potlatches held by Northwest Coast Indians, particularly the Tilingit and Haida. Among these groups, one could not refuse to attend a potlatch or refuse a gift. Potlatches were formal gatherings for the purpose of giving gifts. Not to reciprocate a gift created a "debt," which could lead to actual enslavement of the person. Literally, one became "indebted" to the giver.

Adding to the binding power of the exchange is the idea that the gift contains the spirit of the giver. Consequently, Mauss wrote, the potlatch in societies in Northeast Siberia and West Alaska "produces an effect not only upon men, who vie with one another in generosity, not only upon the things they pass on to one another or consume at it, not only upon the souls of the dead who are present and take part in it, and whose names have been assumed by men, but even upon nature."[57]

It was conflicting ideas between Native Americans and European invaders about giving, receiving, reciprocating, and ownership of land that shaped the economic life of North America. For North American Indians, no single person could own land, but everyone could use land. A clan or tribe might allow the use of land and, in exchange, receive a gift. For Europeans, the gift or money purchased the land. One of the principal sources of gifts for Eastern Native Americans was wampum usually made of shells strung together in patterns. European invaders assumed that wampum was like European money that could be used to purchase goods and land. This confusion over cultural concepts of economic exchange and land contributed to the demise of Native Americans and the evolution of North America from an economically equalitarian society to one of extreme differences in wealth.

Heading east from California in the late 20th century to study the evolution of monetary values in North America, Jerry Martien pondered, "It had always been a question of value. What was the value of a life, what made it worth living? The books and papers in my knapsack, the pictures in my mind, the little money in my pocket—all taking me on an errand of ancient commerce."[58] As I read these lines, I wondered whether an economist, such as the head of the Federal Reserve Alan Greenspan worried about the value of life as he manipulated monetary policy. "But of course he does," I thought, "the basic principle of Austrian economics is that what people consider valuable is better determined by the free exchange of the marketplace rather than the actions of government planners and bureaucrats. Individual choice is the key to determining what people really value. This is the whole basis of the neo-classical revolt against bureaucracy and government economic regulation."[59] The one flaw in this reasoning might be that this form of choice is premised on the pursuit of self-interest and profit in the marketplace. Should self-interest and the profit motive be the moral doctrine of the economic system?

How should value be determined? When Europeans arrived on the eastern shore of North America, they mistook the giving of strings of shells or wampum as monetary exchanges. In their confusion, the New England colonies for 30 years recognized wampum as an official currency which could be used to purchase (in a European sense) goods and pay for tuition at Harvard University. The primary sources for wampum were the shores of Long Island where the colonists promptly put colonial women to work at its eastern end in Montauk making strings of shells. Later, a wampum factory was built in New Jersey. The colonist established official rates of exchange between wampum and European currencies. The mass production of wampum by the colonists drove down its value for the purchase of beaver pelts. In the early 20th century, the New York legislature made the Board of Regents of the State University official keepers of the wampum. Today, wampum belts are stored in a vault under the state capital. To the amazement of Native Americans, Europeans assumed that giving wampum allowed them to purchase land. Thus, the Dutch in their greedy confusion claimed purchase of the island of Manhattan.

What did wampum mean to Native Americans? There are several stories about the origin of wampum. One account is that the Iroquois founder Hayonhwatha was wandering in bereavement over the loss of his family when he came to the shore of a beautiful lake. Waterfowl suddenly flew all at once and the force of their wings caused the water to be displaced, revealing a lake floor covered with shells. He gathered the shells and hung them on strings. As he traveled from village to village, he gave a string to anyone he saw in deep grief. The wampum gift was used to console those bereaving the loss of others. Wampum became part of the condolence ceremony to restore vision, hearing, and speech obstructed by grief and ashes. Later, the wampum belt was used as treaty contract to unite the five tribes of the Iroquois nation. It was used as a ceremonial item to mark tribal and clan agreements and to unite people. Contrary to the European assumption that wampum was mere currency to be used as payment for goods, services, and land, Native Americans imbued wampum with moral meaning.

Most important, wampum represented the three obligations of the gift exchange—reciprocity, giving, and receiving. As Europeans built their moral economy on the concept of private property, Native Americans built it on sharing. This premise did not mean a utopian world free of war and ritual slaughter, but it did mean that in the clan everyone had a moral obligation to share.

Cynically, and without sympathy for the European misunderstanding of the moral economy of Native Americans, Jerry Martien described the evolution of colonial economics: "They began with a gift, and they turned it into money. This is how the New World was 'conquered'—not with a bang, but one crooked deal at a time."[60] Martien's stages of economic evolution are: Corn was used as money and then wampum was used to buy corn; wampum was exchanged for beaver pelts; guns were sold for wampum and gunpowder was used to buy pelts; rum was used as currency to buy pelts; and when the beaver disappeared land was bought with notes of credit for currency.[61]

Martien thought that eventually the moral economy of the colonists deteriorated under the weight of their own greed. For Martien, this begins with the abandonment of the ideal of the family farm for corporate farming. Many colonists believed private property was the basis for the social contract that held society together. The family farm, idealized by Americans such as Thomas Jefferson, was supposed to be the source of republican values. The family farm was another form of moral economy that contrasted sharply with Native American belief in common ownership of land. Agrarian values were to be the strength of the new nation.

However, with the development of the textile industry in the 19th-century, the ideal of the family farm as the source of moral values was slowly replaced by demands that farming become a business that produced surpluses to feed workers. Businesslike farming also freed family members to join the industrial workforce. Daughters left family farms in the early 19th-century to work in textile mills and to teach in the new common school system.

Nineteenth-century America contained many different forms of moral economy. Most Native American tribes still adhered to common ownership and the obligations of gift giving. Rising industrialists rebeled against the concept of the just price and wage. However, Christian charity and responsibility still guided the actions of many of the new industrialists exemplified by the philanthropic works of Andrew Carnegie.

In the 20th century, corporations translated concepts of Christian responsibility into corporate welfarism by providing benefits to workers ranging from cafeterias to afterwork activities such as baseball. Library carts were pushed through the aisles of the National Cash Register Corporation so that workers could take books home. IBM became known as the company that took care of its workers by providing lifetime jobs.[62]

However, by the end of the 20th century, moral responsibility disappeared from economic doctrines as big businesses fired workers and cut back on benefits. Corporate welfarism, the last vestige of Christian charity, collapsed under the weight of greed and the doctrines of Austrian economics. The three obligations of gift giving remained in the cultural patterns of some Native Americans. However, cheated of their lands, many lived in poverty and cultural confusion similar to that identified by Asante for African Americans.

These examples are meant merely to illustrate the importance of considering the effect of economics on human relationships as an important part of understanding the advantages and disadvantages of global economics. Obviously, the actual content of instruction and discussion of the moral aspects of economic systems varies from region to region. However, I argue, that the right to education should guarantee that all students have the right to knowledge and discussion of moral economy.

CONCLUSION: CULTURE AND ECONOMICS

In addition to literacy, numeracy, and human rights, cultural centeredness and the study of moral economy are, I argue, part of the universal definition of education as provided by the right to education. Again, I want to emphasize, these are intended only as basic parts of the elementary and secondary education guaranteed to all children below the ages of 18 years. Under the concept of cultural centeredness all people have the right to know and understand the evolution of their culture within the framework of global culture. Cultural centeredness, as I discussed previously, includes social class, gender, and language. It also includes an understanding of the dynamic and fluid qualities of culture in a constantly changing world. Moral economy could be considered one aspect of cultural centeredness. Everyone has the right to know how economics effects human relationships. As I suggested earlier, the study of the evolution of economic exchanges can provide some insight into the connection between the quality of human life and economic theory and transactions. Rather than studying economics to determine how to be more productive and efficient, the goal is to study economics for the purpose of improving human happiness and to search for alternatives to the good life.

Consequently, cultural centeredness and the study of moral economy are educational methods rather than prescriptions about how the world should be organized. Frankly, I have no plan for the good life. I am still searching. My intent is to provide the right to an education that maximizes the opportunity for all people to engage in this quest. My discussions of past cultures and forms of economic exchange are not for the purpose of holding them up as ideals but to energize thinking about the future. I do not consider the past lives of Native Americans, Polynesians, or Africans superior to those of present cultures. They serve only as alternative examples to unlock the social imagination. Freed from authoritarian forms of political and economic nationalistic education, the right to education provides students with the intellectual tools to mediate the effect of the global economy and culture.

❧ 8 ❧

Summary: The Universal Right to Education

Composed during the transition in the world system from colonialism to a postcolonial society of transnational corporations, global media, international political and economic arrangements, and high-speed information systems, the 1948 Universal Declaration of Human Rights outlined basic rules for governing human conduct. Hurriedly planned and written after World War II to stop any new outbreaks of genocide, imperialism, and ethnocide, the Universal Declaration set the tone for future discussions about global rights. Later generations debated and elaborated on the justification and meaning of the human rights identified in the 1948 declaration.

Since 1948, there have been many discussions about the meaning of "Everyone has the right to education," as specified in Article 26 of the Universal Declaration of Human Rights. After examining these discussions and considering the role of education in the world system, I have composed a general justification for the right to education, a universal concept of education, and basic guidelines for human rights, literacy, numeracy, and cultural education.

In conclusion, I summarize the justifications, definitions, and guidelines for the right to education. In keeping with the 1989 Convention on the Rights of the Child, I define childhood as the stage of development below the age of 18 years. Consequently, the right to education is guaranteed to all people below the age of 18.

JUSTIFICATION

There are two major justifications for the right to education. The first justification is based on the effects of colonialism and the current global culture and economy. This justification, as I have elaborated on throughout this book, can be stated:

A universal right to an education is justified by the necessity for all people to know how the global culture and economy created by colonialism and postcolonialism affects their live, and what benefits or harm might result from them.

The second justification is based on the close relation between education and the general protection of human rights. People must know their rights and how to protect them. Therefore,

A universal right to an education is justified as necessary for understanding and protecting other human rights. This justification acknowledges a close interdependence between the right to education and all other human rights.

EDUCATION AND CHILDREN'S RIGHTS

Simply stated, children cannot benefit from the right to education unless they receive adequate food, medical care, housing, and protection from exploitive labor. Therefore, the right to education justifies children's assistance rights. These rights are:

Universal assistance rights for children, such as government provision of high-quality health care, proper nutrition for normal development, housing, and free schooling, which are justified as necessary for children to exercise their right to an education.

Universal protection rights for children, such as protection against economic and social exploitation, or employment in work harmful to their morals or health or dangerous to life or likely to hamper their normal development, which are justified by being necessary for children to exercise their right to an education.

LIBERTY AND EDUCATION RIGHTS

The right of children to free access to information and freedom of thought is necessary for an education that provides an understanding of the advantages and disadvantages of the global economy and culture and of human rights. Because human rights protect freedom of thought and access to information, an education in human rights requires recognition of these principles. Currently, these principles are being violated by the national and state examinations that control the content of the curriculum and methods of instruction and by human capital theories that define the major purpose of schooling as educating better workers to increase economic growth. Therefore the right to education includes:

Universal liberty rights for children, such as freedom of expression; freedom to seek, receive and impart information and ideas; and freedom of thought.

The universal right to an education that *does not* serve nationalistic or particular political ends by indoctrination, propaganda, or the use of national examinations to control teacher and student learning.

NONDISCRIMINATION AND THE RIGHT TO EDUCATION

Fulfillment of the right to education requires that schooling be made available to all citizens. In addition, human rights doctrines preclude any form of discrimination in the offering of educational services. Therefore, a guiding principle is:

The universal right to an education is guaranteed to all children regardless of race, color, sex, language, social class, religion, or political beliefs.

CULTURE, LANGUAGE, AND EDUCATION RIGHTS

A universal right to education requires recognition of cultural and language differences. Because human rights doctrines are now the major source of protection for minority and indigenous cultures and languages, the exercise of cultural rights must be in accordance with human rights. As I discussed earlier, education can serve as a vehicle for moral discourses about potential conflicts over cultural and human rights, such as abortion and female circumcision.

The right to education includes the following cultural and language rights:

All people have a right to an education in their own language and in methods of teaching and learning appropriate to their own culture.

All people have the right to an education that teaches:

1. An understanding of their own culture and their relation to it.
2. Their mother tongue.
3. The dominant or official language of the nation.
4. An understanding of the effect of the world culture and economy on their own culture and economy.

ENVIRONMENTAL DESTRUCTION AND THE RIGHT TO EDUCATION

Because the right to life is the most fundamental right, protecting the planet from environmental destruction provides another justification for the right to education. The following provides a summary of the relation between the right to education and environmental education:

Environmental Education and the Right to Education

1. Environmental destruction threatens the basic human right of the right to life.

2. The right to education, which includes environmental education, might safeguard the planet.

3. The preservation and growth of the holistic knowledge of nature of indigenous peoples could be a safeguard against planetary devastation.

4. To protect the earth, indigenous peoples' education should include their cultural and scientific traditions and should be according to their cultural practices with instruction in their mother tongues and the official or dominant languages of their nations.

5. Therefore, the right to education, which includes environmental education and respect for the holistic knowledge of indigenous peoples, is necessary for protection of the basic human right of right to life.

HUMAN RIGHTS AND A UNIVERSAL CONCEPT OF EDUCATION

An important justification of the right to education is the necessity of protecting human rights. Therefore, one aspect of a universal concept of education is an education in human rights. Important to the protection of human rights is creating a moral duty to actively protect the human rights of others. This moral duty is an essential part of instruction in human rights. Also, there is a current tendency for human rights education to follow the pattern of traditional nationalistic and indoctrinating forms of schooling. Human rights education must avoid these past practices. Therefore, the following universal guidelines for human rights education begin with a set of cautions:

Human rights education *should avoid* "nationalistic" forms of education designed to win the allegiance of students to organizations that claim protection of human rights, such as UNICEF and the UN. The value of all institutions should be an object of critical exploration and discussion.

Universal Guidelines for Human Rights Education

Cautions

- Human rights education *should avoid* binding human rights with ideas such democracy, the rule of law, equality, tolerance, and solidarity. These should be considered as separate and complex ideas that should be subjected to critical analysis and discussion.

- Human rights education *should avoid* treating human rights documents as sacred texts to be "enshrined" and worshiped. These documents should be presented to students as imperfect beginnings that are open to criticism and improvement.

•. Human rights education *should avoid* cultural insensitivity as highlighted by Eurocentric historical treatments of human rights and assumptions about the cultural appropriateness student activities.

These guidelines also include a list of methods:

Methods

• A critical analysis of the history of human rights documents.

• A critical discussion of human rights documents.

• The use of thematic representations and role playing to generate critical dialogue about human rights situations.

• The use of critical thinking, imagination, and fantasy to generate students' visions of ideal human rights.

• A critical discussion of student created human rights documents as compared with existing documents.

• The use of thematic representations and role playing to generate discussion about the moral duty to protect the rights of all people.

• The use of thematic representations and role playing to generate discussion about the role of public shame and guilt in fostering a moral duty to protect the rights of all people.

UNIVERSAL MINIMUM GUIDELINES FOR LITERACY INSTRUCTION

Minimum guidelines for universal literacy instruction are determined by the justifications used for a universal right to education. In other words, at a minimum, literacy should prepare students to understand and decide upon the advantages and disadvantages of the global culture and economy and to actively protect human rights. Again, I want to stress that these guidelines are intended only to provide universal minimums for literacy.

Universal Guidelines for Literacy Instruction

1. Initial language instruction should be in the mother tongue.

2. Initial language instruction should use words that name the world surrounding students.

3. Initial language instruction should use words associated with human rights.

4. Initial reading material should include the history and cultures of students for the purpose of presenting alternative lifestyles, polit-

ical and economic arrangements, and value systems. This material should not be written to indoctrinate students, but to present possible alternatives to the good life.

5. Initial reading material should present real-life problems that force students to think about their present situation.

UNIVERSAL MINIMUM GUIDELINES FOR NUMERACY INSTRUCTION

Similar to my guidelines for literacy instruction, these guidelines for numeracy instruction are intended to fulfill the requirements for the universal justifications of the right to education. Similar to education in the mother tongue, I emphasize the importance of learning culturally based numbering systems.

Universal Guidelines for Numeracy Instruction

1. Initial numeracy instruction should be in accordance with the culture of students or, stated in terms similar to literacy guidelines, initial numeracy instruction should be in the mother numbering system.

2. Culturally based number systems should be used as a bridge for learning the numbering system of the global economy.

3. Instruction in the dominant-global number system should be linked to concrete social situations involving the exchange of goods and money, government taxes, and the measurement of goods and basic building structures.

4. Instruction should include the operation of electronic calculators and computers.

5. Instruction should include literacy in the language of modern electronic and computers.

6. Instruction should include how numbers are used as means of political, economic, and behavioral control.

CULTURAL CENTEREDNESS, MORAL ECONOMY, AND SOCIAL IMAGINATION

Throughout this book I have stressed the importance of unlocking the critical imagination of people so that they can think about alternatives to existing political, economic, and social structures. I believe that the protection of minority and indigenous cultures and languages provides differing ways of thinking about the world and sources of knowledge for protecting our environment. In addition, as I argued in chapter 7, cultural centeredness sparks imaginative thinking while helping people mediate the effects of the global culture. In the same manner, the study of moral economy or the human relationships involved in economic exchange provides students with tools to imagine differing economic systems and to understand the impact of the global economy.

Throughout this volume, I have stressed that I do not believe that utopia is possible. However, I do believe that a universal right to education that unlocks the doors of human imagination about alternatives to the good life will help to bring us closer to a world that respects human rights and a world in which political and economic systems are organized to promote human happiness. The end goal of all educational systems should be increasing joy for all people.

Notes

Chapter 1

[1] Carol Bellamy, *The State of the World's Children 1999: Education* (New York: UNICEF, 1999), p. 7.

[2] See Frank Levy, *The New Dollars and Dreams: American Incomes and Economic Change* (New York: Russell Sage, 1998).

[3] Bellamy, p. 7.

[4] "Universal Declaration of Human Rights, 1948," *Basic Documents on Human Rights Third Edition,* edited by Ian Brownlie (New York: Oxford University Press, 1992), p. 26.

[5] "EFA Theme Song," *Final Report: World Conference on Education for All: Meeting Basic Learning Needs* (New York: Inter-Agency Commission for the World Conference on Education for All, 1990), p. 121.

[6] Ibid., p. 10.

[7] Ibid., p. 12.

[8] Ibid., p. 10.

[9] "World Declaration on Education for All: Meeting Basic Learning Needs" in *Final Report: World Conference on Education for All*, pp. 42–43.

[10] Ibid., p. 43.

[11] Ibid., p. 43.

[12] John P. Humphrey, *Human Rights & the United Nations: A Great Adventure* (New York: International, 1984), p. 29.

[13] Ibid., p. 25.

[14] Ibid., p. 10.

[15] Ibid., p. 20.

[16] Ibid., p. 20.

[17] Ibid., p. 20.

[18] Jacques Maritain, "Introduction," in *Human Rights: Comments and Interpretations: A Symposium Edited by UNESCO* (Westport, CT: Greenwood Press, 1973), p. 12.

[19] Ibid., p. 12.

[20]Paul Gordon Lauren, *The Evolution of International Human Rights: Visions Seen* (Philadelphia: University of Pennsylvania Press, 1998), p. 5.

[21]"Grounds of an International Declaration of Human Rights," in *Human Rights: Comments and Interpretations: A Symposium Edited by UNESCO* (Westport, CT: Greenwood Press, 1973), pp. 262–263.

[22]"Grounds of an International Declaration of Human Rights," p. 263.

[23]"Memorandum And Questionnaire Circulated by UNESCO on the Theoretical Bases of the Rights of Man," in *Human Rights: Comments and Interpretations*, p. 254.

[24]Ibid., pp. 254–255.

[25]Ibid., p. 255.

[26]Boris Tchechko, "The Conception of the Rights of Man in the U.S.S.R. based on Official Documents," in *Human Rights: Comments and Interpretations*, p. 169.

[27]Ibid., p. 169.

[28]Ibid., pp. 169–170.

[29]Ibid., pp. 160–161.

[30]Sergius Hessen, "The Rights of Man in Liberalism, Socialism, and Communism," in *Human Rights: Comments and Interpretations*, pp. 108–142.

[31]Ibid., p. 127.

[32]Ibid., p. 128.

[33]Ibid., p. 126.

[34]Ibid., p. 138.

[35]Chung-Shu Lo, "Human Rights in the Chinese Tradition," in *Human Rights: Comments and Interpretations*, p. 186.

[36]Ibid., p. 186.

[37]Confucius, *The Analects* (New York: Penguin, 1979), p. 93.

[38]Ibid., p. 140.

[39]Ibid., p. 85.

[40]Ibid., p. 59.

[41]Lo, p. 188.

[42]S. V. Puntambekar, "The Hindu Concept of Human Rights," in Human Rights: Comments and Interpretations, p. 197.

[43]Ibid., p. 195.

[44]Timothy Reagan, *Non-Western Educational Traditions* (Mahwah, NJ: Lawrence Erlbaum Associates, 1996), p. 111.

[45]I. L. Kandel, "Education and Human Rights," in *Human Rights: Comments and Interpretations*, p. 223.

[46]Ibid., p. 224.

[47]Ibid., p. 225.

[48]Ibid., p. 225.

[49]Ibid., p. 225.

[50]Ibid., p. 225.

[51]Ibid., p. 225.

Chapter 2

[1]Enrique Dussel, "Beyond Eurocentrism: The World-System and the Limits of Modernity," in *The Cultures of Globalization*, edited by Frederic Jameson and Masao Miyoshi (Durham: Duke University Press, 1998), p. 9.

[2]Ibid., pp. 11–12.

[3]See Daniel R. Headrick, *The Tools of Empire: Technology and European Imperialism in the Nineteenth Century* (New York: Oxford University Press, 1981), pp. 3–4.

[4]Anthony Pagden, *Lords of All the World: Ideologies of Empire in Spain, Britain and France c.1500–c.1800* (New Haven: Yale University Press, 1995), p. 20.

[5]Pagden, pp. 24–25.

[6]Ibid., pp. 29–30.

[7]Edward W. Said, *Culture and Imperialism* (New York: Vintage Books, 1994), p. 10.

[8]Ibid.

[9]Dussel, p. 12.

[10]See W. O. Lee, *Social Change and Educational Problems in Japan, Singapore and Hong Kong* (New York: St. Martin's Press, 1991).

[11]Thomas Hylland Eriksen, "Multiculturalism, Individualism and Human Rights: Romanticism, the Enlightenment and Lessons from Mauritius," in *Human Rights, Culture & Context: Anthropological Perspectives*, edited by Richard Wilson (London: Pluto Press, 1997), pp. 55–56.

[12]Ibid., p. 52.

[13]Javier Perez de Cuellar, ed., *Our Creative Diversity: Report of the World Commission on Culture and Development* (Paris: UNESCO, 1995), p. 62.

[14]"International Labour Organisation, 1991: Convention No. 169 Concerning Indigenous and Tribal Peoples in Independent Countries," *International Labour Conventions and Recommendations 1919–1991* (Geneva: International Labour Office, 1991), pp. 1436–1447. Retrieved from www.ciesin.org on March 31, 1999, p. 2.

[15]Ibid., p. 2.

[16]Perez de Cuellar, p. 68.

[17]See Darrell Addison Posey, "Can Cultural rights Protect Traditional Cultural Knowledge and Biodiversity?" in *Cultural Rights and Wrongs: A Collection of Essays in the Commemoration of the 50th Anniversary of the Universal Declaration of Human Rights*, edited by Halina Niec (Paris: UNESCO, 1998), p. 44.

[18]A. P. Elkin, "The Rights of Man in Primitive Society," in *Human Rights: Comments and Interpretations*, p. 228.

[19]Perez de Cuellar, pp. 69–70.

[20]Ibid., pp. 228–237.

[21]Ibid., p. 237.

[22]Ibid., p. 228.

[23]Ibid., p. 228.

[24]Ibid., pp. 228–229.

[25]"Universal Declaration of Human Rights, 1948" p. 25.

[26]Ibid., p. 22.

[27]See Lauren, pp. 246–248 and Howard Tolley Jr,. *The U.N. Commission on Human Rights* (Boulder, CO: Westview Press, 1987), pp. 14–29.

[28]"Universal Declaration of Human Rights, 1948" pp. 24–25.

[29]Lauren, pp. 252–254; Tolley, pp. 32–55; Humphrey, pp. 259–260.

[30]"Declaration on the Granting of Independence to Colonial Countries and Peoples, 1960," in *Basic Documents on Human Rights*, pp. 28–29.

[31]"Convention Against Discrimination in Education, 1960," in *Basic Documents on Human Rights*, p. 319.

[32]Ibid., p. 319.

[33]"Convention Against Discrimination in Education, 1960," p. 321.

[34]Tove Skutnabb-Kangas, *Linguistic Genocide in Education—Does Linguistic Diversity Have A Future* (Mahwah, NJ: Lawrence Erlbaum Associates, in press).

[35]Ibid.

[36]"Declaration of the Rights of Persons Belonging to National or Ethnic, Religious and Linguistic Minorities." *Gopher://gopher.un.org:70/00/recess/47/135* (April 31,1999), p. 4.

[37]"International Labour Organization, 1991", pp. 9–10.

[38]Ibid., p. 10.

[39]Richard Wilson, "Human Rights, Culture and Context: An Introduction," in *Human Rights, Culture & Context*, p. 9.

[40]Ericksen, p. 58.

[41]"Declaration on the Rights of Persons Belonging to National or Ethnic, Religious and Linguistic Minorities." *Gopher://gopher.un.org:70/00/ga/reces/47/135* (April 31, 1999), p. 3.

[42]Michael J. Perry, *The Idea of Human Rights: Four Inquiries* (New York: Oxford University Press, 1998), p. 66.

[43]Ibid., p. 75.

[44]See Rodolfo Stavenhagen, "Cultural Rights: A Social Science Perspective," in *Cultural Rights and Wrongs*, pp. 17–19.

[45]The "United Nations Draft Declaration of Indigenous Peoples Human Rights" can be found in Alexander Ewen, *Voice of Indigenous Peoples* (Santa Fe, NM: Clear Light Publishers, 1994), p. 160.

[46]Ibid., p. 162.

[47]Ibid., p. 165.

[48]Ibid., p. 166.

[49]Maenette Kape'ahiokalani Padeken Ah Nee-Benham with Joanne Elizabeth Cooper, *Indigenous Educational Models for Contemporary Practice: In Our Mother's Voice* (Mahwah: Lawrence Erlbaum Associates, in press), p. 19.

[50]Elkin, pp. 226–227.

Chapter 3

1. Quoted by Ann Cvetkovich and Douglas Kellner, "Introduction: Thinking Global and Local," in *Articulating the Global and the Local*, edited by Ann Cvetkovich and Douglas Kellner (Boulder, CO: Westview Press, 1997), p. 4.
2. Ibid., p. 4.
3. Ibid., pp. 4–5.
4. Joel Spring, *Education and the Rise of the Global Economy* (Mahwah, NJ: Lawrence Erlbaum, Associates, 1998), pp. 37–70.
5. For an introduction to current discussions and controversies about globalization, see Richard Barnet and John Cavanagh, *Global Dreams: Imperial Corporations and the New World Order* (New York: Simon & Schuster, 1994); Lester C. Thurow, *The Future of Capitalism: How Today's Economic Forces Shape Tomorrow's World* (New York: William Morrow, 1996); and Rob Wilson and Wimal Dissanayake, eds., *Global/Local: Cultural Production and the Transnational Imaginary* (Durham: Duke University Press, 1996). Also see previously cited works by Ann Cvetkovich and Douglas Kellner, eds., *Articulating the Global* and by Frederic Jameson and Masao Miyoshi, eds., *The Cultures of Globalization*.
6. Walter D. Mignolo, "Globalization, Civilization, and Languages," in *The Cultures of Globalization*, p. 36.
7. Ibid., pp. 39–40.
8. See Braj B. Kachru, *The Alchemy of English: The Spread, Functions, and Models of Non-native Englishes* (Urbana: University of Illinois Press, 1990).
9. Steven Erlanger, "Birthday in a Shelter, 'With Fireworks,'" *The New York Times* (March 16, 1999), p. A1.
10. Quoted in Perez de Cuellar, p. 105.
11. Allan Luke and Carmen Luke, "A Situated Perspective on Cultural Globalisation," in *Globalisation and Educational Policy*, edited by N. Burbules & C. Torres (New York: Routledge, in press), p. 4.
12. Ibid., p. 4.
13. Ibid., p. 6.
14. Ibid., p. 8.
15. Ibid., pp. 9–15.
16. Eriksen, p. 52.
17. Cvetkovich and Kellner, p. 10.
18. Ibid., p. 10.
19. Perez de Cuellar, p. 27.
20. Ibid., p. 27.
21. Ibid., p. 112.
22. Ibid., p. 104.
23. Ibid., p. 113.
24. World Bank, *Priorities and Strategies for Education: A World Bank Review* (Washington, DC: World Bank, 1995). I am using the version avail-

able from http://www.worldbank.org/html/hcovp/PUBLICAT/PRSTR1. htm, p. 2.

[25]Perez de Cuellar, p. 9.

[26]Ibid., p. 22.

[27]Ibid., p. 22.

[28]Ibid., p. 42.

[29]"Understanding Culture: A Precondition for Effective Learning," in *Education for All: Purpose and Context*, pp. 7–19.

[30]Ibid., p. 7.

[31]Ibid., p. 11.

[32]Ibid., p. 11

[33]Perez de Cuellar, p. 22.

[34]Ibid., pp. 25–26.

[35]Ibid., p. 26.

[36]Ibid., p. 41.

[37]After being robbed in Caracas, Venezuela, in 1990, I was standing in a police station paying a bribe to file a police report so that I could obtain a new visa, when suddenly there appeared a police officer dressed in black leather from head to toe. My negotiator, whom I had to hire to deal with the police report, grabbed me and pushed me back against the wall with the other people in the room. Frightened, I asked what was happening. My negotiator informed me that the officer was part of the political police unit—the most feared unit in the country.

[38]Perez de Cuellar, p. 42.

[39]Halina Niec, "Introduction," in *Cultural Rights and Wrongs*, p. xiii.

[40]Posy, p. 43.

[41]Ibid., p. 43.

[42]Ibid., p. 54.

[43]"The Declaration of Belem." *users.ox.ac.uk/~wgtrr/belem.htm* (April 4, 1999), p. 1.

[44]Ibid., p. 1.

[45]"The Mataatua Declaration on Cultural and Intellectual Property Rights of Indigenous Peoples." *users.ox.ac.uk/~wgtrr/mataatua* (April 4, 1999), p. 2.

[46]"Background of the Convention." *www.biodiv.org/conv/BACKGROUND.HTML* (March 31, 1999), pp. 1–2.

[47]"Convention on Biological Diversity." *www.biodiv.org/chm/conv/cbd_text_e.htm* (March 31, 1999), p. 6.

[48]Ibid., p. 8.

Chapter 4

[1]Bellamy, The State of the World's Children 1999 ... , p. 10.

[2]"Convention on the Rights of the Child, 1989," in *Basic Documents on Human Rights*, p. 183.

[3]Ibid., p. 184.

[4]Carol Bellamy, *The State of the World's Children 1998* (Oxford: Oxford University Press, 1998).

[5]Ibid., p. 16.

[6]"Strategies for Eliminating Child Labour: Prevention, Removal and Rehabilitation, Synthesis Document," *International Conference on Child Labour Oslo, October 27–30, 1997* (New York: International Labour Office Geneva United Nations Children's Fund, 1997), pp. 2–4.

[7]Ibid., p. 7.

[8]Ibid., p. 5.

[9]Philip Ngunjiri, "Rights—East Africa: Child Labour on the Rise, *World News, Interpress Service. http://www.oneworld.org* (2/26/99).

[10]"Strategies for Eliminating Child Labour," p. 3.

[11]Mike Woolridge, "World: South Asia: A 'trade in human misery,'" *BBC Online Network, http://news.bbc.co.uk* (2/26/99).

[12]"Strategies for Eliminating Chold Labour," p. 4.

[13]"A Stolen Future: Protecting the Rights of Refugee Children," *Amnesty International. http://www.amnesty.org* (February, 26 1999).

[14]Ibid., p. 2.

[15]Ibid., p. 3.

[16]"World Declaration on Education for All: Meeting Basic Learning Needs", in *Final Report: World Conference on Education for All*, p. 4.

[17]"Education of Homeless Children and Youth," *National Coalition for the Homeless, February 1999, http://nch.ari.net/edchild* (March 3, 1999).

[18]Mauricio Villela, "Sao Paulo/Brasil with S," *Speakin'Out—A Free Tribune for People Who Have Something to Say. Http://brazilonline.com/ spkj.html* (3/3/99).

[19]Lauren, p. 254.

[20]"International Covenant on Civil and Political Rights, 1966," in *Basic Documents on Human Rights*, p. 133.

[21]Ibid., p. 128.

[22]Ibid., p. 117.

[23]Ibid., pp. 117–119.

[24]Freda Troup, *Forbidden Pastures: Education Under Apartheid* (London: International Defense and Aid Fund for South Africa, 1976), p. 20.

[25]"Convention on the Rights of the Child, 1989," in *Basic Documents on Human Rights*, p. 184.

[26]Philip Alston, ed., *The Best Interests of the Child: Reconciling Culture and Human Rights* (Oxford: Oxford University Press, 1994).

[27]Philip Alston, "The Best Interests Principle: Towards A Reconciliation of Culture and Human Rights," in *The Best Interests of the Child*, p. 5.

[28]Ibid., p. 5.

[29]B. Rwezaura, "The Concept of the Child's Best Interests in the Changing Economic and Social Context of Sub-Saharan Africa," in *The Best Interests of the Child*, pp. 82–117.

[30]Ibid., p. 92.

[31]Ian Fisher, "Sometimes a Girl's Best Friend Is Not Her Father," *New York Times on the Web* (March 2, 1999).

[32]Bellamy, *The State of the World's Children 1999*, p. 10.

[33]*African Charter on the Rights and Welfare. http:heiwww.unige.ch*, (February 22, 1999), pp. 1–2.

[34]Ibid., p. 2.

³⁵Ibid., p. 3.

³⁶Savitri Goonesekere, "The Best Interests of the Child: A South Asian Perspective," in *The Best Interests of the Child*, p. 119.

³⁷Goonesekere, p. 124.

³⁸Goonesekere, pp. 144–145.

³⁹Satoshi Minamikata, "The Best Interests of Children and Children's School Experience in Japan: The Parents' Perspective," in *The Best Interests of the Child*, p. 281.

⁴⁰See Spring, *Education and the Rise of the Global Economy*, pp. 37–70.

⁴¹Minamikata, p. 282.

⁴²Ibid., p. 282.

⁴³Ibid., p. 286.

⁴⁴Ibid., p. 286.

⁴⁵Quoted by Byron Marshall, *Learning to Be Modern: Japanese Discourse on Education* (Boulder, CO: Westview Press, 1994), pp. 177–178.

⁴⁶"Universal Declaration of Human Rights," p. 26.

⁴⁷"Convention of the Rights of the Child," p. 194.

Chapter 5

¹"Human Rights Questions: Human Rights Questions, Including Alternative Approaches for Improving the Effective Enjoyment of Human rights and Fundamental Freedoms, Guidelines for National Plans of Action for Human rights Education" (October 20, 1997). *Http://www.unchr.ch/html/menu4/garep/52ga469a1.htm*, (April 14, 1999), p. 1.

²Nancy Flowers and Kristi Rudelius-Palmer, "Part II: The Right to Know Your Rights: An Introduction to Human Rights Education," *Human Rights U.S.A. http://134.84.205.236/H&Npart2introhre.htm (May 13, 1999)*, p. 2.

³Pam Costain, "Part I: Human Rights Fundamentals: What Are Human Rights," *Human Rights U.S.A. Http://134.84.205.236/H&Npart1what.htm (May 13, 1999)*, p. 1.

⁴*Vienna Declaration and Programme of Action. http://www.hri.ca/vienna+5/vdpa.shtml* (April 14, 1999) p. 22.

⁵Ibid., p. 22.

⁶Human Rights Internet, "States Limp Across the Finish Line," *Human Rights Tribune, November 1993, Vienna Declaration and Programme of Action. http://www.hri.ca/vienna+5/1993/stateslimp.shtml* (April 14, 1999).

⁷Human Rights Internet, "Commissioner and International Criminal Court: Two High Profile Issues Struggle in Vienna," *Human Rights Tribune, November 1993, Vienna Declaration and Programme of Action. http://www.hri.ca/vienna+5/1993/2issues.shtml* (April 14, 1999).

⁸Human Rights Internet, "States Limp Across the Finish Line," p. 4.

⁹Ibid., p. 4.

¹⁰Ibid., p. 4.

[11]"High Commissioner for the Promotion and Protection of All Human Rights, 85th Plenary Meeting, 20 December, 1993." *gopher://gopher.undp.org:70/00/undocs/gad/RES/48/141* (April 14, 1999), p. 3.

[12]"United Nations Decade for Human Rights Education," *Resolution Adopted by the General Assembly 49/184. Http://www.unchr.ch/html/ menu4/gares/res49184.htm* (April 14, 1999), p. 1.

[13]Ibid., p. 1.

[14]"Human Rights Questions: Human Rights Questions, Including Alternative Approaches for Improving the Effective Enjoyment of Human Rights and Fundamental Freedoms A/50/698, 27 October 1995." *Gopher://gopher.un.org:70/00/ga/docs/50/plenary/698* (April 14, 1999), p. 2.

[15]"Further Promotion and Encouragement of Human Rights and Fundamental Freedoms, Including the Question of the Programme and Methods of Work of the Commission, Implementation of the Plan of Action for the United Nations Decade for Human Rights Education (1995–2004), Report of the High Commissioner for Human Rights (March 18, 1996)." http://*www.unchr.ch/html/menu4/ chrrep/9651.htm*,(April 14, 1999) p. 12.

[16]Ibid., p. 12.

[17]"Human Rights Questions," p. 3.

[18]Arno Baltin, Mai Kahru, Voldemar Kolga, Urve Laanemets, Aita Manvald, Meedi Neeme, Maaris Raudsepp, Any Toots, and Sulev Valdmaa, *We, The World and Human Rights* (Netherlands: Jann Tonisson Institute, 1997) retrieved from http://erc.hrea.org (May 13, 1999), p. 6.

[19]Ibid., p. 6.

[20]Nick Wilson and Branka Emerdic, *First Steps: A Manual for Starting Human Rights Education* (London: Amnesty International Secretariat, 1996), p. 110.

[21]Ibid., p. 112.

[22]Ibid., p. 21.

[23]"Human Rights Questions," p. 4.

[24]The Commission on Human Rights, "Decade for Human Rights Education: Commission on Human Rights Resolution 1995/47." *http://www.unchr.ch/html/menu4/chrres/9547.htm*; and "United Nations Decade for Human Rights Education: Commission on Human Rights Resolution 1996/44." *http://www.unchr.ch/html/menu4/ chrres/1996.res/44.htm* (April 14, 1999).

[25]"Human Rights Questions: Human Rights Questions, Including Alternative Approaches for Improving the Effective Enjoyment of Human rights and Fundamental Freedoms, Guidelines for National Plans of Action for Human rights Education," p. 4.

[26]Ibid., p. 6.

[27]Jana Ondrackova, with Felisa Tibbitts, "Human Rights and Citizenship Education—A Czech Classroom Experience," in *Case Studies in Human Rights Education: Examples From Central and Eastern Europe, Council of Europe/Human Rights Education Association, 1997.* http://*www.hrea.org* (May 13, 1999).

[28]Felisa Tibbitts, "Research and Evaluation in the Service of Human Rights Education, I: The Russian Experience," in *Case Studies in Human Rights Education*, p. 1.

[29]Ibid., p. 1.

[30]Ibid., p. 1.

[31]Felisa Tibbitts, "An Annotated Primer for Selecting Democratic and Human Rights Education Teaching Materials (August 1997)." *http://www.hrea.org/pubs/Primer/index.html (May 13, 1999)*, p. 2.

[32]"Human Rights Questions: Human Rights Questions, Including Alternative Approaches for Improving the Effective Enjoyment of Human Rights and Fundamental Freedoms, Guidelines for National Plans of Action for Human Rights Education," p. 4.

[33]"Universal Declaration of Human Rights," p. 26.

[34]See Spring, pp. 39–46.

[35]Kaisa Savolainen, ed., *All Human Beings ... Manual for Human Rights Education: The Teacher's Library* (Paris: UNESCO, 1998), p. 11.

[36]Ibid., p. 11.

[37]Ibid., p. 18.

[38]Ibid., p. 18.

[39]Ibid., p. 19.

[40]Ibid., p. 19.

[41]Amy Gutmann, *Democratic Education* (Princeton: Princeton University Press, 1987).

[42]Ibid., p. 76.

[43]Kaisa Savolainen, pp. 39–40.

[44]Ibid., p. 22.

[45]Arno Baltin et al., p. 5.

[46]Kaisa Savolainen, p. 23.

[47]Ibid., p. 116.

[48]Ibid., p. 69.

[49]Ibid., p. 49.

[50]Wilson and Emerdic, p. 44.

[51]Kaisa Savolainen, p. 50.

[52]Ibid., pp. 51–52.

[53]Wilson and Emeerdic, p. 22.

[54]See Lauren, pp. 4–36.

[55]United Nations High Commissioner for Human Rights, *ABC, Teaching Human Rights: Practical Activities for Primary and Secondary Schools* (Geneva: Office of the United Nations High Commissioner for Human Rights, 1998).

[56]Quoted in Kaisa Savolainen, p. 107.

[57]Ibid., p. 107.

[58]Ibid., p. 119.

[59]United Nations High Commissioner for Human Rights, *ABC, Teaching Human Rights*, p. 17.

[60]Ibid., p. 17.

[61]Ibid., p. 16.

[62]Quoted in Kaisa Savolainen, p. 102.

[63]United Nations High Commissioner for Human Rights, *ABC, Teaching Human Rights*, p. 7.

[64]Ibid., p. 8.

[65]Ibid., p. 9.

[66]Ibid., p. 9.

[67]See Joel Spring, *Wheels in the Head: Educational Philosophies of Authority, Freedom, and Culture From Socrates to Human Rights Second Edition* (New York: McGraw-Hill, 1999), pp. 145–157.

[68]"A Child in Domestic Service," in Kaisa Savolainen, p. 81.

[69]Ibid., p. 81.

[70]Ibid., p. 80.

[71]"Being Tortured for One's Opinions," in Kaisa Savolainen, p. 83.

[72]Ibid., p. 83.

[73]Amnesty International, "Learning Activities About the Universal Declaration of Human Rights." *http://erc.hrea.org/Library/activities_ UDHR.html* (May 13, 1999), p. 4.

[74]Arno Baltin, Mai Kahru, Voldemar Kolga, Urve Laanemets, Aita Manvald Meedi Neeme, Maaris Raudsepp, Any Toots, and Sulev Valdmaa, *It's About Me and Human Rights* (Netherlands: Jann Tonisson Institute, 1997). Retrieved from http://erc.hrea.org (May 13, 1999), pp. 9–10.

[75]Ibid., p. 10.

[76]Ibid., p. 13

Chapter 6

[1]See Paulo Freire, *Pedagogy of the Oppressed* (New York: Herder and Herder, 1970).

[2]Spring, *Education and the Rise*, pp. 13–30.

[3]Sally Engle Merry, "Legal Pluralism and Transnational Culture: The Ka Ho'okokolonui Kananka Maoli Tribunal, Hawai'i, 1993," in *Human Rights, Culture & Context*, p. 32.

[4]Maenette K.P. Benham and Ronald H. Heck, *Culture and Educational Policy in Hawai'i* (Mahwah, NJ: Lawrence Erlbaum Associates, 1998), pp. 179–215.

[5]Merry, p. 32.

[6]Benham and Cooper, p. 22.

[7]Ibid., p. 4.

[8]Thomas Banyacya, "The Hopi Message to the United Nations General Assembly," *http:www.alphacde.com/banyacya/un92.html* (February 15, 1999), p. 2.

[9]Ibid., pp. 4–5.

[10]David Noble, *The Religion of Technology: The Divinity of Man and the Spirit of Invention* (New York: Alfred Knopf, 1997).

[11]"An Example: A Treasure Box of Children's Rights." *http:// www.unesco.org/education/hci/eng_man/p23.html* (January 7, 1999), p. 1.

[12]Marcia Ascher and Robert Ascher, "Ethnomathematics," in *Ethnomathematics: Challenging Eurocentrism in Mathematics Education,*

edited by Arthur B. Powell and Marilyn Frankenstein (Albany: State University of New York Press, 1997), p. 28.

[13]*The Republic*, in *The Great Dialogues of Plato*, translated by W. H. D. Rouse (New York: Mentor Books, 1956).

[14]Karl Menninger, *Number Words and Number Symbols: A Cultural History of Numbers* (New York: Dover, 1992), pp. 138–139.

[15]Ibid., p. 138.

[16]Ibid., p. 254.

[17]"Ethnomathematics and Its Place in the History and Pedagogy of Mathematics," in *Ethnomathematics: Challenging Eurocentrism* p. 23.

[18]For a discussion of the human accounting methods of the World Bank and the Organization for Economic Cooperation and Development, see Spring, *Education and the Rise*, pp. 159–190.

[19]William Greider, *One World, Ready or Not: The Manic Logic of Global Capitalism* (New York: Simon & Schuster, 1997), p. 98.

[20]Ibid., pp. 82–83.

[21]Ibid., p. 83.

[22]Ibid., p. 99.

[23]Ibid., p. 99.

[24]Menninger, p. 309.

[25]For a general discussion of Dewey's ideas, see his lectures "The Child and the Curriculum" and "School and Society" in *Dewey on Education* ,edited by Martin Dworkin (New York: Teachers College Press, 1959).

[26]Jerry Lipka with Gerald V. Mohatt and the Ciulistet Group, *Transforming the Culture of Schools: Yup'ik Eskimo Examples* (Mahwah, NJ: Lawrence Erlbaum Associates, 1998), p. 142.

[27]Ibid., pp. 146–149.

[28]Ibid., p. 151.

[29]Ibid., p. 160.

[30]George Gheverghese Joseph, "Foundations of Eurocentrism in Mathematics," in *Ethnomathematics: Challenging Eurocentrism*, p. 61.

[31]Ibid., pp. 61–79.

Chapter 7

[1]For a discussion of differing concepts of culture see Wilson, pp. 1–27.

[2]"With the World Opening Up, Languages Are Losers," *The New York Times* (May 16, 1999), p. 17.

[3]Ibid., p. 17.

[4]Catherine C. Robbins, "Pueblo Indians Receive Remains of Their Ancestors," *The New York Times on the Web, (May 23, 1999)*, p. 1.

[5]See Chapter 2 of Joel Spring, *The Intersection of Cultures* (New York: McGraw-Hill, 2000).

[6]For a study of the cultural adaptation of African Americans to the culture of the power elite, see Richard Zweigenhaft and G. William Domhoff, *Blacks in the White Establishment?: A Study of Race and Class in America* (New Haven: Yale University Press, 1991), and *Diversity in the Power Elite* (New Haven Yale University Press, 1998). For an example of

successful Black professionals who grew up in a household marked by strong Protestant values, see Sarah and A. Elizabeth Delany, *Having Our Say: The Delany Sisters' First 100 Years* (New York: Kodansha International, 1993).

[7]For an example of the continuing crisis in cultural identity of an African-American male who grew up in a wealthy family and attended elite schools, see Jake Lamar, *Bourgeois Blues: An American Memoir* (New York: Plume Books, 1992).

[8]Cornel West, *Race Matters* (New York: Random House, 1993), pp. 22–23.

[9]Ibid., p. 30.

[10]Ibid., p. 29.

[11]Frantz Fanon, *The Wretched of the Earth* (New York: Grove Press, 1968).

[12]Molefi Kete Asante, *The Afrocentric Idea: Revised and Expanded Edition* (Philadelphia: Temple University Press, 1998), p. 7.

[13]Molefi Kete Asante, "Afrocentric Systematics," in *Malcolm X as Cultural Hero & Other Afrocentric Essays* (Trenton, NJ: Africa World Press, 1993), p. 2.

[14]Ibid., p. 2.

[15]Quoted by Molefi Kete Asante in "On Historical Interpretation," in *Malcolm X as Cultural Hero*, p. 20.

[16]Arthur Schlesinger Jr., *The Disuniting of America* (New York: Norton, 1992), and Mary R. Lefkowitz, *How Afrocentrism Became an Excuse to Teach Myth as History* (New York: Free Press, 1992).

[17]Molefi Kete Asante, "On Cultural Nationalism and Criticism" in *Malcolm X as Cultural Hero*, p. 41.

[18]Ibid., p. 41.

[19]Asante, *The Afrocentric Idea*, p. 187.

[20]Nicholas Kristof, "Help! There's a Mausu in My Konpyutaa!" *The New York Times on the Web* (April 4, 1999).

[21]Kachru, *The Alchemy of English: The Spread, Functions, and Models of Non-native Englishes*.

[22]Ibid., p. 2.

[23]Ibid., p. 2.

[24]"The Linguistic Society of America Resolution on the Oakland Ebonics Issue," reprinted by Walt Wolfram, Carolyn Temple Adger, and Donna Christian in *Dialects in Schools and Communities* (Mahwah, NJ: Lawrence Erlbaum Associates, 1999), p. 22.

[25]Ibid., p. 21.

[26]Ibid., p. 22.

[27]Ibid., p. 22.

[28]Asante, *The Afrocentric Idea*, p. 55.

[29]Ibid., p. 55.

[30]"Guatemalan Indians Lament Recognition Measure's Defeat," *The New York Times* (May 18, 1999), p. A8.

[31]Wolfram, Adger, and Christian, p. 24.

[32]Ibid., p. 55.

[33]Ibid., p. 57.

[34]Ibid., p. 85.

[35]See Asante, *The Afrocentric Idea*, pp. 196–207.

³⁶Ibid., p. 200.
³⁷Ibid., p. 200.
³⁸Ibid., p. 205.
³⁹Ibid., p. 209.
⁴⁰Ibid., p. 202
⁴¹Spring, *Education and the Rise,* pp. 70–89, 92–116.
⁴²Quoted in ibid., p. 86.
⁴³Quoted in ibid., p. 84.
⁴⁴Ibid., p. 96.
⁴⁵For instance see ibid., pp. 70–190, and Joel Spring, *The Sorting Machine Revisited: National Educational Policy Since 1945* (White Plains: Longman, 1988).
⁴⁶I discuss the role of the World Bank and the Organization for Economic Development and Cooperation in Spring, *Education and the Rise,* pp. 92–190.
⁴⁷For a discussion of Austrian economics, see Joel Spring, *Political Agenda for Education: From the Christian Coalition to the Green Party* (Mahwah, NJ: Lawrence Erlbaum Associates, 1997), pp. 23–69.
⁴⁸For examples of this political rhetoric and corporate actions, see Hillary Rodham Clinton, *It Takes A Village: And Other Lessons Children Teach Us* (New York: Simon & Schuster, 1996), pp. 285–302.
⁴⁹Marcel Mauss, *The Gift: The Form and Reason for Exchange in Archaic Societies* (New York: Norton, 1990).
⁵⁰Jerry Martien, *Shell Game: A True Account of Beads and Money in North America* (San Francisco: Mercury House, 1996).
⁵¹For various interpretations and criticisms of Mauss's essay, see Nicolas Thomas, *Entangled Objects: Exchange, Material Culture and Colonialism in the Pacific* (Cambridge, MA: Harvard University Press, 1991).
⁵²Mauss, p. 71.
⁵³Quoted in Martien, p. 45.
⁵⁴Ibid., p. 32.
⁵⁵Mauss, p. 13.
⁵⁶Ibid., p. 13.
⁵⁷Ibid., p. 14.
⁵⁸Martien, p. 4.
⁵⁹The classic work in Austrian economics, which contains a laudatory introduction by Milton Friedman, is F. A. Hayek's *The Road to Serfdom* (Chicago: University of Chicago Press, 1994).
⁶⁰Martien, p. 54.
⁶¹Ibid., p. 54.
⁶²For a study of corporate welfarism and education, see Joel Spring, *Education and the Rise of the Corporate State* (Boston: Beacon Press, 1972).

Index

A

"A Stolen Future," 59, 171
"A Treasure Box of Children's Rights,"
    119, 175
Abacus, 124
ABC, Teaching Human Right (United
    Nations), 101, 103, 105-106,
    174-175
Abortion, cultural conflicts over, 34, 102
Absenteeism, classroom, 73
Absolutist state, human rights per, 12-13
Activism, in human rights education,
    80-82, 84-86
    protection role of, 86-89
Adger, 143, 177
Advertising, in cultural hybridization, 42
Africa
    child labor in, 58-59, 67-68
    children's rights in, 64-70
African American Vernacular English
    (AAVE), 140
African Charter on the Rights and Wel-
    fare of the Child, 70, 171-172
African-Americans, cultural adaptation
    of, 133-139, 143-146
Afrocentric perspective
    of cultural centeredness, 136-139
    English sociolects and, 140-142
A.I.C. Girls Primary Boarding School,
    68-69
AIDS (acquired immune deficiency syn-
    drome), 59
Al-Farabi, A. N., 100
Alston, P., 65-66, 171

Alternative systems, *see* Social imagina-
    tion
Amnesty International, 59, 175
    on human rights education, 77,
        82-83, 109
Analysis, cultural diversity of, 97-98
Argot, 139
Art, human rights and, 109-111
Article 26, of Universal Declaration of
    Human Rights, 1-2, 16, 74, 81,
    157
Aryan Nation, 23
Asante, M. K., 133-139, 141, 144-145,
    177-178
Ascher, M., 121, 175
Ascher, R., 121, 175
Assistance rights
    for children, 56, 60-63, 87-88, 158
    claim rights *versus*, 87
ATMs (automated teller machines), fam-
    ily structure and, 123-124
Attitudes
    cultural, economic development and,
        45, 150-155
    in human rights education, 80, 83-86
Authoritarian school systems
    educational rights and, 2, 6, 11-14,
        17
    examples of, 63, 85, 122, 148
Ayala-Lasso, Jose, 80

B

Baltin, A., 81-82, 94, 110-111, 173-175
Banyacya, T., 118, 175
Barnet, R., 41, 169

179

Behavior patterns, cultural centeredness
    and, 136, 143-146
Beliefs
    cultural centeredness and, 131-133,
        136, 143-146
    human rights education and, 85-86,
        101
Bellamy, C., 1, 56-57, 69, 165, 170-171
Benham, Maenette K. P., 37-38, 98,
    116-117, 168, 175
Biculturalism, 30
Bilingualism, 30-33
Biodiversity preservation, see Environ-
    mental preservation
Blind trust, for human relations educa-
    tion, 103
Boarding schools, African, 68-69
Body parts trade, 60
Bondage, of children, 56-59
Book of History (Chinese), 14
Brand names, in cultural hybridization,
    42-43
Bricker, John, 27-28
Bride wealth, 66-69
Brody, Reed, 79
Buddhism, human rights per, 15-16,
    100, 121
Buddy method, for human relations edu-
    cation, 103-104
Burdens, on children
    from global system, 56-60, 65-67,
        69-70, 72
    from rights, 87-88
Bush, George, 150

                        C

Calculators, numeracy and, 124,
    127-128, 162
Call-and-response style, of Ebonics,
    140-141
Capitalism
    education rights per, 10, 12, 15, 129
    moral considerations of, 150-155
Cavanagh, J., 41, 169
Censorship, post-World War II, 73-74,
    136
Census taking, power through, 121-122
Central Station (movie), 60
Chang, P. C., 7
Child abandonment, 71
Child labor
    in Africa, 58-59, 67-68
    world state of, 56-59, 71
Children
    condition of the world's, 55-60, 65,
        69, 71

cultural diversity and best interests
    of, 65-66, 72
as special class of citizens, 61-62,
    157
Children's rights
    for assistance, 56, 60-63, 158
    critical dialogue about, 107-111
    cultural, 63, 65-66
    declarations on, 55-56, 60, 65-66,
        70, 72, 83, 85, 108
    education and, see Education rights
    educational exploitation and, 72-74,
        114-115
    in Japan, 72-74
    justification for universal right to,
        74-75, 114
    for liberty, 55, 63-65
    linguistic, 63, 119, 159
    perfect dreams of, 105-106
    for protection, 3, 56, 60-62, 158
    in sub-Saharan Africa, 66-70
Child-rights advocates, 61, 72
China, human rights in, 13-14, 41, 100
Christian, 143, 177
Christianity, influence of, 21, 67, 89,
    102, 151-152, 155
Chuan Li, 14
Cicero, 21, 121
Circumcision, female, 34, 68
Citizenship
    children's status of, 61-62, 157
    passive, 81-82, 130
Civic education, tradition notions of,
    85-86
Civil rights
    colonialism breakdown and, 27-28
    as global ethic, 48-49
Civilization, expansion of, see Colonial-
    ism
Civilized cultures, universal rights and,
    25-27
Claim rights
    assistance rights versus, 87
    education rights as, 87-89
    human rights protection as, 86-89,
        106
    for indigenous cultures, 27, 152
    liberty rights versus, 87
    principles of, 12-13, 27
Classroom discourse
    as nationalism threat, 85
    universal education concept of,
        128-129
Clinton, Bill, 117, 150
Clinton, H. R., 150, 178
Cold War, impact on human rights, 10,
    27-28, 65, 77
Collectivism, of human rights, 7-9, 47

Colleta, N., 46
Colonialism
    children's burdens of, 56, 65-67, 70, 72
    ethnic mixing of, 22-23
    European spread of, 20-23, 39-41, 99-101, 115-116
    global system from, 20-25, 39-41
    human rights and breakdown of, 27-28, 41
    in human rights education, 99-100
    literacy strategies with, 115-116, 133
    mathematics during, 122
    social dysfunctionalism with, 133-136
Communism
    American hysteria over, 27-28
    education rights per, 10-13
    human rights per, 27-28
Computers
    numeracy and, 124, 127-128, 162
    sociolect terms for, 139
Conflict resolution, peaceful
    as global ethic, 48-49
    human rights education and, 78-80, 83-84
Confucianism, human rights per, 14-15, 73, 100, 166
Consumerism, 119
Control, political, see Power imbalance
Convention Against Discrimination in Education, 3, 29-30, 168
Convention on Biologic Diversity, 52, 114, 170
Convention on the Rights of the Child, 74, 170-172
    declarations of, 55-56, 60, 65-66, 70, 72, 157
    human rights education and, 83, 85, 108
Cooper, J. E., 37-38, 117, 168, 175
Cooperation, human rights education on, 95-97
Corporations
    transnational
        labor force strategies in, 123
        power of, 40-41, 77-78
    welfare role of, 155
Costain, P., 77, 172
Counterculture youth, 43
Creolization, 22, 33, 43, 142
Criminal court, international, 79
Critical dialogue, in human rights education, 106-111
Critical thought
    for alternative systems, see Social imagination

in human relations education, 101-104, 106-111
in human rights education, 81, 93, 96, 98, 101, 105-106, 161
Cultural centeredness
    linguistics as key, 132-133, 139-143
    as managed process, 146-147
    meaning of, 132-139, 162-163
    nationalism versus, 131, 133, 146-147
    perspective component of, 136-139
    social imagination and, 131-132, 162-162
    values and, 133-138, 143-146
Cultural diversity
    children's interests and, 65-66
    colonial expansion of, 22-25, 28, 41
    convergence of, 9-11, 146-147
    as human right, 50-53
    human rights education on, 94, 97-101
    indigenous, see Indigenous cultures
    minority, see Minority cultures
    in number usage, 121-127
    universal education and, 2-3, 5
    universal rights per, 13-17, 19, 47
Cultural ethnocide, influencing factors, 25, 37-38, 49, 56, 79
Cultural freedom
    developmental principles of, 47, 146-149, 159
    education rights and, 47, 53-54, 159
Cultural goods, as exports, 44
Cultural hybridization
    causes of, 41-45
    economic development through, 45-46
Cultural imperialism, 33
Cultural instruction, in human rights education, 94, 97-101
Cultural relativism, 32-33
Cultural rights
    for children, 63, 65-66
    Elkin's manifesto on, 25-27, 35, 37-38
    as human rights, 4-6, 8-9
    conflicts with, 32-35
Cultural Rights and Wrongs (UNESCO), 50
Cultural unity
    within economic diversity, 146-155
    as managed process, 146-147
    of minority cultures, see Cultural centeredness
Curriculum, minimum guidelines for, 1, 3, 114, 127, 158-163
Cvetkovich, A., 40, 43-44, 169

D

D'Ambrosio, U., 122, 176
Death rates, of children, 56-58
Debate, as human right, 81, 93, 97
Decade for Human Rights Education,
        Plan of Action for, 79-86, 90,
        173
Declaration of Belem, 51, 170
Declaration of the Rights of Man, 100
Declaration of the Rights of Persons Be-
        longing to National or Ethnic,
        Religious and Linguistic Minor-
        ities, 31, 33, 168
Declaration on Education for All, 5-6,
        60, 171
Declaration on the Granting of Independ-
        ence to Colonial Countries and
        Peoples, 28, 168
Democracy
    education rights per, 10-13, 15
    global ethics and, 48-49
    human rights education and, 77-78,
        81, 84, 86
        limits on, 92
        Manual guidelines for, 90-93,
            95-96
Democratic professionalism, 92
Development
    economic, *see* Economic develop-
        ment
    human, *see* Human development
    of personality, *see* Personality devel-
        opment
    societal, *see* Social imagination; Sus-
        tainable development
Dewey, J., 124-125, 176
Dialects, cultural centeredness through,
        139-140
Discourse
    classroom, 85, 128-129
    critical, in human rights, 106-111
    moral, 34-35
Discrimination, educational
    definition of, 29
    efforts against, 3, 29-30, 33-35
    universal justification and, 7-9, 159
Domhoff, G. W., 134, 176
Dominant cultures
    language knowledge in, 133, 139-140,
        142-143, 159
    as oppressor, 133-138, 146
Dominant-global number system,
        125-128, 162
Draft Declaration of Indigenous Peoples
        Rights, 30, 35-36, 168
Dussel, E., 20, 22, 167

E

Earth Day, 85
Earth Summit, 52
Ebonics, cultural centeredness through,
        133-134, 140-142
Economic development
    Cold War's impact on, 27-28
    cultural change and, 45-46
    cultural freedom and, 47, 146-149,
        159
    education for, 5-6, 47
    moral issues of, 149-155, 163
    of world, *see* Global system
Economic doctrines, impact on human
        relations, 150-155
Economic exploitation, numeracy impact
        on, 123-124, 127
Economic morality, the good life and,
        149-155, 163
Economic nationalism, 147-149
Economic rights, as human right, 12-13,
        27
Economic unity
    within the global system, 146-149
    morality considerations of, 149-155,
        163
Education
    children's rights and, 3, 55-75, 114,
        158
    economic purposes of, 5-6
    human welfare relationship to, 1, 3
    indoctrination function of, 9-12, 17,
        35, 64
    totalitarian control of, 63, 122
    universal concept of, 1-6, 17,
            114-115, 127-129, 157-158
        human rights and moral duties,
            76-113, 160-163
        literacy and numeracy, 114-130,
            161-162
Education of Homeless Children and
        Youth Act (1987), 60, 171
Education rights
    for biodiversity preservation, 50-53
    for children
        critical dialogue about, 110-111,
            114
        declarations for, 60-63, 158-159
        in India and Sri Lanka, 70-72
        in Japan, 72-74
        privileged children, 53-54
        in sub-Saharan Africa, 66-70
        universal justification for, 3, 55,
            74-75, 157-158
    as claim rights, 87-89

Elkin's manifesto on, 25-27, 35,
    37-38
in global system
    biodiversity considerations, 50-53
    cultural freedom and, 47, 53-54,
        159
    ethical considerations, 47-49
    mediation of, 1, 3, 19, 38, 43, 131
liberty rights as, 55, 63-65, 87-88,
    158-159
minimum guidelines for filling, 1, 3,
    114, 127, 158-163
for minority cultures, 2-3, 5, 17, 30,
    35-36
per Article 26, 1-2, 16, 74, 81, 157
universal definition of
    colonial independence and, 28
    cultural diversity and, 15-18
    original debates on, 1-2, 5-6
    search efforts for, 6-9
universal justification of
    children's rights and, 3, 55-75,
        114, 157-158
    conditions required for, 7, 19, 114
    cultural convergence in, 9-11
    cultural differences in, 4-6
    framework for, 1-5, 157-158
    human rights in, 7-10, 15-18,
        160-161
    implementation cautions, 114-115
    for literacy, 127-129, 159,
        161-162
    for numeracy, 127-129, 162
    socialist state and, 11-13, 129
    World Declaration Preamble for,
        5-6
universal summary of, 157-163
Educational exploitation, children's
    rights and, 72-74
EFA, see World Conference on Educa-
    tion for All
Elimination of Violence Against Women,
    34
Elkin, A. P., 19-20, 25-28, 30, 35, 37-38,
    168
Emerdic, B., 82-83, 96, 100, 109,
    173-174
Emotional bonding, to economic enter-
    prise, 147-149
Emotional detachment, 97-98
Emotions, cultural diversity of, 97-98,
    117
Engels, Friedrich, 40
England, colonial expansion of, 22-23,
    41, 115-116
English language
    as official language, 33, 41, 115-116
    sociolects of, 140-142

Environmental preservation
    education rights for, 50-53, 84, 114,
        159-160
    holistic knowledge for, 52-53, 118,
        160
    technology impact on, 117-118
Equality
    human relations education on,
        103-104
    human rights education on, 93-97
    racial, see Racial equality
Eriksen, T. H., 22-23, 33, 43, 167-169
Erlanger, S., 42, 169
Estonia, 81
Ethics, see Global ethics
Ethnic cleansing, see Cultural ethnocide
Ethnic mixing, with colonialism, 22-23
Ethnobiology, 51
Ethnomathematics, 122, 176
Eurocentric perspective
    of cultural centeredness, 136-139
    of human rights, 12, 15, 17, 97
    in human rights education, 97-100
    in numeracy instruction, 126-127
European colonialism
    global system from, 20-23, 39-41
    in human rights education, 99-101
European Enlightenment, 15, 99, 119
European Union, for managed cultural
    centeredness, 146-148
Ewen, A., 35-36, 168
Examinations
    national educational, 72-73, 148-149
    standardized mathematical, 122
Exploitation, see specific type
Exports, cultural goods as, 44
Expression, freedom of, see Speech
        rights
External efficiency, economic, 148

F

Family structure and function
    children's rights per, 56, 58, 60-63,
        65-66
    in India, 70-72
    in sub-Saharan Africa, 66-70
    number usage impact on, 123-124
Fanon, F., 135, 177
Farming, cultural values related to,
    154-155
Fascism, 23
Final Report (EFA Theme Song), 4-6, 165
Financial markets, globalization of,
    40-41
First International Congress on
    Ethnobiology, 51

Fisher, I., 69, 171
Flowers, N., 77, 172
France, colonial expansion of, 22-23, 41,
    100
Free market, see Capitalism
Freedom, right of, see Liberty rights
Freire, P., 106-108, 115, 175
Friedman, M., 153, 178

G

Genocide, of indigenous people, 25,
    37-38, 49, 56
Ghost Dance traditions, 100
Gift exchange, obligations of, 152-155
Giving, as gift exchange obligation,
    152-155
Global ethics, education rights and,
    47-49
Global system (culture and economy)
    children's burdens of, 56-60, 65-67,
        70, 72
    cultural freedom principles for, 47,
        146-149
    cultural relationship of, 2-3, 19, 30,
        35, 38, 126
    economic morality and, 149-155
    economic unity models for, 147-149
    educational rights in
        biodiversity considerations, 50-53
        cultural freedom and, 47, 53-54,
            159
        ethical considerations, 47-49
        mediation of, 1, 3, 19, 38, 43, 131
    evolution of, 20-23, 39-41
    literacy role in, 115, 118-120,
        161-162
    mediation of, see also Cultural cen-
        teredness
    rights to, 1, 3, 19, 38, 43, 55, 131
    universal guidelines for, 76-78,
        114-115, 119-120
    numbers role in, 122-128
    self-determination within, 35, 37-38,
        119-120
    social dysfunctionalism with,
        133-136
    transnational corporations in, 40-41,
        77-78, 123, 155
Globalization, see also Global system
    stages of, 41
Good life, the, see also Utopia
    economic morality and, 149-155
    reflections on, 119, 129-130, 162
Goonesekere, S., 71-72, 172
Government systems, see also specific
    type

educational rights and, 1, 4-6, 11-13,
    17
    as global ethic, 48-49
    human rights per, 7-13
Greenspan, Alan, 153
Greider, W., 123-124, 176
"Grounds of an International Declaration
    of Human Rights," 10, 166
"Guatemalan Indians Lament Recogni-
    tion Measure's Defeat," 142,
    177
Guidelines for National Plans of Action
    for Human Rights Education,
    76, 84, 86, 172
Guilt, as moral imperative of human
    rights, 89, 92, 106, 161
Gutmann, A., 91-92, 174

H

Hammurabi, King of Babylon, 10, 100
Harmony, as cultural value, 144-145
Hassan, Prince of Jordan, 4
Hawaii
    cultural comparisons of, 25, 97-98
    language restoration of, 116-117
Headrick, D. R., 21, 167
Health
    children's status of, 55-60
    education relationship to, 1, 3
Hean, Teo Chee, 146
Heck, R. H., 98, 116, 175
Henderson, Jeffrey, 123
Hessen, S., 12-13, 166
High Commissioner for Human Rights,
    79-80, 84, 86, 101, 103,
    105-106, 173-175
Hinduism, human rights per, 15-16
History
    human rights education epochs for,
        96-101
    literacy instruction and, 116-118
HIV (human immunodeficiency virus),
    58-59
Holistic knowledge, environmental, of in-
    digenous people, 52-53, 118,
    160
Homelessness, in children, 56-58, 60
Human capital accounting, 122, 148-149
Human development, economic develop-
    ment versus, 46
Human needs, universal, 33-34
Human relations education
    critical dialogue about, 106-111
    critical thought and, 101-104
    economic morality in, 149-155
    language role, 115-117

Human reproduction, cultural differences in, 104
Human resource model, of schooling, 148-149
Human responsibilities
  as global ethic, 48-49
  human rights education on, 77, 82, 106
Human rights
  art and, 109-111
  biodiversity preservation as, 50-53
  Cold War impact on, 10, 27-28, 65, 77
  colonialism breakdown and, 27-28
  in communism *versus* liberalism, 11-13
  declarations for, 25-27, 31-32, 35-36
  Eurocentric perspective of, 12, 15, 17
  evolution of, 100, 105
  as global ethic, 48-49, 76-78
  liberty rights as, 3, 6, 10, 12-13, 17
  linguistics as, 7, 9, 30-32, 119-120, 159
  moral duties and, 86-89, 92-93, 130
  protection of, 86-89, 106, 130
  as universal
    cultural rights as conflict of, 13-17, 32-35
    in education debates, 7-10, 15-17, 35-36, 76-78
    educational guidelines for, 111-113
    linguistic rights as conflict of, 30-35
    moral imperative of, 86-89, 92-93, 130
  Vienna World Conference on, 78-79, 82-83, 90
  violations of, 82, 130
Human Rights Commission, of United Nations, 7-9, 79, 83, 173
Human rights doctrines
  creative opportunities of, 33, 84, 86
  of UNESCO, 4, 9-10, 16-17, 50
Human rights documents, critical review of, 100, 105-106, 160-161
Human rights education
  activist objective, 80-82, 84-86
    protection role of, 86-89
  Amnesty International's role, 77, 82-83, 109
  attitudinal objective, 80, 84-86
  basic principles of, 3, 5-6, 17, 50-53, 160
  beliefs component, 85-86
  critical dialogue about, 106-111
  critical thought instruction in, 93, 96, 98, 101-106

cultural instruction in, 94, 97-101
democracy instruction in, 90-93, 95-96
equality component of, 93-97
indoctrination function of, 90-97
knowledge component, 85-86
manuals for, 82, 89-104, 109
National Plans of Action for, 76, 84, 86
nationalistic instruction in, 93-97
per United Nations, 76, 78-86
Universal Declaration of Human Rights role, 81, 87-88, 93, 99, 105, 110
universal guidelines for, 76-78, 111-113, 160-161
values component, 85-86, 94, 96
Human Rights Education Association, 85
Human Rights Internet, 79, 172
"Human Rights Questions," 76, 80-81, 83-84, 86, 172-174
Human welfare, education relationship to, 1, 3
Humphrey, J. P., 7-9, 165
Hybridization, *see* Cultural hybridization

I

Illiteracy, statistics on, 1
Imagination, *see* Social imagination
Imaginative reflection, 119, 129-130
Immigration
  globalization role of, 43, 138
  minority culture evolution and, 23-24, 144
Imperialism, expansion of, 21-22, 41, 99-100
Improvisation, in cultural adaptations, 141
India, children's rights in, 70-72
Indigenous cultures
  cultural centeredness and, 132-133, 142
  discrimination against, 3, 29-30, 33-35
  economic development role of, 46
  educational rights of, 2-3, 5, 17
    Draft Declaration for, 30, 35-36, 168
  evolution in multicultural societies, 22-25
  genocide of, 25, 37-38, 49, 56
  holistic environmental knowledge of, 52-53, 118, 160
  language rights of, 30-31, 33, 116-118, 120, 126, 128, 142, 159, 162
  property rights of, 51-52

selected world statistics on, 24-25
Individualism, in human rights, 7-10,
    47, 66-67, 95, 145
Indoctrination
    through education, 9-12, 17, 35, 64,
        159
    of human rights, 90-97
    of spiritual values, 102
    by United Nations, 78-80, 83-84
Industrialization, impact of, 99, 154-155
Infanticide, 71
Information
    freedom of access to, 3, 17, 55, 64,
        88, 158
    technological advancements in, see
        Technology
Integrated Framework of Action on Edu-
    cation for Peace, Human Rights
    and Democracy, 91
Intellect, cultural diversity of, 97-98
Internal efficiency, economic, 148
International Conference on the Cultural
    and Intellectual Property Rights
    of Indigenous Peoples, 51
International Convenant on Civil and Po-
    litical Rights (1966), 60-63, 99,
    171
International Convenant on Economic,
    Social, and Cultural Rights
    (1966), 60-63, 70, 105
International Convention on the Elimina-
    tion of all Forms of Racial Dis-
    crimination, 29-30, 61
International Labor Office
    child labor estimates of, 57-59
    cultural definitions of, 24-25
    linguistics position of, 31-32
International Labour Organisation,
    24-25, 31-32, 167-168
International Law Commission, human
    rights and, 79
International organizations, see Corpo-
    rations
International Year for the World's Indige-
    nous Peoples, 51
Islam, human rights in, 4, 22, 79, 100,
    102, 123
It's About Me and Human Rights
    (Dutch), 110

J

Japan
    children's rights in, 72-74
    colonial expansion of, 40
Jargon, 139
Jefferson, Thomas, 154
Job training, 114

Joseph, G. G., 126-127, 176
Judaism, human rights per, 100, 102, 121
Juisha, Kitaoka, 73

K

Kachru, B., 41, 140, 169, 177
Kahru, M., 81-82, 94, 110-111, 173-174
Kalakaua, King of Hawaii, 117
Kamakahi, Dennis, 117
Kandel, I. L., 17-18, 35, 55, 166
Katakana, 139
Kellner, D., 40, 43-44, 169
Kidd, R., 46
Kinship groups, children's rights in,
    66-70
Knowledge
    cultural diversity of, 97-98
    human rights education and, 85-86,
        128
Kolga, V., 81-82, 94, 110-111, 173-175
Kristof, N., 139, 177

L

Laanemets, U., 81-82, 94, 110-111,
    173-175
Labor market
    economic nationalism model of,
        147-149
    globalization impact on, 56-59, 123
Lamar, J., 134, 177
Land ownership, see Property rights
Language, see Linguistics; specific lan-
        guage
Lauren, P. G., 9-10, 28, 61, 100, 166,
        168, 171, 174
Lawsuits, over African children, 67-68
Learning disabilities, in children, 57
Lee, W. O., 22, 167
Lefkowitz, M. R., 137, 177
Levy, F., 1, 165
Liberalism, education rights per, 11-13
Liberation, of female workers, 123-124
Liberty rights
    for children, 55, 63-65, 87-88,
        158-159
    claim rights versus, 87
    developmental advantages of, 47
    as human right, 3, 6, 10, 12-13, 17
Lie, T, 8
Lili'uokalani, Queen of Hawaii, 117
Linguistic Society of America, 140, 177
Linguistics
    colonial expansion of, 22, 28, 41,
        116-118
    cultural centeredness through,
        132-133, 139-143

as human right, 7, 9, 30-32
  for children, 63, 119, 159
  conflicts with, 32-35
power through, 41, 116-120, 139
sociolects in, 139-143
universal education and, 2, 128, 159
Lipka, J., 125-126, 176
Literacy instruction
  basic guidelines for, 3, 5-6, 115
  during colonialism, 115-116, 133
  empowerment through, 119-120
  through history, 116-118
  universal guidelines for, 115-120,
      128-129, 161-162
Lo, C. S., 13-15, 166
Loong, Lee Hsien, 146
Luke, A., 43, 169
Luke, C., 43, 169

M

Magna Carta (England), 7, 100
Malaysian culture, numeracy impact on,
    123-124
Malik, Charles, 7-8
Malnutrition, in children, 56-57
Mandela, Nelson, 42
Manual for Human Rights Education
    (UNESCO), 89-104, 119
  critical thought instruction per, 93,
      96, 101-104
  cultural instruction per, 94, 97-101
  democracy instruction per, 90-93,
      95-96
  nationalistic instruction per, 93-97
Manvald, A., 81-82, 94, 110-111,
    173-175
Maritain, J., 9, 15-16, 27, 165
Marriage
  children's rights for, 66-68, 71, 104
  equality in, 103-104
Marshall, B., 74, 172
Martien, J., 150-151, 153-154, 178
Marx, Karl, 10, 40
Mataatua Declaration, 51-52, 170
Mathematics
  education on, *see* Numeracy instruction
  Eurocentric approach to, 126-127
  power through, 122, 127
Mauss, M., 150-152, 178
McCulture, 42-45
Measurements, numeracy instruction
    and, 126
Media
  cultural centeredness and, 133,
      135-136
  in cultural hybridization, 42-45

"Memorandum and Questionnaire Circu-
    lated by UNESCO on the Theo-
    retical Bases of the Rights of
    Man," 10-11, 166
Menninger, K., 121-122, 124, 176
Merry, S. E., 116, 175
Messianic vision, 119
Mexican Americans, 23
Michaelis, J., 96
Mignolo, W. D., 41, 169
Minamikata, S., 72-73, 172
Minority cultures
  discrimination against, 3, 29-30,
      33-35
  educational rights of, 2-3, 30
  evolution in multicultural societies,
      22-25
  indigenous cultures *versus*, 24-25
  protection of, 7-9, 32-34, 48-49
  selected world statistics on, 24-25
  in universal justification debates, 7-9
Minors, *see* Children
Mintz, Sidney, 136
Monetary transactions, cultural values
    related to, 151-155
Moral discourse, across cultural bound-
    aries, 34-35
Moral economy, perspectives of,
    149-156, 162-163
Moral values (duties)
  basic education for, 3-4
  in economic trade, 149-155, 163
  as global ethic, 48-49, 73-74
  human rights protection as, 86-89
  postcolonial considerations of, 69-70
  as universal concept, 76-78, 162-163
    in justification debate, 9-10, 34-35
  Mortality rates, education relation-
      ship to, 1
Moslem, *see* Islam
Mother tongue, instruction in, 30, 33,
    116-118, 126, 142
  universal guidelines for, 31, 120, 128,
      159, 162
Music, cultural applications of, 43, 117,
    141, 145

N

Names, in language instruction,
    119-120, 142, 161
Nation state, 40, 78
Nationalism
  cultural centeredness *versus*, 131,
      133, 146-147
  economic *versus* political, 147-149
  human rights education on, 84-86,
      93-97, 159

Nationalization
     of testing, rights violations in, 72-73,
          122, 148-149, 159
     of textbooks, 73-74
Nation-building, 9, 33, 40
Native Americans
     cultural adaptation of, 25, 42, 49,
          132, 137, 142, 151
     number meaning for, 121, 125-126
     trade with, moral issues of, 150-155
Native tongue, see Mother tongue
Nazism, 63, 84
NDP, see United Nations Development
     Programme
Neeme, M., 81-82, 94, 110-111, 173-175
Negativism, cultural destruction from,
          134-135
Negotiation, fair, as global ethic, 48-49
Ngunjiri, P., 58, 171
Niec, H., 50, 170
Nihilism, in cultural destruction,
          134-135
Noble, D., 119, 175
Nonauthoritarian school systems, 2-3, 85
Nondiscrimination, principles of, 92-93,
          159
Nonexclusionary educational rights, 30
Nonrepression, principles of, 92-93
Number symbols, instruction with,
          125-126
Numbers
     contemporary uses of, 122-124, 127
     culturally diverse uses of, 121-127
Numeracy instruction
     basic guidelines for, 3, 5-6
     cultural resurrection through,
          125-126
     methodology comparisons, 124-126
     universal guidelines for, 120-129, 162

O

Ondrackova, J., 85, 173
Opinions, human rights education and,
          85-86, 101
Organization for African Unity, 70
Organization for Economic Cooperation
          and Development (OECD), 45,
          122, 146-148

P

Pagden, A., 21, 167
Paradise, see Utopia
Parliamentary government, 95
Partners in Human Rights Education, 77
Passive citizenship, 81-82, 84, 123

Patriotism, human rights education on,
          84-86, 94, 101
Payne, Douglas, 79
Peacekeeping, human rights education
          on, 78-80, 83-84
Perez de Cuellar, J., 23-27, 42, 44-48,
          58, 167-170
Permission, in human rights education,
          82-83
Perry, M. J., 33-34, 168
Personalism, as cultural value, 145
Personality development
     cultural differences in, 97-98
     freedom of, 26-27, 84
Pi (movie), 121
Pidgin, 139
Pledging, of children, 67-69
Political prisoners, 6, 109
Political systems, see Government sys-
          tems
Posey, D. A., 25, 50-51, 167, 170
Possession, spirituality and, 145
Postcolonialism
     African children's rights during,
          69-70
     global system from, 20, 22-23, 32,
          39-41
Poverty
     child labor and, 57-60
     international definition of, 58
Power imbalance
     from colonialism, 40-41, 116-118
     human rights and, 77-78
     language and, 116-118
     numbers and, 121-122, 126-127
Price, Richard, 136
Primitive cultures, universal rights and,
          25-27
Privileged children, education rights for,
          53-54
Prodi, Romano, 146
Profit motive, as economic doctrine, 153
Property rights
     of indigenous cultures, 51-52
     moral economics of, 152-155
Protection rights, for children, 3, 56,
          60-62, 158
Protectionism, of minority cultures, 7-9,
          32-34, 48-49
Protestant ethic, 96
Puntambekar, S. V., 13, 15-16, 166

Q

Questioning attitudes, see Critical
          thought

R

Racial equality, in education, 29-30, 63
Racial Harmony Day, 22
Racial separatism (purity), 23, 35, 63, 134, 137
Racism, cultural destruction from, 133-135, 145
Rage, in cultural destruction, 134-135
Raudsepp, M., 81-82, 94, 110-111, 173-175
Reading material, in language instruction, 119-120
Reagan, Ronald, 96
Reagan, T., 16, 166
Receiving, as gift exchange obligation, 152-155
Reciprocity, as gift exchange obligation, 152-155
Relationships
    cultural diversity of, 97-98
    education on, see Human relations education
Religion, see Spiritual values
Representative government, 95
Right to education, see Education rights
"Rights of Primitive Man," 19-20, 26-27
Robbins, C. C., 132, 176
Role playing, educational applications of, 85, 104, 108-109, 161
Roman Empire, expansionism of, 21-22
Roosevelt, Eleanor, 7
Rudelius-Palmer, K., 77, 172
Rule of law
    human rights education and, 78, 81, 84, 86, 97
    principles of, 12-13
Rushdie, Salman, 43-44
Rwezaura, B., 66-68, 171

S

Said, E. W., 21-22, 167
Savolainen, K., 90-91, 94-97, 101-102, 104, 107-109, 174
Schlesinger, A., Jr., 137, 177
Self-destruction, cultural, 134-135
Self-determination, cultural, 35, 37-38, 99
Self-esteem, 135
Self-hatred, 135
Self-images, negative, 134-135
Self-interest, as economic doctrine, 153
Self-love, 134
Self-respect, as educational goal, 135
Self-worth, 134
Sexual exploitation, of children, 59

Shame, as moral imperative of human rights, 89, 93, 106, 161
Singapore, cultural issues in, 22, 146-147
Sisterhood/brotherhood, human rights education on, 95-96
Skepticism, see Critical thought
Skutnabb-Kangas, T., 30-31, 168
Slang, 139, 143
Slavery
    of children, 56-59
    cultural adaptations with, 22, 133-139, 143-146
    gift exchange and, 152
Smith, Adam, 40
Social class, cultural centeredness and, 132-134, 137, 143
Social imagination
    critical thought for, 106-111, 161
    cultural centeredness and, 131-132, 162-162
    key to unlocking, 2-3, 55
    literacy instruction and, 115, 117, 119-120, 129-130, 161-162
    Manual guidelines for, 91-93
    numeracy instruction and, 126, 129-130, 162
Social justice, education on, 6, 77-78
Social practices
    cultural differences in, 33-35
    numeracy instruction and, 125-127
Social rights
    education rights per, 11-13, 17
    in human rights, 7-9, 12
    per socialist state, 11-13
Social studies, education epochs for, 96-101
Socialism, education rights per, 11-13, 129
Societal development, see Social imagination; Sustainable development
Sociolects
    cultural centeredness through, 139-142
    social class affiliation of, 143
Socrates, 121, 176
Solidarity, human rights education on, 95-96, 102
Soroban, 124
Spain, colonial expansion of, 20, 39, 41, 99
Spanish language, evolutionary influences on, 116, 142
Speech rights
    cultural diversity of, 97-98
    education and, 3, 6, 10, 12, 17, 28, 64, 73, 111, 128, 158
    Manual guidelines for, 91-92

Spiritual values
  colonial expansion of, 21-22, 40
  cultural centeredness and, 145
  cultural differences in, 13-16, 121
  economic role of, 45, 151-152, 155
  education and, 4, 29-30, 33, 102
  as moral imperative of human rights,
      89, 102
  technology and, 118-119
Spring, J., 40, 48, 72, 89, 107, 116,
      122, 133, 146, 148, 150, 155,
      169-170, 172, 174-176, 178
Sri Lanka, children's rights in, 70-72
Stalinism, 11, 13, 15, 87, 95
State of the World's Children report
      (United Nations), 56-60, 65,
      69, 71
State regulation, as economic system,
      150
State testing, limitations for, 148-149
Statistical methods, dictates for, 122
Stavenhagen, R., 35, 168
"Strategies for Eliminating Child La-
      bour," 57-59, 171
Student dramatization, see Role playing
Sub-Commission on Prevention of Dis-
      crimination and Protection of
      Minorities, 34-35
Subjugated cultures, adaptations of,
      133-138
Sudicism, as cultural value, 144
Suicide, in children, 73
Sustainable development
  human rights education on, 77-78,
      81, 84, 86
  rights necessary for, 47

T

Taxation, power through, 121-122, 162
Tchechko, B., 11-13, 166
Teachers' education, human rights and,
      17
Technology
  in cultural hybridization, 40, 42-45,
      119
  environmental issues with, 117-118
  in numeracy instruction, 124,
      127-128, 162
Television, in cultural hybridization,
      42-45
Tepliakov, Valentin, 8
Textbooks, nationalization of, 73-74
Thematic representations of life, educa-
      tional applications of, 106-111,
      161
Thought, freedom of, see also Critical
      thought

instruction guidelines for, 91-93, 111,
      118, 122, 128-129
Tibbitts, F., 85-86, 173-174
Toots, A., 81-82, 94, 110-111, 173-175
Totalitarianism, 63, 122
Trade
  globally managed, 146-147
  moral considerations of, 150-155
  numeracy instruction and, 122, 125,
      127
Trade routes, global evolution of, 20-22
Trilingualism, 31
Triple Refuge (Buddha), 16
Troup, F., 64, 171
Trust, human relations education on,
      103

U

"Understanding Culture," 46, 170
United Nations
  on children's rights, 55-56, 60-63,
      70, 74
  human rights education per, 76,
      78-86, 90
  human rights efforts of, 1, 7-9, 34,
      79, 83, 173
  indoctrination by, 78-80, 83-84
  International Labor Office of, 24-25,
      31-32, 57-59
  linguistics position of, 30-32
  membership influences, 28, 40
United Nations Children's Fund
      (UNICEF), 4, 108
  State of the World's Children report,
      56-60, 65, 69, 71
United Nations Commission on Human
      Rights, 7-9, 79, 83, 173
United Nations Decade for Human
      Rights Education, 79-86, 90,
      173
United Nations Development Programme
      (NDP), 4
United Nations Educational, Scientific,
      and Cultural Organization
      (UNESCO)
  human rights doctrine of, 4, 9-10,
      16-17, 50
  human rights education manual,
      89-104
Universal Covenant of Linguistic Human
      Rights, 30-32
Universal Declaration of Human Rights
      (1948), 165, 168, 172, 174
  assistance rights per, 87-88
  cultural practices and, 13-17, 19, 100
  education rights per, 1-2, 16, 74, 81,
      157

human rights education and, 81, 87-88, 93, 99, 105, 110
implementation challenges of, 27-28, 40, 61
original debates about, 2-4, 6-7, 148, 157
U.S. Declaration of Independence, 100
Utopia, sources of, 93, 105-106, 163

V

Valdmaa, S., 81-82, 94, 110-111, 173-175
Values
cultural centeredness and, 133-138, 143-146
economic doctrines impact on, 150-155
human rights education and, 85-86, 94, 96
Vienna Declaration and Programme of Action, 78, 172
Vienna World Conference on Human Rights, 78-79, 82-83, 90
Villela, M., 60, 171
Vocational education, 114

W

Wages
child labor and, 57-59
education relationship to, 1, 12
Wampum, cultural values related to, 153-154
War
children's burdens of, 59-60, 69
textbook censorship of, 74, 136
Web of life, 50, 128
Welfarism, 1, 3, 155
West, C., 134-135, 177
Western history, education bias of, 97-99

Wilson, N., 82-83, 96, 100, 109, 173-174
Wilson, R., 32, 131, 168, 176
Winthrop, John, 151
"With the World Opening Up, Languages are Losers," 132, 176
Wolfram, 143, 177
Women's rights, numeracy impact on, 123-124
Woolridge, M., 59, 171
Words, in language instruction, 119-120, 142, 161
World Bank, 4, 45, 58, 122, 148, 169
World Commission on Culture and Development, 23, 25, 44-45, 47, 50
World Conference on Education for All (EFA), 6, 165
Declaration of, 5-6
definition debates of, 4-5
failures of, 46
World Conference on Human Rights (Vienna), 78-79, 82-83, 90
World culture, see Global system
World Directory of Minorities (1990), 23
World economy, see Global system
World War II
censorship after, 73-74, 136
globalization after, 4, 22, 40-41, 73, 118
in human rights education, 99-100, 157

Y

Yup'ik Eskimos, cultural resurrection of, 125-126

Z

Zweigenhaft, R., 134, 176

DATE DUE

SE 27 '03			
MY 17 '06			
5/5 08			
		WITHDRAWN	

DEMCO 38-296